The Great Pacific War

A HISTORY OF THE AMERICAN–JAPANESE CAMPAIGN OF 1931–1933

BY

HECTOR C. BYWATER

ASSOCIATE OF INST. NAV. ARCH.,
ASSOCIATE MEMBER OF U.S. NAV. INST.

AUTHOR OF "SEA POWER IN THE PACIFIC"

This edition of *The Great Pacific War* was first published in 1925.

Hector Bywater (1884–1940) began working as a reporter for the
New York Herald at the age of 19. Engaged as a spy by the British
during World War I, he was later hired by the Baltimore Sun to
cover the Disarmament Conference of 1921 in Washington, D.C.
A brilliant military analyst, he correctly predicted the methods
Japan would use to gain control over vast territories and the
means whereby the United States would eventually regain
control of the South Pacific. Bywater died in London in 1940
under mysterious circumstances.

Thank you for purchasing an Applewood Book.
Applewood reprints America's lively classics—
books from the past that are still of interest
to modern readers. For a free copy of our
current catalog, write to:
Applewood Books
P.O. Box 365
Bedford, MA 01730

ISBN 1-55709-557-4

Library of Congress Control Number: 2001097622

1 3 5 7 9 10 8 6 4 2

PRINTED IN CANADA

PREFACE

ALTHOUGH this book portrays the course of an imaginary war between the United States and Japan, it has not been written to support the view that such a conflict is either close at hand or inevitable. No doubt there are elements of danger in the immigration controversy, while further causes of friction may attend the growth of American commercial enterprise in the Far East. For the moment, however, the Pacific horizon is fairly free from clouds. But if war between the two nations is happily improbable, it remains a contingency that cannot be dismissed as wholly impossible.

In a previous volume, "Sea Power in the Pacific," I discussed at some length the formidable problems of strategy that would confront the United States in the event of hostilities with Japan. To naval officers the peculiar character of those problems had, of course, long been evident, but their recital appears to have aroused considerable interest among the public at large. To develop the theme further it was necessary to have recourse to the medium of fiction.

In the present book I have sought to demonstrate that, notwithstanding the handicaps of distance and, on America's side, the want of naval stations in the western area of the Pacific, means might still be found of establishing contact between the main belligerent forces and thus forcing matters to a decisive issue. It is often averred that war between the United States and Japan is out of the question, if only because their respective fleets, divided as they are by thousands of miles of ocean and with no intermediate bases of supply, could never get sufficiently close to engage. This, however, is probably a delusion, as I have endeavoured to show.

In foreshadowing the strategic moves and counter-moves of the supposititious campaign, it has been my aim to keep well within the bounds of reasonable possibility, and not to sacrifice reality for the sake of dramatic effect. It would have been easy, for example, to bring the Japanese battle fleet to Hawaii, or even to the American seaboard. I might even have conveyed whole Japanese army corps to San Francisco and allowed them to overrun the Pacific Slope. But to do so would have been to expose the narrative to the well-merited ridicule of informed critics.

Service readers may take exception to the account of the Bonins expedition, on the ground that so foolhardy an undertaking would never for a moment commend itself to the merest tyro in naval strategy. I submit, however, that the enterprise in question would be no more hazardous and unsound than certain operations which were seriously advocated by professional strategists during the world war of 1914–18. Moreover, at a time of national crisis any scheme which promises to achieve major results at small cost must inevitably make a strong appeal to political leaders, who have not infrequently been known to sanction military operations in the teeth of the best professional advice.

Particulars of the American and Japanese combatant forces are based upon the latest and most reliable information from both countries. Japanese submarines are designated in accordance with the new system promulgated by the Imperial Navy Department in November, 1924. The descriptions of islands, harbours, and channels, in common with all other topographical details, have been carefully checked, nor has the influence of weather conditions in certain regions of the Pacific escaped attention. Most names of merchant ships appearing in the text are actually borne by vessels now afloat. The account of cruiser and submarine raids on commerce has been compiled with due regard to existing trade routes and sea traffic. In fine, no effort has been spared to ensure technical accuracy throughout the narrative.

All persons named in the book, whether American or Japanese, are fictitious, no attempt having been made to draw individuals " from the life."

I am indebted to Mr. Francis E. McMurtrie, a co-editor of " Fighting Ships," the well-known naval annual, for valuable aid in the preparation of this story. His wide knowledge of maritime affairs was placed unreservedly at my disposal, and it is due to his practical interest that the original plan of the book was extended to include chapters descriptive of the trade war and other subsidiary but instructive operations beyond the principal zone of hostilities.

I have only to add that, to the best of my knowledge, this book constitutes the first attempt that has been made to forecast the progress of a future naval war in the Pacific from the Western point of view, though at least two Japanese works on the same subject have appeared within recent years.

HECTOR C. BYWATER.

April, 1925.

CONTENTS

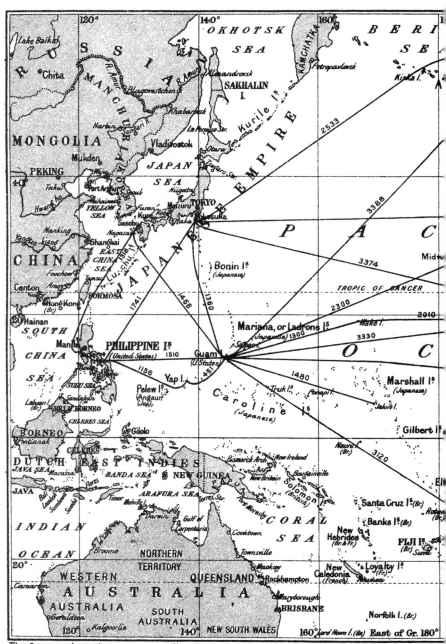

The figures along the routes are distances in Nautical Miles

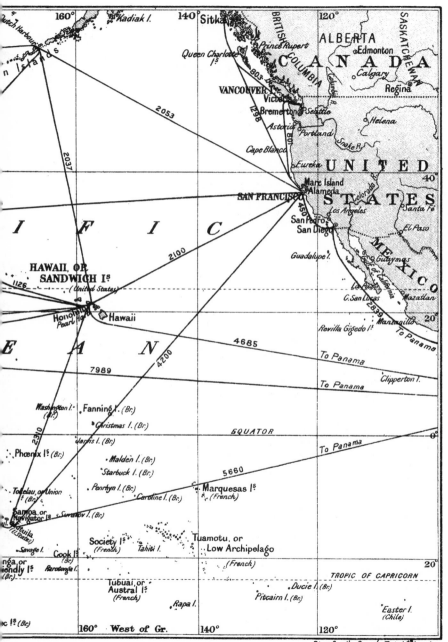

THE GREAT PACIFIC WAR

CHAPTER I

Causes that led to the War—Japan's endeavours to control China—
China takes a step towards unification—Friction over an American
concession—Situation complicated by a Communist agitation in
Japan—Japanese Government decides on war with the United
States as a solution for domestic difficulties

A PISTOL shot fired at Sarajevo in June, 1914, touched
off the European powder magazine, causing an explosion
that convulsed the earth. It might be said with equal
truth that a bomb bursting in Tokyo on January 5,
1931, gave the signal for the recent tremendous conflict
between the United States and Japan, the echoes of
which have scarcely died away. Thanks to the documentary evidence now available, it is possible to trace, link
by link, the connection between this attempt on the life
of Prince Kawamura, the Japanese Prime Minister, and
the subsequent events which culminated in the Pacific
War; but to do so we must first briefly review what had
been happening in Japan and elsewhere in the Far East
during the preceding ten years. While to most of the
nations embroiled therein the World War of 1914–18
had proved an unmitigated curse, to one at least it had
brought wealth, prosperity, and increased political
influence. Alone among all the belligerents, Japan
emerged from the struggle with a substantial balance on
the credit side. In the space of four years her industrial
system developed beyond all expectations, her foreign
trade increased fourfold, and her gold reserve tenfold.
Since she had taken only a nominal share in the actual
fighting, her losses had been trivial, yet they were richly

B

compensated by the possession of all the former German Pacific islands north of the Equator. Moreover, she had made the most of her opportunities in China while the rest of the world was preoccupied with war. Over some of the richest provinces of that ancient Empire she ruled with all the authority of a proprietor. China itself, disunited, racked, and plundered by selfish factions, with a puppet central government and a horde of venal politicians who kept the treasury in a chronic state of emptiness, was in no condition to resist the encroachment of her virile neighbour. The " 21 Demands " which Japan put forward in 1915 showed how far she was prepared to go in her resolve to make the best part of Chinese territory an appanage of Nippon. Nor did Japanese imperialism encounter any serious check till 1921. In that year the Washington Conference met, and the attitude of the Western Powers, though not unfriendly, was such as to convince the statesmen of Tokyo that some modification of their policy towards China was advisable in the interest of Japan herself. Certain covenants were therefore negotiated, aiming at the maintenance of the " open door," and the granting of equal opportunities to all who wished to trade with China or assist in developing her economic resources. But it soon became evident that Japan had no intention of allowing others to share the privileges she claimed on the Asiatic mainland. The process of " freezing out " foreign interests in those parts of China under her domination went on as before, though by methods less overt and brusque than had hitherto been practised. Periodical outbreaks of civil warfare gave her a pretext for keeping troops at strategic points in Chinese territory. Her capitalists and merchants enjoyed a virtual monopoly in Southern Manchuria, besides holding a controlling interest in the mines, railways and industries of Eastern Inner Mongolia. The province of Fukien had been brought within the ever-widening sphere of Japanese influence, and even the coal and iron mines of the Yangtse Valley were exploited to a large extent by Japanese nationals. To a casual observer, therefore, it seemed as though nothing could prevent Japan from becoming, by the process of transition from " peaceful penetration " to permanent occupation, the supreme arbiter of China's destiny, political as well as economic. But for the attainment of this object it was essential that China should remain disunited and impotent. National unification, the setting up of a strong central government which could speak and act for China as an entity, and, if need be, mobilise all the national resources in defence of national interests—such a development would mean the end of foreign ascendancy. Japan, knowing this well, had shown herself unsympathetic towards every movement in the direction of coalition. It was to her interest that the policy of *divide et impera* should be pursued by fomenting internal discord. She was credited with having secretly supported with arms and money the various *Tu'chuns,* or local war lords, whose private feuds kept the country in a perennial ferment and effectually hindered the establishment of national unity. So dissension and disorder held sway till 1929, with the state of China going from bad to worse; but in that year arose the star of General Wang Tsu, scholar, soldier, and patriot, whose name bids fair to go down to posterity as the regenerator of his country. As a youth Wang Tsu had graduated at an American University, where his intellectual gifts had earned him something of a reputation. Returning to China, he took up the practice of law at Hankow, and was engaged in that peaceful pursuit when civil war broke out early in 1929, following the attempt of Tu-Shih-kuan, a military adventurer from Shansi, to march on Peking and proclaim himself dictator. Wang Tsu, who had joined the Northern Army in March as a volunteer, soon revealed himself as a military genius with a talent for leadership. Rising by sheer force of personality to commanding rank, he was found a few months later leading the right wing of General Min's army, which inflicted a smashing defeat on Tu Shih-kuan at Ho-kian. Shortly after this battle General Min was disabled by sickness, whereupon the government at Peking, yielding to the wish of the army, appointed

Wang Tsu as his successor. The new commander-in-chief lost no time in showing his mettle. Following up the discomfited Tu Shih-kuan, he fell upon that luckless adventurer and scattered his army to the winds, Tu himself being killed. Then, turning in his tracks with a speed seldom paralleled in Oriental warfare, Wang marched his troops 200 miles in twelve days and attacked Li Ping-hui, the Manchurian ruler who had supported Tu, routing him with heavy loss. It is interesting to note that even at this early date Wang had struck a blow at Japanese interests, to which Li Ping-hui was known to be attached.

Flushed with success, the victorious general returned to Peking and placed himself at the disposal of the Government, at the same time requesting that he be given a free hand to deal with any other satrap who chose to defy the central authority. President Huang Sen, a well-meaning statesman who now saw his long-cherished dream of unity within reach, sent out invitations to the military governors of each province to assemble at Peking for the purpose of discussing a new scheme of federation, hinting that failure to comply would be followed by a visit from the redoubtable Wang Tsu and his ever-victorious army. The hint was not lost. By 1930 all the provincial governors had repaired to the capital, and it was evident that agreement would be reached on the vital point of unification. Even the sluggish patriotism of the provincial governors was stirred by the prospect of putting an end to that foreign dictation which they had endured for so long; and for the first time since the revolution, all parties in China found themselves working amicably together with one common object—in this case the eradication of Japanese influence from every part of the Chinese dominions. Such, then, was the position at the dawn of 1930. Japan looked on with growing concern, as well she might, having by this time convinced herself, rightly or wrongly, that her whole future—nay, her very existence, was bound up with the exploitation of China. She had come to regard the resources of that country as her own by divine right.

Without Chinese minerals her industrial machine could not be kept going; it required to be fed with a constant supply of the coal, iron, copper and tin from the mines of Shansi, Shantung and Manchuria. Without Chinese foodstuffs her people would go hungry, for the domestic supply had long since ceased to cover the needs of an ever-growing population. The proportion of imported food had now increased to more than one-third, of which the greater part came from China. Since the discovery of rich oil-fields in Shansi province in 1926, and her acquisition of prior rights over the same, Japan had largely reorganised her industries and communications on an oil-fuel basis, and any stoppage or interference with this supply would be disastrous. For these reasons it was necessary at all costs to maintain her grip on China, and no one familiar with the circumstances ever doubted that she would take drastic measures rather than relax it. But she had another and even more imperative motive for holding her own in China. In the event of war with a Great Power she could not carry on for a month without Chinese supplies, and since China—smarting under the memory of years of tyranny—would be at best a malevolent neutral in such a war, nothing was more certain than that the stream of foodstuffs and raw materials from the mainland would be cut off unless Japan were in control of the source. Japanese strategists therefore had reason on their side when they endeavoured by every means to strengthen their grasp on the most productive provinces of the neighbouring country, for if these were lost Japan would be at the mercy of any foe who was powerful at sea. But in thus pursuing a policy which aimed at the virtual enslavement of China, she had inevitably drawn upon herself the hostility of other Powers. Japan, in fact, had been looked at askance for some years past as a nation whose avowed militaristic tendencies were a danger to world peace. Her intolerant attitude towards other foreign interests in East Asia had repeatedly evoked protests from the Western Governments, though by this time it was clear to everyone that nothing short of military action would avail to turn her from her purpose. And she was much too formidable to be challenged with impunity. In the opinion of the best judges, her strategic position made her almost impregnable to attack, for her fleet held absolute command of the Western Pacific, and the lack of bases in that area seemingly rendered it impossible for any hostile fleet to menace her shores. Moreover, with an active army of 250,000 men, and a trained reserve of two millions, she was strong enough to hold her own against any force that could be brought against her from the neighbouring Continent. And so it happened that up to the period at which our narrative begins Japan's ascendency on the Asiatic Continent, antagonistic though it was to all other interests in that region, had not been seriously contested. In the autumn of 1930 an incident had occurred which seemed not unlikely to bring matters to a head. In October the Peking Government granted to an American syndicate, headed by Mr. Waldo Sayers, the well-known New York financier, a concession to work the Green Mountain iron and coal fields of Kiangsi, an upper province of the Yangtsze Valley, where exceptionally rich deposits had been located by American prospectors. Japan forthwith addressed a protest to Peking, pointing out that since the district referred to was one in which Japanese interests had hitherto been recognised as paramount, the validity of this concession to the nationals of another Power could not be admitted by her. The Chinese Government, in reply, pointed out that Kiangsi province was not mentioned as a Japanese enclave in any existing convention or treaty between the two countries, so that the Government was fully justified in granting such a concession to the American syndicate. The Japanese rejoinder to this note was brusque, and even threatening, but Peking stood firm. There the matter rested for the moment while Mr. Sayers continued his preparations for developing the concession, though the Japanese Press boasted in violent language that neither he nor any other foreigner would be permitted to raise a ton of coal or iron from the Kiangsi mines.

Concurrent events in Japan itself had already begun to turn the thoughts of her rulers into dangerous channels. A succession of harsh laws had utterly failed to check the spread of radical doctrines which had taken root among the masses some twenty years beforehand. Large sections of the people were imbued with Communistic ideas, and organised labour was loudly demanding a voice in the conduct of national affairs. It was clear that the old order was changing, but the representatives of that order were in no mood to accept the inevitable. Honestly believing as they did that the advent of democratic government would herald the ruin of their country, they were prepared to go to any lengths rather than submit to such an innovation. It is true that manhood suffrage had been conceded in 1925 after years of fruitless agitation by the Liberal parties, but this, as everyone had foreseen, made little difference to the system of government, which remained in essence just as much an autocracy as before. The Japanese Parliament, having no real executive power, was little more than a debating club. The group of Elder Statesmen whose labours had raised Japan to the rank of a Great Power, had passed away, but in their stead the military chiefs still reigned supreme. It was not to be expected that they would stand idle while the shadow of revolution darkened the land and threatened the eclipse of everything they and their caste stood for. Many years before, a writer on Asiatic affairs had predicted what their decision would be in such an event. " It is a cardinal principle of the ruling element in Japan," he observed, "that a people which is kept preoccupied with trouble abroad will have neither the time nor the inclination to brood over its domestic grievances. That these men, in whom the feudal spirit still burns fiercely beneath a veneer of Western civilisation, will remain passive in face of this growing menace to their power and their most sacred traditions, is not to be believed. On the contrary, it is virtually certain that they will shrink from no course of action which is calculated to stem the rising tide of rebellion and anarchy.

On an earlier occasion, when the domestic situation was far less grave, they did not scruple to plunge the country into war with China. What more likely than that the same expedient will be adopted in the present emergency? Patriotism is still a virtue in Japan, and there is little doubt but that all the best elements in the nation would support a policy of war if they believed the alternative to be social chaos." At the period we are now dealing with the social situation in Japan was far more acute than it had been when the above forecast was penned. Communist agitators were hard at work in all the great industrial centres; mass meetings at which sedition was preached were held without any attempt at concealment, and the police were openly defied. In November, 1930, an attempt to arrest two prominent Communists, Watanabe and Onzu, who were addressing a Labour Convention at Osaka, provoked a riot, in which several police officials and more than a score of civilians were killed. So threatening was the temper of the crowd on this occasion that troops were called out. In the following month Watanabe was arrested at Tokyo, and the authorities announced that he would be severely dealt with. Organised labour at once took up the challenge; indignation meetings were held in all parts of the country, and resolutions passed demanding the immediate release of the prisoner and the dismissal of the Minister for Home Affairs, Mr. Sasaki, who had ordered the arrest to be made. Failing compliance with these demands, the Labour spokesmen threatened a general strike. There were those in the Cabinet who urged upon the Premier, Prince Kawamura, the wisdom of setting Watanabe at liberty in view of the ugly temper of the populace. But the Prince refused to listen to such advice. He would countenance no parleying with the mob, he said. It was the duty of the Government to maintain law and order, and they were determined to take all necessary measures to that end. When the Premier's answer became known there was a violent outburst of fury among the workers. A general strike was declared on January 2, 1931, and so swift was the response that in less than twenty-four hours the industrial system of the country was all but paralysed. Riots broke out simultaneously at so many points in Tokyo and the provinces that the police were powerless to cope with them. Strong detachments of military were hurried to the chief cities, with instructions to suppress all disturbance with an iron hand. On the night of January 4 the residences of the Premier and Home Minister were attacked by a huge crowd, which broke through the cordon of troops and did a great deal of damage before it was dispersed by rifle fire. The bodies of those killed by the fusillade were then carried through the streets on litters, to the mournful strains of the " Hymn of Revolution." Parliament was to meet next morning, and at an early hour a throng numbering at least one hundred thousand persons gathered in the neighbourhood of the Diet buildings. Ministers and Deputies, under a strong escort of police and troops, reached their places in safety, but the noise of the vast multitude outside made it difficult to proceed with the business of the day. Replying to interpellations in both Chambers, the Government announced that the situation was well in hand, and that should the strike continue troops would be drafted to carry on essential public services; furthermore, that force would be employed without stint against those evil-minded persons who were seeking to overthrow the Constitution. As the Premier was passing out through the lobby of the Upper Chamber a man in the uniform of an usher hurled a bomb. Although the explosion was violent Prince Kawamura escaped serious injury, but two Deputies with him were killed outright, and there were numerous casualties among bystanders in the lobby. The assassin, on being apprehended, was found to be a young student who had gained admission to the building by donning the uniform of an usher from one of the Ministries. That same evening a conference took place at Prince Kawamura's villa, at which, in addition to the senior members of the Cabinet, General Oka, chief of the General Staff, was present. Contradictory versions of what transpired at this momentous gathering have been circulated, but in view of subsequent events it appears certain that the Premier laid bare his drastic plan for " bringing the people to their senses," as he termed it, and there and then secured the consent of his colleagues to its immediate application. So much, indeed, is admitted by the Japanese historian, Dr. Ikeda, whose recent volume, " Political Antecedents of the American War," contains what purports to be an accurate summary of the proceedings at this emergency meeting of the Cabinet. The following extracts from this work, which was published at Tokyo in 1934, are illuminating :

" Prince Kawamura, having received his visitors, announced that they would await the arrival of the chief of the General Staff before opening the discussion, as military questions of the highest importance were involved. The Foreign Minister, Baron Fukuhara; the Naval Minister, Admiral Oshima; the War Minister, General Ofuji, and other members of the Cabinet were already present. When General Oka arrived the Premier at once declared the meeting in session and began an address. ' The country stands in imminent danger,' he said. ' As you are aware, the revolt is spreading more rapidly than we can cope with it, and the ringleaders, conscious of their strength, are daily becoming more defiant. I have been advised from certain quarters to parley with them, but that to my mind would be a fatal course, for it would lead them to think that their tactics of intimidation had succeeded and they would be encouraged to raise all manner of impossible demands. On the other hand, to stamp out this menace we should need to employ the most ruthless measures; blood would flow in streams; and when all was over the populace, cowed though they might be for the time being, would be more than ever inclined to lend an ear to seditious teaching. Nor is that all. Before deciding to make unrestricted use of troops to crush this revolt we must be sure that the spirit of the army is proof against the insidious propaganda of the revolutionaries, and I fear that we have no such assurance. The War Minister informs me that two battalions of the 85th infantry regiment at Nagoya refused to entrain for Tokyo, declaring that they would not fire on their own people, and although the mutineers have been severely dealt with the divisional commander reports that acts of disobedience have occurred in other regiments. Only this evening a despatch has been received from Kanazawa, reporting a mutinous outbreak among the troops of that division. We shall therefore do well not to place too great a strain on the loyalty of the army. Now, gentlemen, it seems to me that the only alternative to civil war is a diversion abroad, which would inflame the declining patriotism of the people and provide them with something to think about in place of their imaginary grievances. There can be no doubt that at the first threat of foreign aggression all sections of the community would forget their differences and rally to the support of the Government. It has always happened before; it will surely happen again. And, as a matter of fact, such a threat already exists. The recent epidemic of militarism in China has not subsided; on the contrary it is increasing, and at any moment we may be forced to defend our vital interests in that country at the point of the sword. We have positive evidence that American money, arms, and equipment are pouring into China for the purpose of enabling her to attack us, and now comes this affair of the Sayers concession to prove, if proof were needed, that America is stealthily manœuvring to destroy our privileged position in those lands which we have brought under our economic sway by the labour and sacrifice of years. If we elect to wait until America and her Chinese confederates are ready to strike, we may find ourselves driven out of the Continent, including Korea; and that, of course, would mean the end of Japan as a Power that counts in world affairs. I therefore propose that we make clear without delay our firm resolve to tolerate no foreign interference with our rights. This will not necessarily mean war, but if war should result I think we could face it calmly. The staffs of the army and navy are in complete agreement on that point. The military position *vis-à-vis* China is favourable at the moment, but it will, of course, turn more and more against us as the reorganisation of the Chinese army progresses. The naval position, I am assured, is such that a conflict with America could be entered into with every prospect of a happy issue. For the rest, we have a gold reserve that experts declare to be adequate for the contingency in view; provided our communications with the Continent are kept open there will be no shortage of essential supplies, and our industry is now sufficiently organised and developed to produce all the material necessary for a campaign of some duration. Finally there is no reason to suppose that we should have to deal with any enemies other than China and America. Our relations with other Powers are on a footing that rules out the possibility of their taking up arms against us unless their interests were directly molested, which we should be particularly careful to avoid. And now let us consider the advantages we should derive from a favourable issue of this struggle in defence of our national existence. In the first place it would scotch, if not completely kill, the demon of anarchy who has been rearing his head in our country of late. Chastened in the hard school of war, our people would turn aside from the baneful doctrines which foreign agitators have been propagating, and revert to their former allegiance. For a generation at least the country would be purged of the revolutionary poison which has invaded its system. Secondly, our position in China would become impregnable, and we could henceforth continue the development of its resources without fear of interruption. Thirdly, we could set up impassable barriers against the extension of those Western influences, moral as well as material, which have wrought so much harm in the past to the peoples of Asia, and which, if allowed to spread, will end by bringing the whole Continent under the domination of the white race. Fourthly, we should obtain new territories in the Pacific which, by reason of their admirable climate, fertility, and rich resources, would offer the best possible field for settlement by our surplus population. I have now placed before you quite frankly the problem with which we are confronted, and would ask you to judge which of the two alternatives it is our duty to adopt; but before coming to a decision it would be advisable to hear the reports of the Ministers of Army and Navy.'

" Admiral Oshima, General Ofuji, and General Oka were then successively called upon to express their views, which generally confirmed the favourable account which the Premier had given of the outlook from the naval and military points of view. After a discussion lasting several hours all the Ministers, excepting only Mr. Sasaki (Home Affairs), agreed that a strong foreign policy offered the best means of uniting the nation and putting an end to the grave domestic troubles then in progress. Mr. Sasaki dissented, but expressed his readiness to resign if his views did not harmonise with those of the rest of the Cabinet. At this the meeting broke up, Prince Kawamura bidding his colleagues farewell with the significant words : ' Gentlemen, the necessary steps will be taken to give effect to our common decision.' At 6 p.m. secret orders were issued to put in force Sections 1, 2 and 4A of the War Emergency Plan."

It should be noted in connection with the foregoing that, while Dr. Ikeda has incurred some odium in Japan by reason of his liberal opinions, his general veracity as an historian has never been questioned; and we may consequently accept his account of this fateful Cabinet meeting on January 5, 1931, as being in the main accurate.

CHAPTER II

Diplomatic correspondence preceding hostilities—Radio and cable communications interrupted—Dangerous weakness of U.S. Asiatic Squadron—Captain Appleton, Assistant Chief of Naval Operations Bureau, resigns as a protest—Japanese steamer blows up in Panama Canal, suspending communication between Atlantic and Pacific—Question of employing submarines against merchant vessels raised—Bad news of the Asiatic Squadron

EVENTS now marched swiftly to their appointed end. Rioting continued in the capital and elsewhere during the 6th and 7th, and as the troops were repeatedly compelled to use their weapons, the tale of casualties mounted steadily. With Japan, as it seemed, on the verge of revolution, her friends and enemies alike waited breathlessly for the *dénouement*. But suddenly the whole complexion of affairs underwent a marked change. Speaking in the Diet on January 10, the Foreign Minister announced in solemn tones that a critical situation had arisen in China, the gravity of which was enhanced by the unlooked-for intervention of a third Power. Baron Fukuhara then reviewed the negotiations which had taken place with regard to the Sayers concession, reminded his hearers that the Chinese Government had lately adopted a tone which was difficult to reconcile with peaceful intentions and added : " In order to make our position quite clear we have informed the United States Government that, since the question at issue concerns only ourselves and China we do not propose to make the Sayers concession a subject of diplomatic negotiation with any other Power." Appreciating to the full the significance of these words, the deputies gave way to patriotic fervour, their cheers quite drowning for the moment the tumult of the crowd which still surged about the precincts of the Diet. An hour or so later, when the evening papers appeared with a report of the Foreign Minister's speech under flaring headlines, and the people read that little Japan had figuratively snapped its fingers under the nose of the American Colossus, they speedily verified the Premier's prediction by forgetting all about those grievances which they had come out to ventilate. Serried masses of workmen still paraded the streets, but in place of the " Hymn of Revolution " many of them were now chanting the martial songs which their fathers had sung on the eve of battle, and the air was full of " Banzais." That night the labour chiefs held an emergency meeting, at which they decided to annul the general strike and suspend their campaign against the Government until the foreign crisis was at an end. A few of the leaders were against this course, arguing that the crisis had been deliberately manufactured to turn the thoughts of the people away from their wrongs, and that action by the workers was more necessary than ever now that the imperialists were seeking to plunge the country into war. These counsels, however, were not listened to. Not only was the strike declared at an end, but the meeting passed resolutions pledging the trade unions to support the Government in any reasonable measures it might take to safeguard the country against foreign aggression. Prince Kawamura's scheme had, so far, proved completely successful. Revolution had been averted for the moment, but unless the fires of patriotism were kept burning a reaction might set in and the forces of disorder again become supreme. The Press was therefore encouraged to inflame racial passion by recalling the American attitude on Japanese immigration. In a few days a violent anti-American campaign was in full blast. Fuel was added to the blaze by the receipt of a strong note from Washington, which not only upheld the validity of the Sayers concession, but declined to recognise Japan's claims to favoured treatment in the district concerned, and expressed " profound surprise " at the tone of the Foreign

Minister's speech in the Diet. Contrary to all diplomatic precedent, the Japanese Government at once communicated the contents of this note to the Press, which naturally hailed it as further evidence of America's aggressive intentions. In a further note, dated February 4, the United States proposed that the dispute over the Sayers concession be submitted to arbitration, as provided for in the Nine-Power Treaty negotiated at Washington in February, 1922. Japan, however, declined the proposal on the ground that the question at issue concerned her sovereign rights, and was therefore not a fit subject for submission to an international tribunal. Undeterred by this rebuff, the United States Government was continuing its efforts to promote an amicable solution when an incident occurred which gave a fresh impetus to the war fever in Japan. On February 15 a New York paper stated, with an air of authority, that all American warships in the Atlantic had received urgent orders to pass through the Panama Canal and join up with the Pacific Fleet at Hawaii, from whence the combined force would make a cruise to the Philippines. This report was instantly contradicted by the Navy Department in an official *communiqué*. A few ships, it was stated, had certainly been ordered to the Pacific, but only in line with ordinary routine, and the report of a naval cruise to the Philippines was absolutely unfounded. But the mischief was done. The original message had been flashed to Japan, where it caused the wildest excitement; while for some reason, never satisfactorily explained, the Navy Department's denial was held up for several days. Before it reached Tokyo—or at any rate before its receipt was officially admitted there—the Government addressed a sharp Note to Washington, protesting against naval movements " which could only be interpreted as a menace to Japan." The Note went on to declare that American transports were known to be under orders to proceed to the Philippines with cargoes of guns and naval mines, and added that unless these ships were immediately recalled " the Imperial Government will be

c

forced to conclude that the intentions of the United States Government are not of a friendly character." It was now clear to all that Japan was bent, if not on provoking war, at least on subjecting the United States to a diplomatic humiliation that would not only reduce American prestige in the Far East to zero, but at the same time force that country to acknowledge, in so many words, Japan's complete ascendency in China and her monopoly of Chinese resources. The gravity of the issue was fully appreciated at Washington, but the authorities were determined to prevent the catastrophe of war if this were possible without the sacrifice of national honour. In a long and courteously-worded Note the Japanese Government was urged to reconsider the arbitration proposal, and assured that the United States would scrupulously refrain from taking any action, military or otherwise, that could in any way be construed as prejudicial to Japanese interests. The Sayers concession, as well as all other American undertakings in the disputed Chinese territory, would be regarded as in abeyance pending the decision of the arbitration court. The Note concluded by recalling the traditional friendship between the two nations, " which the United States Government most earnestly desires shall continue unimpaired, and which it will do its utmost to preserve." But forces were already at work against which all the arts of diplomacy were powerless. Japan, having definitely resolved to unsheath the sword, was in no mood to draw back at the eleventh hour. Her reply to the last American Note was curt, and while professing peaceful sentiments, reiterated the demand that no reinforcements of any kind whether of ships, troops, or material, should be dispatched to the American stations west of Hawaii. " The Imperial Government," added Baron Fukuhara, " assumes that the transports already *en route* to Manila will be ordered back immediately; failing which it must reserve the right to take such measures as may be expedient in the interest of national defence." There were some members of the Cabinet at Washington who would have yielded to this ultimatum

—for such in effect it was—rather than involve their country in war; but by this time public opinion was taking a hand in the matter. Devotion to peace is inherent in the American temperament; but so also is a passionate patriotism, which at moments of national crisis is apt to override every other consideration. If in this instance the Japanese demands had contained the smallest element of justice or equity, had they even been presented in a less bellicose manner, public opinion in the United States would have been unconquerably opposed to war, and the Government might have made almost any sacrifice of interests in the Far East without incurring the anger of its people. As it was, however, Japan's truculence had the desired effect. The State Department's last Note to Tokyo was condemned in nearly all quarters as being far too mildly worded, the Press with few exceptions urging the Government to inform Japan in plain terms that the limit of American patience had been reached. More than this, it demanded that all requisite steps be taken without delay to protect American interests in Asia. Special emphasis was laid on the necessity of putting the Philippines into a state of defence. Confronted with this evidence of the nation's resolve to defend its rights at all costs, the Government had no option but to adopt a stiffer attitude towards Japan. This it did by notifying Tokyo that the latter's demand for the recall of the transports *en route* to Manila could not be entertained. At this date, February 28, the ships in question, *Beaufort* and *Newport News*, were half-way across the Pacific, and destroyers of the U.S. Asiatic fleet had been ordered to meet them at a point 1000 miles east of Manila, to convoy them safely over the last stage of their journey. Concurrently with this Note to Japan, Admiral Ribley, commanding the Asiatic Fleet, was instructed to assemble all units of his command at Cavite, the principal naval base in the Philippines, there to await further orders. The political situation, he was informed, was serious enough to justify the taking of special measures for the safety of his command. Not until long afterwards was it known that the issue of these orders to Admiral Ribley had occasioned a serious dispute at the Navy Department, and led to the retirement of Captain Appleton, the Assistant Chief of Naval Operations, an officer of brilliant attainments, whose appointment to this important post a year earlier had evoked some heart-burnings, it being usually held by a flag officer. The Asiatic fleet was less of a fighting organisation than a squadron for "showing the flag"; excepting the destroyers and submarines it was composed of obsolete ships with limited military value. Besides the flagship *Missoula*, an armoured cruiser more than twenty years old, it comprised the *Frederick*, an older and smaller vessel of the same type; three slow and ancient light cruisers—*Galveston, Denver,* and *Cleveland;* the small airplane-carrier *Curtiss;* ten destroyers, three light mine-layers, twelve submarines, and various non-combatant auxiliaries. As the larger ships of this squadron could offer no serious resistance in case of attack by the Japanese fleet, and must inevitably be destroyed if they were brought to action, Captain Appleton urged their immediate recall to Hawaii. The destroyers and submarines he proposed to leave in the Western Pacific, as they were well fitted to co-operate in the defence of the Philippines. But this plan did not commend itself to Admiral Morrison, the Chief of Naval Operations, who rated the military power of the Asiatic fleet more highly than his subordinate and believed that, if concentrated, it could put up a good fight against anything short of the Japanese battle fleet. Declining to accept responsibility for orders which he regarded as the forerunner of certain disaster, Captain Appleton resigned his post and applied for a sea command. This, however, he did not receive till some time after, when events had fully vindicated the accuracy of his judgment. His successor as Assistant Chief of Operations was Rear-Admiral Hubbard. On March 2 a message was received from Admiral Ribley acknowledging the Department's orders, but requesting the prompt dispatch of reinforcements for his fleet, and indicating deficiencies in reserve ammunition and other warlike stores. This proved to be the last communication from him. A day later the cable ceased to work, and repeated radio messages, both direct from the high-power stations on the West coast and relayed from Samoa, failed to elicit an answer. Nor could contact be made with Guam, though in normal circumstances the radio plant at that island could send over a distance of ten thousand miles. From the silence that now descended on the Western Pacific it was only too plain that some radio installation of maximum power was being used to jamb all signals from the American stations, nor could there be any doubt as to who was responsible for this interference. The only conclusion possible was that Japan had cast her vote for war and was already engaged in acts of hostility. This belief was universally held at Washington on the evening of March 3. But it was not until March 5 that the Japanese Ambassador, Count Sakatani, applied for his passports, and by that time things had happened which made the Japanese declaration of war a somewhat superfluous formality. Late in February, when the gravity of the situation could no longer be ignored, the majority of the warships then in the Atlantic and Caribbean had been ordered to join the flag of the Commander-in-Chief in the Pacific, Admiral Robert J. Dallinger. Needless to say, these orders were not made public, but the volume of naval traffic through the Panama Canal showed clearly enough that a big concentration of strength in the Pacific was in progress. Ordinary commercial traffic still went on, however, as the United States Government, still hoping for peace, was careful to abstain from any action that might be interpreted as preparation for war. But special precautions were observed by the Canal authorities during this period of crisis, all mercantile ships, American as well as foreign, having to undergo inspection before being permitted to enter the waterway. At dawn on March 3 a large Japanese cargo steamer, the *Akashi Maru*, owned by the Osaka Shosen Kaisha, arrived off Colon, where she was boarded by an American guard boat. She proved to be from Hamburg to Kobe, with a consignment of heavy machinery and railroad material. Her papers were quite in order, nothing of a suspicious nature was discovered by the inspecting party, and as no instructions had been received to hold up Japanese ships, it was decided to let the vessel pass through. The captain was told, however, that an armed guard would remain on board his ship while it was in the Canal zone, and as he raised no objection to this a party of four marines, under a corporal, were detailed to accompany the *Akashi Maru* as far as Panama. The huge freighter, of nearly 12,000 tons dead weight, was worked through the first locks and entered Gatun Lake eight miles astern of the American cruiser *Huron,* which had preceded her through the Gatun locks. Once out in the lake she steamed at her full speed of 13 knots, making such good headway that at Bas Obispo, where the channel enters the famous Culebra Cut, she had reduced the distance between herself and the cruiser to five miles. It has always been thought that she wished to involve the *Huron* in the catastrophe about to occur; but in this she failed, for the American warship escaped injury of any kind. The *Akashi Maru* was approximately midway in the Cut when a thunderous explosion was heard, and a gigantic column of water, smoke, and dust shot up to the sky. Blending with the echoes of this terrific detonation was heard a roaring sound, of which the sinister import was but too well known to those familiar with the Canal. The shock of the explosion had dislodged millions of tons of earth from the steep sides of the Culebra ravine, causing a landslide of infinitely greater dimensions than any that had been previously experienced. When a party of Canal officials reached the scene of the disaster, an extraordinary spectacle met their gaze. A thick pall of dust still hung over the Cut, both sides of which had collapsed for a distance of nearly a thousand yards. Where a broad channel of water had existed half an hour before was now a solid rampart of earth twenty-five feet high. This, of course, was the bed of the Canal, which had been forced up by the overwhelming pressure of the adjoining hills. Of

the Japanese steamer that had caused the havoc, not a
vestige remained.   It seemed impossible that a great
ship could be utterly blotted out in the space of a few
seconds, yet so it was.   Fragments of her structure were
eventually picked up miles from the scene of the explosion, but the ship herself and all on board had vanished
completely.   It needed only a cursory glance to perceive the appalling extent of the damage.   Landslides
were of not infrequent occurrence in the Cut, and special
machinery was held ready to cope with them.   But
no such cataclysm as this had ever happened before.
Months must elapse ere a channel could be cut through
the mountainous *débris,* and meanwhile the Canal would
remain blocked at the very period when its use promised
to be of vital importance to the United States.   The
mystery of the explosion which produced this fateful
result has never been fully cleared up.   The Japanese
Government disclaimed all knowledge of the cause, con-
tenting itself with the suggestion that the oil fuel of the
Akashi Maru might have caught fire and destroyed the
ship—a theory dismissed by experts as too childish to
be worth a moment's notice.   In their opinion nothing
less than an immense quantity of high-explosives could
have caused so tremendous a detonation.   One of their
number attributed it to at least a thousand tons of
dynamite or blasting powder, and other estimates of the
quantity of explosive were considerably higher.   Inquiry
into the movements of the *Akashi Maru* showed her to
have arrived at Hamburg on January 15, 1931, from
Kobe, with a mixed cargo, all of which was thought to
have been discharged at the German port   She had then
taken on board a full consignment of locomotives and
heavy machinery, but there was no record of any
explosives having been delivered to the ship at Hamburg.
She sailed for Japan on February 5, and had thus taken
twenty-six days to cover the run of 5,000 miles to
Colon—an unusually long time for a ship with an
economical speed of 10 knots.   According to reports by
other vessels on the route at approximately the same
time, very little bad weather had been met with.   The

long duration of the *Akashi Maru's* voyage lent colour
to the theory that she had been met at sea by some ship
which had transferred a large quantity of explosives to
the big freighter. This view was generally accepted,
though no plausible explanation was forthcoming as to
how a thousand tons of dynamite could have been stowed
away without displacing cargo already in the hold, and
in such a way as to remain hidden from the officials who
had inspected the ship at Colon. The only other theory
which in any way squared with the facts was that the
explosives had been deposited on the bed of Culebra
Cut by a Japanese steamer which had passed through
several days, or even several weeks, previously, and that
the *Akashi Maru* had detonated the charge by some
pre-arranged method. But whether those on board
had deliberately sacrificed themselves and their ship,
or whether, owing to some miscalculation, the explosion
had been premature, remains to this day an open question. Not only the Japanese Government, but the
owners of the ship and their agents both in Japan and
Europe, have consistently denied all knowledge of the
facts or collusion in what was palpably a deep-laid plot
for the blocking of the canal on the very eve of war.
It is certain, at all events, that the United States Government would have made this outrage a *casus belli*, even if
Japan had refrained from committing other acts of
hostility. From the American point of view, the
disabling of the Canal was a calamity of the first magnitude, which threatened to ruin all the plans on which
the strategical employment of the Navy had been based.
While the greater part of the fleet was already in the
Pacific, a number of important ships were still in the
other ocean, and would now have to make a journey of
13,000 miles before reaching their war bases on the
West coast. This, however, was by no means the most
serious consequence of the disaster. For several months,
at least, it ruled out all the Atlantic coast navy yards as
a factor of immediate value in the prosecution of the
war. The entire Fleet in the Pacific would have to
depend on the resources of local yards for its mainten-

ance, and these were notoriously ill-equipped to supply
the needs of a great naval force.   Until the Canal was
repaired, vast quantities of fuel, stores, and other war
material required by the fleet must be shipped to the
West Coast *via* Cape Horn, a voyage of nearly two months
for the average cargo steamer, since the railroads would
be able to undertake but a relatively small part of this
traffic.   It was therefore of supreme importance to get
the Canal in working order again as quickly as possible.
To excavate a passage sufficiently deep and wide for the
largest ships would be a task of at least four months,
according to the original forecast; actually, owing to
further landslides which seemed to mock at the superhuman efforts put forth by all concerned, the work was
not finished for six and a half months.   But meanwhile
grave loss and disaster were to be suffered in consequence of the initial blow which Japan had delivered at
her antagonist, as will appear in due course.   An incident
now occurred which, though trivial in itself, was destined
to have far-reaching consequences on the naval campaign
about to open.   Following the news of the Culebra Cut
explosion, all merchant ships in the Canal, or awaiting
admission at Balboa and Colon, were ordered to anchor
under the guns of the coast batteries, pending a thorough
search of each vessel, regardless of the flag it flew.   There
was a not unnatural suspicion that some further outrage
might be contemplated, for the purpose of intensifying
the damage already caused to the Canal.   A rigid censorship was placed on all communications from the Canal
Zone, and no message was allowed to be sent which made
any reference to the disaster.   The idea was to keep the
news secret for a few days, not only for military reasons,
but to enable all incoming ships to be held up and
searched, on the chance of finding another hidden cargo
of explosives.   It was, of course, probable that Japan
had already taken measures to notify her shipping of
the outbreak of war, in which case they would give the
Canal Zone a wide berth; but, on the other hand, there
was a bare possibility that some vessel, bent upon
mischief, would enter the trap which had been set.

As a further precaution, destroyers, submarines, and aircraft attached to the Canal Zone defences were ordered to patrol the Atlantic and Pacific within a radius of two hundred miles from Colon and Panama respectively. Their mission was to keep a vigilant watch over the approaches to the Canal, and if any vessel, finding itself under observation, sought to escape, to bring the suspect into port for examination. At 8 a.m. on March 5 the United States submarine *S 4*, being then 150 miles north of Colon, sighted a large merchant steamer which displayed no colours. The vessel was steering due east, and therefore heading away from the Canal, but the fact that it altered course and appeared to increase speed on observing the submarine impressed Lieutenant Bradlow, commanding *S 4*, as a suspicious circumstance. He therefore raised speed to 15 knots, and finding the steamer took no notice of his signal to heave-to, fired a blank shot from the 4-inch gun mounted on the deck of the submarine. Neither this nor a second blank charge had any effect, while the thick smoke pouring from the funnels of the mysterious vessel showed that her captain did not mean to be caught if he could help it. What with the thick weather that limited visibility to a couple of miles, and the high speed at which the unknown ship was now steaming, Lieutenant Bradlow saw nothing for it but to take sterner measures if the chase were not to get clear away, and to permit that would have been contrary to his orders. So he caused a shell to be fired across the steamer's bows. It pitched into the water less than a hundred yards ahead, but not the slightest attention was paid even to this peremptory summons. The mist was now so thick that the profile of the steamer could scarcely be made out; the submarine, though running at her best speed, could not overhaul the swift quarry, and the only way of compelling her to obey orders was to open fire in real earnest. This was done, but to avoid needless damage the first two shells were unfused. The first round fell short, though near enough to send a shower of water over the steamer's forecastle; the second, flying high tore away a boat and demolished part of the deckhouse. This proved to be enough, for the stranger promptly hove-to, at the same time hoisting the Japanese flag. In response to a megaphone hail from the submarine, which had now come within speaking distance, the captain announced his ship to be the *Nikko Maru*, of the Nippon Yusen Kaisha, with passengers and cargo from New York to Valparaiso and Yokohama. His ordinary route, he added, would have taken him through the Canal, but having some hours previously intercepted a radio message which announced war between Japan and the United States to be imminent, he had decided to make for a Brazilian port to obtain instructions from his owners. He ended by protesting vehemently against the action of the submarine in firing into him, claiming to be well within his rights in trying to escape, as submarine attacks on merchant shipping were forbidden by international law. At this point Lieutenant Bradlow broke off the parley by ordering the steamer to shape a course for Colon, and this was done under protest, the *S 4* following astern with her gun trained on the prize, the short voyage being accomplished without further incident. As soon as the *Nikko Maru* reached Colon she was boarded and thoroughly searched, but nothing of a suspicious nature was found. Nevertheless, having been captured after war had broken out, she was held as lawful prize, and eventually put into service as a United States fleet auxiliary. On receiving a detailed report of the circumstances from Lieutenant Bradlow, through the officer commanding in the Canal Zone, the Navy Department officially approved his action. It was realised, however, that a dangerous precedent had been set, of which the enemy would not be slow to take advantage. Evidence of this was soon forthcoming in the shape of an official message from Tokyo, which announced to the world that since a United States submarine, in direct contravention of the Five-Power Treaty signed at Washington in 1922, had molested and fired on an unarmed Japanese merchant steamer, and since this illegal act on the part of the commander of the submarine had not been disavowed by the United States authorities, the Japanese Government had no option but to regard the said Treaty as null and void, and would, accordingly, reserve to itself the right to employ its own submarines in any way it saw fit. This led to much controversy among international jurists as to whether the action of *S 4* did, in fact, constitute a breach of the Treaty regulating the procedure of submarines with regard to merchant vessels. The pertinent clauses of the Treaty were as follows :

(1) A merchant vessel must be ordered to submit to visit and search to determine its character before it can be seized.

A merchant vessel must not be attacked unless it refuse to submit to visit and search after warning, or to proceed as directed after seizure. . . .

(2) The belligerent submarines are not under any circumstances exempt from the universal rules above stated ; and if a submarine cannot capture a merchant vessel in conformity with these rules the existing law of nations requires it to desist from attack and from seizure, and to permit the merchant vessel to proceed unmolested.

The Signatory Powers recognise the practical impossibility of using submarines as commerce destroyers without violating, as they were violated in the recent war of 1914–18, the requirements universally accepted by civilised nations for the protection of the lives of neutrals and non-combatants, and to the end that the prohibition of the use of submarines as commerce destroyers shall be universally accepted as a part of the law of nations, they now accept that prohibition as henceforth binding as between themselves, and they invite all other nations to adhere thereto.

It will be seen that the rules laid down as above were to some extent contradictory. On the one hand, a submarine was authorised by implication to detain, visit, and search a merchant vessel, and equally by implication to attack such a vessel if it refused to submit to visit and search. On the other hand, the submarine was expressly forbidden to persist with the attack if it seemed impossible to capture the merchant vessel without endangering the lives of non-combatants on board. Finally, the Signatory Powers, of whom the United States was one, had in the concluding paragraph virtually bound themselves not to employ submarines against merchant vessels under any circumstances whatever. It could be, and was, argued on behalf of the United States that the case of the *S 4* and the *Nikko Maru* was an exceptional one. Only a few hours previously a merchant vessel under the Japanese flag had been the means of inflicting serious damage on the Panama Canal, and while the Japanese Government might deny complicity in this outrage, the fact remained that a merchant-man, owned and manned by its nationals, had committed a flagrant act of war. It was but natural, therefore, that all other Japanese vessels in the vicinity of the Canal should fall under grave suspicion and be regarded as active enemies until the contrary had been proved. For this reason the United States held itself justified in taking the measures that had been taken against the *Nikko Maru*, whose behaviour when requested to stop and submit to search had been highly suspicious. That the ship had been intercepted by a submarine instead of a surface patrol vessel was a fortuitous circumstance that did not affect the main issue. The United States Government concluded by maintaining that the Treaty in question was still valid, and would continue to be observed by its own submarines till further notice. The controversy thus initiated endured as long as the war itself, but Japan always insisted that the shots fired by *S 4* had automatically cancelled the embargo on submarines as commerce destroyers, and from that time forward did not scruple to use her underwater boats for attacking enemy merchant ships. For the moment, however, public interest was centred on a matter of more immediate concern—the fate of those gallant men who were called upon to defend America's overseas possessions against crushing odds.   From March 3 to March 7 not a word of news reached Washington from that quarter of the world.   It was as though an impenetrable screen had been established round a great area of the Western Pacific to hide the tragedy being enacted in those distant waters.   Late on March 8 the silence was broken by a press cable from Hong Kong to London, transmitted to New York.   This stated that rumours were current in the Chinese ports of a great naval battle having been fought off the Philippines between the Japanese and American fleets, and ending in the total destruction of the latter.   A few hours later came another cable from the same source, containing news of the direst import. A Dutch steamer from Batavia to Hong Kong had reported by radio that she had picked up, 200 miles west of Manila, seven survivors of the American destroyer *Crosby*, who had been found clinging to wreckage from their lost ship.   Being in the last stage of exhaustion they were unable to give coherent details of what had occurred, and could only say that their ship had been sunk, " along with all the rest," in action with " the whole Japanese fleet."   Further particulars were promised in a later cable, but before this arrived the dread news of disaster was confirmed by a brief but pregnant official bulletin from Tokyo, which is here quoted in full :

" In the forenoon of March 6 our South Sea naval forces, under the command of Vice-Admiral Hiraga, encountered the American Asiatic Squadron outside Manila Bay.   By skilful manœuvres it was brought to action under favourable conditions, the battle lasting three hours.   The enemy force was totally destroyed, in spite of a brave defence.   We sank five cruisers, one large auxiliary, nine destroyers and several submarines.   Two store ships were sunk and one was captured.   A number of prisoners have been taken.   Our losses are small.   Operations in the Southern Seas are continuing to our advantage.

Japanese war bulletins have never erred on the side
of verbosity, but as a rule they are very much to the
point. This one was no exception. It told in plain
terms of the annihilation of the only American naval
force in the Far East, and, consequently, the only force
which had been available for the floating defence of the
Philippines. The islands, being thus deprived of all
means of protection by naval power, were now exposed
to the full force of Japanese attack. It is true that some
resistance could be offered by the shore batteries and
mine-fields, but that these could long withstand a determined onslaught by such forces as the enemy would be
certain to bring against them, no one in Washington
believed. Tragedies have often been foreseen before
they actually occurred, but the feelings they evoke are
none the less poignant on that account. The bad news
from the Far East sent a wave of grief over the United
States. For the time being little heed was paid to the
peril which menaced the Philippines. The country was
thinking of those thousands of gallant seamen who had
gone to their doom, fighting to the last against tremendous odds, with the old flag still flying as the waters closed
above the torn and battered hulls of their ships. But
the first thrill of horror was succeeded by a stern resolve
to see this struggle through to the bitter end. However
protracted the war might be, however costly in blood
and treasure, it would be waged with the combined might
of the whole nation until the sword was struck from the
enemy's grasp and he was forced to sue for peace.
And it was in that spirit that the American people waited
for further details of the tragedy of Manila, which to
them, if not to their leaders, had come like a bolt from
the blue.

CHAPTER III

U.S. Asiatic Squadron attacked by superior Japanese fleet—Majority of the American ships destroyed—Japanese prepare to invade Philippines—U.S. preparations to receive them

IT is clear from the private letters of Rear-Admiral Ribley, made public after his death, that he fully recognised the desperate situation in which his squadron would be placed if it had to await attack by the Japanese fleet. In a letter dated March 3, 1931, he wrote: " I have been ordered to concentrate at Manila, to assist the land defences in repelling the Japanese invasion which is momentarily expected. We have had no news from home since yesterday, as all radio messages taken in are incoherent and unreadable, and the cable went out of business last night. Consequently we do not know if war has been declared; but apart from this interference with our communications, which can only be the work of the Japanese, there is something in the air which tells us the fight is about to begin. Of course, with our handful of old ships we cannot do much against Japanese dreadnoughts, but we shall sell our lives dearly. I do not take my orders to mean that I am to remain in Manila Bay itself. That would be to repeat the suicidal blunder of the Spaniards in 1898. So the whole squadron is to leave as soon as we have coaled, which I expect will be about noon to-morrow. I shall then cruise off the coast and await developments. Our aircraft should give us early warning of the enemy's approach. If he is accompanied by troop transports, we shall try and sink as many of these as we possibly can before going under. But I am afraid he will not

32

bring troops along until he has disposed of our squadron. If only we had a couple of fast, well-armed ships, we might make a fight for it, but as things are we are in a tight corner; but at any rate we will keep the flag flying to the last." In modern naval warfare there is not much room for the " fighting chance " which in former days sometimes enabled brave men to win victory in the teeth of fearful odds. The fleet which has the best ships and the heaviest guns is practically certain to win once battle has been joined, provided its officers and men are up to the average standard of efficiency. Courage of the highest order, dauntless resolution, superlative seamanship—all these qualities count for little against a crushing preponderance of material. It should therefore have been obvious to Admiral Morrison, the Chief of Naval Operations, that in ordering the Asiatic fleet to remain in the Philippines he was dooming it to destruction. As we now know, a belief was cherished in Washington that, as at Chemulpo in 1904, the Japanese would make a combined naval and military attack on the islands, in which case they would have to bring crowded transports with the fleet. If that were done the American squadron, small though it was, might be able to inflict sufficient damage to compensate for its own destruction. But this theory of a combined attack postulated a very imperfect knowledge of the laws of strategy on the part of the Japanese. In all their previous campaigns they had shown themselves well acquainted with those laws, and there was no reason to suppose they would ignore them now. If they did attempt to throw troops ashore in the Philippines before the American squadron had been disposed of, it could only be because they feared the arrival of reinforcements from the United States, and wished to make themselves masters of the islands before these could come on the scene. But, in fact, there was no such imperative need for haste. At least three weeks must elapse ere a large American fleet, attended by its slow fuel ships and other essential auxiliaries, could cross the Pacific even if it steamed

D

all the way at its highest collective speed and was not
molested *en route*. But although they doubted whether
the American battle fleet would be despatched to Asiatic
waters, the Japanese had made all preparations to
receive it, and could count with confidence on delaying
its arrival until they had worked their will in the Philippines. So when Vice-Admiral Hiraga steamed south
to settle accounts with the American Asiatic fleet he
took no military transports with him. His force consisted of three battle-cruisers—*Kongo* (flagship), *Hiyei*,
and *Kirishima ;* six light cruisers, twenty-four destroyers
and the airplane carrier *Hosho*. The speed of the
slowest ship was 25 knots. The disparity between this
fleet and the American squadron was immense. Admiral
Ribley's two armoured cruisers had a nominal speed of
22 knots, but so long as the squadron kept together
its pace must be regulated by that of the slowest unit,
and the three old cruisers of the " Denver " class were
not good for more than 15 knots. In gun power the
Japanese superiority was overwhelming. Counting only
heavy pieces, they had twenty-four 14-inch guns,
which could range up to 24,000 yards; to which the
Americans could oppose but four 10-inch and four 8-inch
guns, whose extreme range was 15,000 yards. As the
three old " Denver " cruisers simply did not count as
fighting units, the only other vessels that could play
any useful *rôle* in action were the ten destroyers, three
light mine-layers, and twelve submarines. There was
also the airplane carrier *Curtiss*, a 22-knot ship which
carried fourteen planes, six of which were equipped for
torpedo attack. Had Admiral Ribley chosen to remain
inside Manila Bay he would probably have been safe
for the time being, for the Japanese, knowing 12-inch
guns to be mounted in the batteries of Corregidor
which guard the entrance, would have hesitated to
send in their big ships. But if the squadron stayed at
Manila there was very little chance of its ever coming
out again, as the enemy would be sure to seal the channel
with mines laid by submarines, besides keeping a strong
blockading force near at hand. And with the American

squadron safely bottled up there would be nothing to
stop the Japanese transports from putting to sea. The
investment of Port Arthur in 1904 had provided ample
warning of what would follow. Landing, as it was
expected to do, at points on the coast of Luzon well
away from the batteries at Manila, the invading army
would advance towards that city and bring the bay
under artillery fire, making it a deathtrap for the
American ships. As the garrison of Luzon, including
native troops, did not exceed 17,000 men, they could
not hope to fight more than a delaying action against
an army of 80,000, which was the minimum number
the Japanese were expected to send. When all these
facts are given due weight, Admiral Ribley's decision
to meet the enemy outside Manila is seen to have been
the soundest one that was possible under the circumstances. So long as his ships remained above water
they constituted a " fleet in being," and therefore a
hindrance—albeit a feeble one—to invasion. At dusk
on March 5 an American airplane sighted the smoke
of a large fleet 200 miles due west of Cape Bogeador.
On approaching to reconnoitre more closely it was
chased and fired on by three machines marked with
the Japanese cockade, and only escaped by its superior
speed. The first shots of the war were thus fired in
the clouds. A radio message from the air scout notified
Admiral Ribley of the enemy's approach. Other
American planes which went up before dawn on the
6th soon made contact with the Japanese fleet. At
5 a.m. it was observed west of Lingayen Bay, steering
S.S.E. The three battle-cruisers were in line ahead,
with the light cruisers and destroyers screening them
from submarine attack. Astern of the third battle-
cruiser was the airplane carrier, *Hosho*, several of whose
chaser machines were flying ahead of the fleet. In view
of the necessity of conserving all aircraft for defence
purposes, the American pilots had been ordered to
avoid action, and this they did, confining themselves
to long-distance observation of the enemy's movements. Admiral Ribley by now had made his dis-

positions.   At 8 a.m. he was 10 miles N.W. of Lubang Island.   His squadron was complete save for the *Cleveland*, this cruiser having been sent back to Cavite on account of engine trouble, which reduced her speed to 10 knots.   Six submarines, detached the previous evening, were now patrolling independently off the south-west coast of Luzon, with orders to attack the enemy's large ships if a good opportunity offered.   The other six submarines were cruising between Subig Bay and Verde Island.   A report came in from the air scouts at 9.15 that the Japanese fleet was firing heavily at some unseen target, probably a submarine.   The thunder of the guns was clearly audible in the American ships, where the men waited with tense nerves for the first sight of their foe.   Two Japanese airplanes were now seen approaching at high speed, one of which dropped a bomb as it crossed the American ships. This missile struck the water some 200 yards astern of the flagship.   Planes from the *Curtiss*, which had been patrolling on the 8,000 foot level for the past hour, intercepted and shot down one of the enemy machines. At 10.20 smoke was visible from the control top of the *Missoula*, and a few minutes later the dim shapes of the Japanese battle-cruisers loomed on the horizon. Graphic accounts of the action that now took place have been published since the war by survivors of the American squadron.   The following is an abridged version of the narrative by Lieutenant Elkins, who was present in the flagship *Missoula* as aide to Admiral Ribley :—

> " We were leading the line, if you could call that a ' line ' which included but two ships, our own and the *Frederick*.   The *Galveston*, *Denver*, and *Curtiss*, being ships of no fighting power, were steaming 4,000 yards away on our port beam, where we thought they would be safe from ' overs,' and yet near enough, as the Admiral grimly remarked, ' to pick us up if we go swimming.'   The destroyers were ahead of us in two groups, to port

and starboard, where they were in a position to engage the Japanese torpedo craft if these should try to attack. At 10.30 the control top gave us the range as 24,000 yards. The Admiral and I were at this time standing on the after bridge. So clear was the atmosphere that the silhouettes of the Japanese ships were sharply defined, and with our glasses we could even see the big guns in the battle-cruisers being trained. Our information was that their 14-inch had an extreme range of 23,000 yards, but this must have been an underestimate, for the first shots came when our instruments registered 24,000 yards, and they fell pretty close. As we were watching the leading ship, which we took to be the *Kongo*, we saw a single flash from her forward turret. Some 45 seconds later there was a roaring sound like an express train, and a giant spout rose from the sea about 600 yards to starboard. After this the enemy was silent for a couple of minutes, during which we turned several points to port to keep the range open as much as possible, our destroyers meanwhile having put up a big smoke screen. At 10.45 the *Kongo* let us have a 4-gun salvo, and a moment later the other two battle-cruisers joined in. The air was full of noise as the huge 1400-pounder projectiles roared overhead. They missed us clean, though the splash of one shell was close enough to wet the quarterdeck. We were just going into the conning-tower when I turned to look back at the *Frederick*, and at that instant saw a sheet of flame burst from her side. She must have been hit amidships in the 6-inch battery by a high-explosive shell which detonated just inside the thin armour. As I watched, two more shells burst aboard her, both well forward, but I could not wait to see what damage had been done. We had not yet been hit, for the enemy seemed to be concentrating on the *Frederick*, which he may have mistaken for the flagship. The range was now 21,000 yards—far too long for our pop-guns; but the strain of being under heavy fire without the ability to reply was so wearing that the Admiral gave orders for our after 10-inch turret to try a few shots, ' just to quieten the men,' as he put it. Needless to say, the spotter reported all rounds short of the target, but it was certainly some relief to hear our guns going. We received our first hit at 10.53, a shell coming in obliquely a few feet from the bows but well above the water-line, exploding with sufficient force to blow up a considerable stretch of the forecastle deck. A report now came from the top that the *Frederick* was in difficulties, with two funnels shot away and heavily on fire aft. Although still on an even keel she was low in the water, and must have been badly hit on or below her armour belt. Now as the enemy, with his far superior speed, could have closed the range and finished us off long before this had he so desired, it was evident that he was treating the affair as a long-range battle shoot to give his gunners practice. But this did not suit the Admiral's book. If we were not to perish ignominiously, without striking a single blow before we went, our only chance was to steam in until our guns would bear, taking the risk of getting smashed up while so doing. We accordingly turned to starboard and worked up to our full speed of 21 knots. Whether the unexpectedness of this manœuvre took the enemy by surprise, or whether he thought he would let us rush on to destruction, I cannot tell; but it is certain that we got to within 15,000 yards of his line without being seriously hit. Both our turrets were now firing with the utmost rapidity, and even the 6-inch starboard battery joined in, though in their case it was probably wasted ammunition. We got at least one hit on the *Kongo*, for I saw a big explosion at the base of her second funnel, and she seemed to sheer a little out of line. But this was as far as we were allowed to go. Thinking he had given us enough rope, the Japanese admiral must have decided to end the game without further ado. What followed is beyond description; all around us the sea spouted and boiled; there were half a dozen terrific explosions in as many seconds; I heard one appalling crash as if a giant redwood tree had toppled athwart our deck; then there was a blaze of light, another ear-splitting crash, and everything came to an end for me. When I recovered my senses I was being dragged into a boat from the destroyer *Hulbert*. They told me the flagship had foundered at 11.30, having been practically blown to pieces. There were only six survivors besides myself. The Admiral had gone down with the ship; probably he had been killed by the shell that knocked me senseless. Someone must have dragged me out of the conning-tower, but I never discovered who it was. From our boat we could see the Japanese sweeping up the remnants of our squadron. Shortly before the flagship went down, the *Frederick* had blown up with all hands. We could see the *Denver* lying over on her beam ends, on fire from stem to stern. Near by was the *Galveston* in action with Japanese light cruisers, which were absolutely pumping shell into her. Even as we watched she put her bows deep under, the stern came up, and she took her last dive. About 4 miles ahead a fierce fight was raging between five of our destroyers and thrice that number of enemy boats, but we could see little of the details. We heard afterwards that only four of the thirteen destroyers and light mine-layers that came out with us ever got back to Cavite. While watching this scene we heard the drone of airplanes above us, and looking up saw four machines which someone in the boat said were ours. They were, in fact, torpedo-planes from the *Curtiss*, which ship, seeing herself about to be attacked by Japanese cruisers, had flown off all the planes then on deck. The *Curtiss* was sunk by gunfire shortly afterwards, but meanwhile her planes were having a last try for the enemy. We could see them making straight for the Japanese battle-cruisers, which were just visible from the boat. As we heard subsequently, two were shot down before reaching their objective; but one of the remaining machines got her torpedo fairly home on the *Hiyei*, while the other, by great good luck, torpedoed and sank the scout cruiser *Tatsuta*. The *Hiyei*, though seriously damaged, appears to have returned to Japan under her own steam. At 2.30 p.m. the Japanese destroyer *Yanagi* bore down on our boat and took us on board, whence we were transferred that evening to the battle-cruiser *Kirishima*, and treated with all proper courtesy. Such was the Battle of Lubang, as I saw it. Our squadron had been wiped out, and upwards of 2,500 gallant comrades had fallen, but at least we could say that we had upheld the honour of the flag. The only Japanese ships sunk were the *Tatsuta* and two destroyers. Their casualties throughout the fleet were returned as 600. But considering the enormous disparity between their force and ours it was remarkable that they suffered any loss at all."

During the action itself none of the American submarines had found an opportunity to attack. But at 10 o'clock the same night, submarines *S 18* and *S 23*, being then in company some 30 miles S.S.W. of Subig Bay, observed several large ships steaming towards them and promptly dived to attack. These were the Japanese battle-cruisers going north again, at low speed, on account of injuries to the *Hiyei*. In spite of a strong destroyer screen both submarines carried out their attack, firing six torpedoes in all. One of these struck the *Kirishima*, but so far forward that the damage was inconsiderable. Two torpedoes from *S 18*, aimed at the *Kongo*, passed astern of her and hit the large destroyer *Hamakaze*, which sank in a few minutes.

Although many depth charges were dropped, both submarines made good their escape.

The destruction of Admiral Ribley's squadron left the way open for the invasion of the Philippines. Ere yet the last battered American ship had vanished from sight a radio message from the Japanese Commander-in-Chief set in motion the fleet of transports which had been lying at Kure and other ports for some days past, with a hundred thousand fighting men on board. The whole convoy, with its naval and air escort, was under way at dusk on March 6. Steaming south at a speed of 12 knots, it was timed to reach the shores of Luzon in four and a half days. And except for a few destroyers and submarines the nearest American warships were at Hawaii, nearly five thousand miles distant. The invading force outnumbered the American garrison in Luzon by at least six to one, it had a proportionate superiority in artillery and other equipment, and there were the guns of half the Japanese fleet to cover its landing. In case of need, reinforcements in men and material could be rushed from Japan in 20-knot ships in the space of three days, or from the advanced base at Formosa in thirty-six hours. Everything, therefore, favoured the Japanese enterprise. It has since been admitted that active preparations for the conquest of the Philippines had begun in the third week of February : well in advance, that is, of the actual declaration of war. The Army Transport Section at Tokyo had on its books upwards of 100 vessels with a sea speed of 14 knots or more, all of which could be requisitioned by the Government if required. But to do this would have caused a serious dislocation of the shipping industry, while the sudden withdrawal of all the fastest Japanese merchant ships from their ordinary routes must have inevitably aroused suspicion abroad and led to the inference that some great military undertaking was in view. It was accordingly decided not to use fast ships for the transport of the Philippine Expeditionary Force, but to employ instead the requisite number of slower vessels, with a collective speed of 12 knots.

This, of course, entailed a longer passage, but calculating on the destruction of the United States Asiatic squadron, and knowing that American reinforcements from the Eastern Pacific, in the unlikely event of their coming at all, could not arrive for several weeks, the Japanese military command was ready to accept the slight delay involved by the use of slower transports. The Expeditionary Force was composed of five divisions, with an approximate strength of 100,000 men. A Japanese division is usually made up of two brigades of infantry, one regiment each of cavalry and artillery, one battalion each of engineers and train, together with chemical warfare (gas) and motor machine-gun sections. Four tank regiments accompanied the expedition, with a total of thirty light " Atsuta " tanks, which could travel over level ground at 12 miles an hour. Large motor-propelled barges or pontoons were carried on board the transports for landing tanks and artillery. The heaviest guns were 8-inch howitzers and 14-centimetre high-velocity pieces for long-range bombardment. Besides the naval aircraft carrier *Matsushima,* which had been detailed to sail with the convoy and had a complement of 20 planes, five transports were loaded up with army aircraft, the total number of planes at the disposal of the invaders being well over 180. While some of the larger vessels carried as many as 3,000 men, the average capacity of the transports was 2,000. As landings on a supposed hostile coast had been practised year after year as a regular feature of Japanese army manœuvres, this operation was one with which officers and men were perfectly familiar. All necessary equipment for such work—boats, barges, pontoons, and portable jetties—had been in readiness at the military depôts for years. In the same way the tactical problems of co-operation between an invading army and its supporting fleet had been thoroughly worked out long beforehand. In their wars with Russia in 1904–05 and with China ten years earlier, the Japanese had shown remarkable skill in throwing large bodies of troops ashore with speed and safety. This time, of course, the landing was likely to be opposed, but as the American garrison was small, and could have no fore-knowledge of the exact place where the troops would be disembarked, the resistance was not expected to be of a very formidable nature. To the Japanese general staff the defences of the Philippines were an open book. Every yard of the ground had been personally surveyed and mapped by Japanese officers. Not only was the site and armament of every existing battery known with exactitude, but every position where a new battery might be placed was clearly marked on the large-scale maps prepared at the Imperial Staff College in Tokyo. At no time had a landing been con-templated in the near vicinity of Manila. Strong batteries, equipped with 12-inch rifles on disappearing mounts, were in position on the island of Corregidor, while others crowned the headlands on either side of the 12-mile entrance to the bay. As these pieces could sweep the sea over a radius of many miles, it would have been madness to expose warships, let alone crowded transports, to their devastating fire. To silence them by naval bombardment was out of the question. Their massive concrete emplacements were shell-proof : nothing short of a direct hit on the gun itself or its mounting would be effective, and as the piece showed above the parapet only for a few seconds at a time, it offered a hopeless target. Against bomb attack from the air the batteries were protected by strong shields of steel. Nor were these guns the only peril that menaced hostile ships seeking to penetrate the bay. Lying across the entrance were several rows of mines, through which no channel could be swept so long as the batteries on the heights remained in American hands. At Subig Bay, some forty miles up the coast, other batteries and mine-fields were in position, but this place, within which the old American naval station of Olongapo was situated, was also given a wide berth. With so many other landing places available, where no fixed defences existed, the Japanese saw no reason for exposing their ships to the guns and mines of fortified harbours. The chief danger, they perceived, would come from the American aircraft, and, as events were to prove, their information as to the number of these was at fault. According to the last report from Japanese agents, not more than fifty serviceable planes were in the islands at the end of February. But on the 25th of that month a transport had arrived at Manila bringing thirty machines of a new and powerful type. These, as we shall see, played a very important part in the defence of Luzon. The American military force did not exceed 17,000 all told. Eight thousand of these were United States regulars—infantry, artillery, and engineers—two thousand were marines, and the remainder native troops, Philippine scouts and militia. There were ten field batteries of four guns each, three mountain batteries, and a dozen mobile 6-inch guns on caterpillar mounts. The artillery establishment was completed by six 8-inch guns on railway mounts, which could be sent at a good speed to any point along the line and fired direct from the rails. It was hoped by means of these guns to bring the enemy ships under heavy fire if they attempted to disembark troops along the north-west coast of the island, to which the railroad ran parallel. Finally, there were the surviving four destroyers and twelve submarines, whose officers and men (now under the orders of Captain Gurner of the *Cleveland*) were burning to avenge their fallen comrades of the cruiser squadron. When news of the disaster to Rear-Admiral Ribley's command reached Manila the same evening (March 6), it was patent to everyone that an invasion was impending. The blow might fall at any moment, for nothing seemed more probable than that the transports of the invading army were already approaching the coast. Actually, as we know, their sailing from Kure had been deferred until news of the American squadron's destruction reached Japan; but of this fact the defenders were naturally ignorant. All that night, and throughout the days and nights that followed, aircraft and submarines maintained between them a sleepless watch over the northern approaches to Luzon. As there was no telling from which quarter the invaders would appear, the submarine flotilla was divided, five boats remaining on the west coast, five going to form a line of patrol east of Cape Engaño, and the remaining two (*S 11* and *S 15*) being sent north to cruise in the Balingtang Channel, through which the Japanese transports might be expected to pass on their way south.

CHAPTER IV

MARCH, 1931

Japanese transports attacked by American aircraft and submarines on reaching Philippines—Landings effected despite heavy casualties—Desperate resistance of American Army—Surrender of Manila—A few light craft escape—Philippines entirely conquered by the Japanese—Absence of news from Guam causes concern in the United States

EARLY on the morning of March 11 American airplanes from Luzon sighted several warships 50 miles N.W. of Santa Cruz, steaming S.E. They were soon identified as the battle cruisers *Kongo* and *Haruna*, with many smaller vessels. This squadron was so well screened by its destroyers and light cruisers that no chance of submarine attack was offered, even had any of the American boats been in the immediate neighbourhood. Since these ships were evidently the vanguard of the fleet which was to cover the landing of the invading army, all U.S. aircraft within call of the Santa Cruz area were immediately ordered to attack. But a few minutes after this order had been issued, a radio signal from the station at Cape Engaño reported that a large fleet of ships had been sighted by aircraft 50 miles east of that point, making for the southward. Almost before this message had been read and its significance noted, a further report came in, announcing the approach of " a large fleet " towards Cape Bolinao. There could be no doubt as to the portent of these messages. The Japanese obviously designed to make landings on both sides of the island, no doubt simultaneously, thereby compelling the garrison to split up its meagre forces and resist an onslaught by overwhelming numbers at two points on the coast, one in the east and the other

46

in the west. General O'Neill, the Commander-in-Chief of the U.S. military forces, lost no time in taking what steps he could to meet this emergency. The order for airplanes to attack the enemy warships off Santa Cruz was negatived; every machine must be held ready to launch itself against the transports. At the same time all submarines were called up by Captain Gurner and given the position of the three enemy formations which had been sighted. If the ships seen off Cape Bolinao were transports, as appeared probable, they were most likely making for Lingayen Gulf, within which good landing beaches were to be found. To meet the contingency of a descent at one or more of these points, two of the 8-inch railroad guns were rushed north up the line as fast as a locomotive could take them, while aircraft were concentrated at Dagupan. The destination of the vessels which had passed Cape Engaño might be any one of the half-dozen bays or inlets on the eastern littoral, but it was rightly conjectured that they were making for some point well to the south, since Manila must surely be the ultimate objective of any force landed. At 11 a.m. on March 11, the Japanese warships already mentioned approached Santa Cruz until within easy range and fired a few shells into the town, destroying the telegraph station and several houses. This bombardment was so obviously a ruse to draw the defenders away from other parts of the coast that it failed in its purpose. Receiving no answer to their fire, the ships steamed south at high speed, leaving several of their escort planes to engage an American airman who had come out from Iba to keep the squadron under observation. For a time it was thought to be making for Manila, but it soon turned north again and was lost to sight. And now, for the first time, the enemy showed his hand. At 3 p.m. a flight of American planes patrolling between Cape Bolinao and San Fernando was suddenly and fiercely attacked by Japanese machines. While this combat was in progress, more enemy planes came over the land, passed up the river, and heavily bombed the aerodrome at Dagupan. They were followed by Japanese cruisers and destroyers, which approached to within a few thousand yards of Lingayen, firing salvos of gas and high explosive shell into the American positions, and being fired at in return by field guns and howitzers. As dusk was almost at hand, it looked as though the enemy meant to make his landing under cover of darkness. At 5 o'clock aircraft sighted two lines of transports steaming up the bay behind a dense wall of smoke, put up by destroyers which preceded them. This was the moment for which the American airmen held in reserve had been impatiently waiting. Twenty of them were already soaring at 10,000 feet, and as many more left the ground as soon as the signal was given. A few minutes later, and all were driving straight for the Japanese transports through a terrific barrage of shell from the anti-aircraft guns of the warships. The enemy planes that tried to stay their headlong course were evaded as far as possible; for there was more urgent business in hand than duelling in mid-air. Once past the smoke screen the transports were in full view—twenty-four big ships, all crowded with men, slowly advancing up the bay in two columns line abreast. Planing down in wide spirals the American flyers discharged their bombs at a height of only a few thousand feet. This brought them within range of machine-gun and rifle fire, so that the air was alive with bullets. But nothing could stop men who had resolved to do the utmost harm to the enemy, cost what it might to themselves. Clear above the thud of anti-aircraft guns and the rattle of small-arms came the crash of detonating bombs. The largest transport in the first column was the N.Y.K. steamer *Sado Maru*, her decks brown with masses of khaki-clad troops. As the first plane crossed the line three 500-pounder demolition bombs plunged into this ship, and in an instant she was transformed into a floating shambles. Hundreds of men were blown to fragments, as many more lay in ghastly heaps, maimed and shattered by the explosions, while a pillar of dense smoke rising amidships told of a fire caused by one of the bombs which had burst below deck in a compartment filled with inflammable stores. Of the ten other transports in which bombs took effect, all suffered terrible casualties. The *Wakasa Maru* was so badly holed that she foundered in a few minutes, with the loss of half her complement of 2,200 soldiers. In another ship, the *Tsubari Maru*, phosphorus bombs set fire to large petrol tanks in the hold, flames from which speedily enveloped the hull from end to end, driving all the men overboard. Besides the casualties to *personnel*, much damage was inflicted on the equipment, boats, and other landing gear which lay on the decks of the transports. It was afterwards claimed by the aviators who carried out this first attack that if a hundred machines had been available, instead of only forty, the Japanese transport fleet would have been practically wiped out and the landing frustrated; nor, in view of the extensive havoc they caused, could this claim be disputed. Even as it was, the enemy had lost more than 6,000 men killed and wounded or drowned; much of his equipment was destroyed, and so many boats and barges were smashed that the process of getting the troops ashore was delayed for several hours. But the American airmen had shot their bolt. Considering the low altitude from which they had attacked and the intensity of the fire brought to bear against them, it was a miracle that any one of the forty machines returned. Twenty-five of them were brought down, seven more were so badly damaged that they crashed on landing, and only eight got back to the aerodrome in a fit state to ascend again. But though a shrewd blow had been delivered at the enemy, his advance was not arrested. Still screened from the view of the defenders ashore, the transports moved steadily in behind a rolling barrage of smoke. And now an iron hail smote the American trenches as the battleships lying well out in the gulf sent salvo after salvo of heavy shell screaming over the transports, this long-range covering fire being directed with great precision by spotting aircraft. But the defenders, on their

E

part, were not idle. Somewhere behind that opaque wall of smoke the transports were coming on; perhaps they were even now transferring their men to boats for the final dash ashore. Targets might be invisible for the moment, but they were there all the same, and every gun was brought into action against them. At this time the two 8-inch railway pieces were up the line 20 miles north-east of Dagupan, and were thus in a position to open a flanking fire on the transports as the latter steamed further in to the shore. Fire had been already opened on several ships that loomed dimly through the smoke, and the two guns were being moved south again to keep them bearing, when a stretch of the railroad line was found to have been torn up near San Fabian by the explosion of a ground mine. This damage, which could not have been done more than an hour beforehand, was clearly the work of spies. It had the effect of eliminating the two most powerful guns possessed by the defence, for they were unable to come further south, and the point where they were held up by the broken line was too far removed from the landing beaches to permit of effective fire. By now the Japanese disembarkation was in full swing. Night had fallen, and although the smoke screen was thinning, as the vessels that made it were now in shoal water and had to turn back, it was still dense enough to baffle the American searchlights and star shell. On the stroke of 8 o'clock the first party of invaders broke through the screen and headed straight for the beach. On they came in boats towed by launches and in motor barges, which hurled smoke bombs from mortars in the bows. The battleships out in the gulf had now suspended their fire, but light cruisers and destroyers offshore still kept up a brisk cannonade. The American trenches and batteries had been bombarded incessantly for four hours, and had suffered heavily during this period; but if the enemy counted on meeting with no resistance he was sharply undeceived. As the first boats emerged from the pall of smoke they came under a tornado of fire from artillery and machine-guns. Many were sunk;

others, in which the occupants had all been stricken down, drifted aimlessly about; but the rest pushed on doggedly until the keels grounded on the beach, when the little men in khaki tumbled over the side and came plunging through the surf, holding rifles and cartridge pouches above their heads, and uttering staccato war cries. Scourged by a cross-fire that cut men down in swathes, the human wave came steadily on, spreading up the foreshore, now lapping the American front trenches, and then flowing over them. Fresh boatloads landed, another flame-tipped wave surged up the beach, and the barrage fire from the smaller warships in the offing was lifted as the attack penetrated deeper inland. In rather less than an hour after the first troops had come ashore the enemy had gained a firm foothold over a wide front, and by now his guns and light tanks were landing across the pontoon bridges which the engineers had laid out with extraordinary speed. All four lines of American trenches were in Japanese hands. Having been hastily thrown up only a few days previously, when Dagupan was first suggested as a likely venue for the enemy's landing, they were badly sited and too shallow, nor was there enough wire to protect the entire front. Such entanglements as there were had been breached at half a dozen points by the naval bombardment, which had also levelled the trenches in many parts. Nevertheless, behind these wretched defences the American troops and their Filipino comrades had fought so stoutly that the invaders lost 2,000 men in storming them. The Americans had also suffered severely, both from the bombardment and the subsequent attack : of the 5,000 officers and men who had waited for the enemy that afternoon, only 2,000 were left unwounded. Colonel Abney, the senior surviving officer, realising the futility of further resistance, now decided to disengage and retreat towards the south, where he could join up with General O'Neill's force that was covering Manila. But the withdrawal did not proceed unmolested. All that night as the weary men tramped along the Tarlac road they were harassed by

Japanese airplanes, which lighted up the scene with magnesium flares, dropped numerous bombs, and sometimes swooped down to use their machine-guns. With daybreak came the first Japanese tanks, five of which overtook the rearguard and had cut it to pieces before they were driven off by field guns. As the Americans retreated they tore up the railroad behind them. It had been damaged at several places by enemy aircraft, and two trains which left Calasiao shortly before midnight were now lying wrecked between San Carlos and Malasiqui, having been bombed at close range. While these events were happening in the north the second Japanese fleet of twenty-five transports had been steaming down the east coast of Luzon. At 9 a.m. on March 12th it was off Polillo Island, with its escort of cruisers, torpedo-boats, and aircraft. For more than 50 miles the armada had been shadowed by two United States submarines, *S 11* and *S 15*, but so far there had been no opportunity to attack. Leaving Polillo on the starboard hand, the fleet turned to the west and ran past Jomalig Island. As this movement was being executed one of the leading transports appeared to develop engine-room trouble, for she suddenly sheered out of station and was all but rammed by her next astern, the whole line being thrown momentarily into confusion. This gave the watchful submarines their chance. Diving to periscope depth they came within a thousand yards before making their attack. Eight torpedoes were launched before the enemy had the least inkling of his danger. Set for a high-speed run at short range the deadly missiles travelled straight and true for the mark, and six muffled explosions showed that that number at least had got home. Four of the transports were hit at this first discharge. The *Sendai Maru*, with two torpedoes in her hull, listed heavily to port and was plainly doomed. Ahead of her, the *Osaka Maru* lay helpless with her propellers blown away and a second torpedo in the boiler-room. Further down the line the *Hanno Maru* and *Aso Maru* were both in difficulties, the first-named down by the head, the second with a gaping rent in her side amidships. The latter was eventually beached and repaired. While two of the Japanese destroyers went alongside the sinking *Sendai Maru* to take off her troops, the others raced madly about in search of the hidden submarines, their depth charges throwing up vast geysers on every hand. But immediately after making their attack the submarines had dived to 150 feet, reloading their torpedo tubes as they went. The *S 11*, although badly shaken by a depth charge which exploded near enough to throw everyone in the boat off his feet, was kept well under control, and ten minutes later was " browning " the rear transports with four more torpedoes. As she did so, *S 15* came into action a mile ahead, and again the thunder of detonating torpedoes reverberated over the sea. This time three ships were hit. One sank in a few minutes, before anything could be done to save the troops on board; another showed signs of settling by the stern, while the third, though her engines were disabled, did not appear to be mortally injured. Just as *S 15* fired her last torpedo a Japanese destroyer sped down the track of air bubbles at 35 knots and let go two depth charges. The concussion was so powerful that the submarine was lifted almost bodily out of the water, and as she broke surface her hull was instantly riddled with shell from the destroyer's guns. The hatch was thrown open, and one man scrambled out, but at that moment more projectiles crashed through the sides of the wounded vessel and with a last convulsive plunge she vanished for ever. The sole survivor, a young seaman, was picked up by one of the destroyers. In the meantime *S 11*, ignorant of the fate of her consort, had again dived to reload her tubes. Her commanding officer, Lieutenant Hockley, must have known the imminent danger he courted by remaining in the vicinity, now that the Japanese destroyers were racing about in all directions and lynx-eyed watchers in the airplanes overhead were scanning the sea. But doubtless he knew, also, the vital importance of doing as much harm as possible to the invading force before it reached land. Be that as it may, he decided to expend his last four torpedoes before leaving the scene. As his submerged speed was too low to permit him to overtake the uninjured transports, which were now far ahead, steaming for dear life, he turned his attention to the damaged ships. On the first of these he got two hits. Then a depth charge shook the boat so violently that a bad leak was started—or so it was surmised—and she was compelled to come to the surface. She rose rather more than a mile away from the nearest destroyer, and owing to the excitement of the hunt, or more probably to the mist which still partly shrouded the water, she was not immediately observed by her pursuers. And now followed what the Japanese themselves acclaimed as one of the most heroic deeds of the war. Had Lieutenant Hockley so desired, he and his men might have surrendered with perfect safety, for the Japanese were chivalrous warriors who would assuredly have treated such doughty foemen with all honour. The submarine was disabled, since it could neither dive nor travel on the surface; but one weapon remained, and with it the chance of striking a last blow at the enemy. There is not the least doubt that Lieutenant Hockley and his crew deliberately elected to seize this chance, which, of course, meant certain death to one and all of them. No sooner, then, did the submarine break surface than the hatches were thrown open, ammunition was handed up from below, and the 4-inch gun opened rapid fire on the nearest transport. If those on board the Japanese destroyers were amazed at this unexpected attack, they did not lose their presence of mind. In a flash, two of them had spun round and were charging straight down on the audacious submarine, which lay motionless on the surface, her gun belching forth shell after shell. It took barely two minutes for the Japanese greyhounds to cover the intervening distance, yet in that brief space of time the submarine fired many more rounds from her gun, and even scored a hit on the foremost destroyer. As a display of iron nerve and consummate courage, that of the gunners of *S 11*, who continued to work their piece as coolly as though at target practice, while every second brought the onrushing death nearer, has rarely been equalled, never surpassed. The only accounts we have of this heroic drama of the sea are from Japanese eye-witnesses, who, however, have done ample justice to it. One of the destroyer officers tells the following story of the last moments of *S 11*:— " As we raced on at full speed, the submarine, which up to then had fired at the transport *Ilsen Maru*, now trained her single gun on us, and let us have two shells, which killed several men. She fired again but missed, and then we were upon her. There were many sailors on deck, including those at the gun, and an officer stood on the conning-tower with his arms folded. They had no idea of surrendering, for a fresh charge was being placed in the gun just as we struck the vessel. Our sharp prow drove deep into the plating just abaft the conning-tower, cutting the submarine almost in two. She sank like a stone, and the momentum of our rush carried us some distance before we could return to the spot, which was marked by large air-bubbles and a widening patch of oil. One survivor was seen and picked up unconscious, only to die soon afterwards in spite of all our surgeon could do. The others must have been drawn down by the suction, for we never saw them after the collision. Thus perished a gallant ship and her crew ! " But seldom has an act of self-sacrifice in war borne richer fruit. These two submarines of medium size had inflicted terrible punishment on the Japanese convoy. Five transports had been sunk or reduced to sinking condition ; two more were so badly damaged that they had to be taken in tow after the troops on board had been transferred to other ships. The *Hanno Maru*, torpedoed in the initial attack, would have remained afloat had it not been for the shells fired into her later on by the *S 11*, whose gun had been served with deadly effect. How many troops were lost in this daring submarine raid is still a matter for conjecture. The Japanese admitted that 2,000 were drowned, but the actual number, it is believed, was considerably higher. In any case it unquestionably delayed the second landing, and this might have had important consequences had the American forces in Luzon been in greater strength; for the thunder of guns and torpedoes off Jomalig had attracted American air scouts, who judged from the southerly course of the Japanese convoy that it was making for Lamon Bay, and promptly radio-phoned a message to that effect. As soon as this intelligence reached headquarters at Manila a flying column of 4,000 troops, with two field-gun batteries, was sent by railroad to Pagbilao and Laguimanoc, while aircraft were held ready to fly out from Cavite when word came that the transports were approaching land. No mine fields had been laid in Lamon Bay, nor did time permit of this deficiency being remedied. All that could be done was to throw up trenches at certain points inland upon which the invaders might be expected to converge, and dispose the handful of troops to best advantage. There was obviously no chance of stemming the tide of invasion at the seashore, for not only were the Japanese transports estimated to have 50,000 troops on board, but the barrage fire of their escorting vessels would speedily overwhelm the feeble American artillery. In these circumstances, it seemed the soundest strategy to concentrate the defence at Calamba, where the Japanese, marching inland on their way to Manila, would have to pass through a narrow defile. Active opposition at the point of landing was accordingly left to the airmen. It was 5 p.m. on March 12 before the first Japanese warships steamed into Lamon Bay between Calbalete and Alabat Islands. They were heralded by strong squadrons of combat and bombing planes, which penetrated inland with the evident purpose of engaging such American machines as might be up, and so distracting their attention from the transports. Finding no one to oppose them, some of the Japanese aircraft cruised above the landing places at Port Lampon, while others reconnoitred the American position at

Pagbilao and dropped bombs. Still unconvinced that the landing would not be resisted, the destroyers approached to within 2,000 yards of the shore and poured a hot fire into the wooded heights overlooking the port. Not until this cannonade had continued for half-an-hour without drawing a single shot in reply did the transports begin to move in. It was then that the single American air scout, who had maintained his position at an altitude of four miles without being observed, flashed the news to the twenty waiting planes at Pagsanjan. A few minutes later found all of them up and heading for the sea at their maximum speed. But on this occasion the Japanese must have anticipated just such an attack, for they were not caught napping. As the American flyers passed over the coast a strong formation of hostile planes met and engaged them with the utmost fury. A wild *mêlée* now ensued, in which half the American machines were destroyed or sent down out of control, though not without disabling several of their opponents. Ten broke through the enemy formation and sped on towards the transports, coming as they did so under a well-aimed fire from naval anti-aircraft guns, which brought down three more. This left but seven planes in action. Nor were they able to attack under conditions so advantageous as those which their colleagues at Lingayan had turned to such good account on the previous night. Here the transports, being still some distance out, were moving at their best speed : moreover, they had enough sea room to zigzag, and thus hamper the airmen's aim. This notwithstanding, one of them was sunk and three others were damaged by bombs, so that, at a narrow estimate, a thousand or more of the invading troops had been placed *hors de combat*. But on the American side nothing more could be done to hinder the landing. With their naval escort still shelling the deserted heights, and under a strong aerial screen, the transports moved in to discharge their living cargoes. Having no opposition to contend with, the disembarkation proceeded with great rapidity. At dawn on the 13th at least 30,000

troops were ashore, with most of their light artillery
and tanks, and a few hours later the landing was complete. Of the Japanese advance inland, and of the
sanguinary action fought at Calamba, which ended in
the virtual annihilation of the small American force
after a stubborn resistance, it is unnecessary to speak at
any length. The defenders did all that brave men could
have done; but, outnumbered as they were by ten to
one, their position was hopeless from the start. In the
two landings at Lingayan and Lamon respectively and
in the subsequent fighting ashore, the invaders had
suffered, perhaps, 15,000 casualties, a loss out of all
proportion to the size of the defending force. But the
Japanese still had over 80,000 men in the two armies
which were now advancing on Manila simultaneously
from north and south. During the next few days there
were innumerable skirmishes, many of them unrecorded,
between the Japanese advance guards and small parties
of American sharpshooters. But the inevitable end
came on March 19, when General O'Neill, with less than
2,000 fit men left under his command, was forced to
capitulate in order to spare Manila the horrors of bombardment. Although severely censured at the time by
American critics who were ignorant of the circumstances,
this decision was, without doubt, both wise and morally
courageous. Further resistance had become absolutely
impossible; to have attempted it would not only have
led to the useless sacrifice of the few Americans who
remained alive, but brought death and destruction to
the teeming populace of Manila. Five days before the
capitulation, the American destroyers and submarines
in Manila Bay were ordered to break out to Guam.
The majority got through safely, but submarine *S 10*
was blown up on a Japanese mine, and the destroyer
Osborne was chased and sunk by light cruisers. The
old cruiser *Cleveland*, being too slow to run the gauntlet
of the blockading fleet, was scuttled by her crew, as
was *S 19*, whose machinery was out of order. Very
little war booty remained for the victors, General
O'Neill having ordered the demolition of all military

material, such as guns, airplanes, etc., on the eve of the surrender. The Japanese troops, under General Kimura, entered the city on March 20. In recognition of their gallant defence, the American Commander-in-Chief and his staff were permitted to retain their swords.

On the previous day a Japanese expeditionary force, consisting of two divisions—about 50,000 men—had landed at Sindangan Bay, on the island of Mindanao, and was advancing on Zamboanga. As the garrison of Mindanao did not exceed 5,000 men, including militia and constabulary, no effectual resistance could be offered to the invasion. In the course of the same week the islands of Samar and Panay were occupied by smaller Japanese detachments. Cavite, the naval station near Manila, became the headquarters of a submarine flotilla from Sasebo, and more of these vessels were based at Davao Bay (Mindanao). In addition, about 500 military aircraft were assigned to strategic bases in the Archipelago. By the end of March Japan could thus claim to have achieved the first of her war aims : the capture of the Philippines, which had been in the possession of the United States for thirty years. American strategists, knowing the vulnerability of these islands on account of their comparative proximity to Japan and their remoteness from the nearest developed American naval base, had always calculated on their speedy fall in the event of war with Japan; but to the nation at large the disaster, if not unexpected, nevertheless came as a heavy blow. Grave fears were entertained at first for the safety of American civilians in Luzon, Mindanao, and elsewhere, but such apprehensions proved to be groundless. Once in occupation of the islands the Japanese exercised great moderation in their treatment of the inhabitants, foreigners as well as natives. American civilians were allowed to pursue their ordinary avocations on giving a pledge to abstain from all interference with the new *régime*, and except for a few recalcitrants, who were removed to Japan, the bulk of them chose to remain at their posts, confident as they were that the

United States would take early steps to eject the intruders and recover possession of her property. As invariably happens in times of national crisis, there were plenty of amateur strategists who bitterly assailed their Government for its supineness in failing to send a relieving force across the Pacific while the invasion was in progress. They did not realise that had the American fleet entered the Western Pacific at this juncture it would, in all likelihood, never have returned. Japan had not sent her armies on their errand of conquest without taking measures to protect them from interference. Before a single transport left Japanese harbours a cordon had been established across every line of approach to the waters of the South-West Pacific. At Port Lloyd, in the Bonin Islands, lay the main body of the Japanese fleet. From the Marshall, Caroline, and Mariana islands Japanese cruisers, submarines, and aircraft maintained watch and ward over the South Seas. Had any large American force advanced westward from Hawaii it must speedily have been detected, whereupon the Japanese patrol craft would have been called up from every quarter to harry it like a pack of wolves. Compelled to travel at low speed in order not to outdistance its indispensable supply ships and auxiliaries, the fleet would have been exposed day and night to attack by Japanese submarines, and, as it got further to the west, to raids by aircraft. If a ship were damaged in any way that prevented it from keeping up with the rest of the fleet, its fate would be sealed. The chances were that a considerable portion of the fleet would be destroyed on its westward voyage, and even if the greater part of the ships got through in safety there would be no friendly base awaiting them at the end of their long journey. They would find themselves in hostile waters, short of fuel, and unable to obtain fresh supplies. Every day they remained in the Western Pacific would increase their peril and bring them nearer to disaster. With their numbers depleted by the campaign of attrition waged by submarines, aircraft, and mine-layers, they would be liable to be brought to action by the Japanese battle fleet, which could strike with full force at its selected moment. No wonder that the American naval authorities, with a clear appreciation of all these circumstances, hesitated to send the fleet to what they believed would prove certain destruction. Nor must it be forgotten that for a full fortnight after the outbreak of war they remained absolutely in the dark as to what was passing in the Western Pacific. Owing to interference by high-power Japanese installations, no radio messages from the Philippines got through. The station at Guam had been silent since March 4. It was therefore impossible to tell whether the American flag was still flying at Manila or Guam. True, the simultaneous fall of both places within a few hours of the beginning of hostilities was a contingency that seemed outside the sphere of possibility; but on the other hand it was not improbable that Japanese expeditions had been approaching the islands long before war was formally declared, and had effected landings both at Manila and Guam while the American Government was yet in doubt as to whether hostilities had begun. In point of fact Guam remained in American hands up to April 3, so that a fleet sailing from Hawaii immediately after Japan had made plain her warlike intentions could have reached the island well before that date, provided it was not delayed by attacks *en route*—a very unlikely supposition. But the American naval chiefs, knowing nothing of this, rightly refused to send the fleet west until they had gained some intelligence of the actual situation there. To do so would have been an act of blatant folly. The silence of Guam can be briefly explained. A flight of Japanese war planes, evidently from Saipan, had appeared over the island on March 4 and dropped several tons of bombs on the radio station at Machanao, completely demolishing it and bringing down the masts. As the damage was far too extensive to be capable of repair with the facilities available locally, and cable communication had failed since the previous day, Guam was completely isolated. Its subsequent fate will be described in due course, but before proceeding with the narrative of events in the actual zone of war, some reference must be made to the resources which the two antagonists had at their command in this opening phase of the struggle.

CHAPTER V

MARCH, 1931

Strength of U.S. and Japanese armed forces at outset of war—Difficulties imposed by vast distance between the two countries—Position of Guam described

WHILE the Washington Naval Limitation Treaty of 1922 had put a stop to the competitive building of capital ships and aircraft carriers, it imposed no limit on the multiplication of smaller craft, whose relative war value had been proportionately increased by the restriction of battleship tonnage. And so, from 1922 onward, a certain rivalry developed between the maritime Powers, each aiming to build up a fleet of so-called " auxiliary " vessels adapted to the new tactics of mosquito warfare, which had already begun to trench upon the traditional *guerre d'escadre*, and seemed likely in the end to supersede it altogether. Japan had set the pace a few months after the Washington Conference by adopting a large programme of cruiser construction. It was designed to cover her requirements up to the year 1928, at which date she expected to have, in addition to her battle fleet of ten capital ships, the following ancillary craft: twenty-five fast cruisers, all capable of steaming at 33 knots, and ranging in size from 3,500 to 10,000 tons; approximately one hundred destroyers of seagoing dimensions, and eighty submarines. Generous provision was also made for fuel ships, ammunition carriers, parent vessels for the destroyer and submarine flotillas, repair ships, and other auxiliary vessels required for the replenishment and maintenance of a modern fleet at sea. But late in the year 1925, following on the adoption of a new programme of cruiser construction by the United States, Japan had considered it necessary to enlarge her own building scheme in order, as she claimed, to preserve the balance of power. Accordingly, eight more cruisers and twenty extra submarines were projected, for completion in 1930. In actual fact, however, the construction of these vessels proceeded so rapidly that all, or nearly all, were ready for service a full year in advance of the date originally named. Meanwhile the United States, in fear of being outdistanced in small naval tonnage, made a new effort in 1927, when Congress, after prolonged debate, appropriated funds for the building of four cruisers and twenty-four large scouting submarines. The Japanese retort was to introduce a supplementary Bill providing for the completion by 1933 of five more cruisers and an unspecified number of submarines. Most of these vessels had been commenced before the outbreak of war. Thus, in the eight years succeeding the Washington Conference, the fleets of both Powers had been substantially reinforced. On two occasions within this period the U.S. Government had proposed the holding of a new Conference to check the growth of minor naval armaments. But the response was not deemed sufficiently encouraging to justify the matter being pressed. The position on the eve of the war was that Japan had a pronounced superiority in every type of small fighting ship except the destroyer. She had ready a fleet of thirty-three swift cruisers, with five others on the stocks; besides 100 submarines, mostly of ocean-going dimensions, and from twenty-five to thirty more under construction. Only in destroyers was she outnumbered, possessing as she did not more than a hundred of these, against an American total of 275, though the majority of her boats were of a later and more powerful design. In airplane carriers the Japanese fleet was slightly inferior, for the Washington Treaty had restricted her aggregate in this class to 81,000 tons, while permitting the United States 135,000 tons. The latter, by converting two battle cruisers for aircraft duty, had locked up 66,000 tons of its quota in two ships, and invested the balance in three carriers of 23,000 tons each, making five ships in all. Japan had followed much the same policy by rebuilding the former capital ships *Kaga* and *Akagi* as aircraft carriers with a displacement of 27,000 tons each. This left her a balance of only 27,000 tons, which she had utilised by building the *Hosho*, of 9,500 tons, and three ships of slightly under 6,000 tons each. The *Kaga* and *Akagi* could steam at 24 and 28 knots respectively, and carry fifty planes apiece. The *Hosho* had a speed of 25 knots and an equipment of twenty planes. Each of the three smaller vessels was designed for a speed of 28 knots and had fifteen planes on board. In all, therefore, Japan had six ships of good speed fitted for the transport of aircraft.

Japanese submarines were of three classes : Medium boats, of 700 to 1,100 tons, with radii of 7,000 to 9,000 miles; large boats, of from 1,500 to 2,500 tons, with radius equal to the medium type; and submersible cruisers. These last-named had been introduced into the Japanese Navy in 1925. Built from designs prepared in Germany, six had been completed on the outbreak of war, and two others were under construction. Owing to the profound secrecy observed concerning this type, its apparently formidable qualities were but little known outside Japan. In 1924 a Japanese naval mission visiting Europe had acquired from Professor Otto Schramm, of Berlin (one of Germany's leading experts in submarine construction), a complete set of drawings for an underwater cruiser of dimensions far exceeding those of the largest submarine then in existence. At the same time German engineers were engaged to supervise in Japan the building of these giant craft and their engines. The first vessel was laid down at Kure dockyard in the spring of 1925. With a length of 405 feet and a breadth of 45 feet, the surface displacement was 7,080 tons. Diesel engines of 29,000 horse power gave a speed of 23 knots on surface, and electro-motors a velocity of 11 knots when submerged. Forward of the conning tower was a low turret containing a pair of 8-inch 250-pounder guns. This turret

F

was rotated by electrical power, and the guns had a clear field of fire in every direction save astern. Three 4-inch rapid-fire guns were also mounted. On deck there were two torpedo tubes, with eight more built into the hull below the water line. For each 8-inch gun 500 rounds of ammunition were provided, and for each of the ten tubes four torpedoes. Thick armour plate covered the turret, the conning tower, and the whole of the deck that was visible when the ship was running on the surface. This carapace of steel made her invulnerable to all but the heaviest gunfire. The hull was exceptionally strong, for the purpose of resisting bomb or depth-charge attack. Sufficient oil could be stored in the tanks for a voyage of 24,000 miles at moderate speed. In spite of her enormous weight and great length, the ship, when manned by a highly trained crew, was supposed to be no more difficult to handle than a submarine only one-tenth her size. In deep water she could dive in less than two minutes. This remarkable vessel was named *Nagasaki*. Five others of similar design were laid down before she had finished her trials, but one of these was a mine-layer, carrying in place of the two heavy guns a few light rapid fire pieces, together with 2,500 mines. No other navy possessed underwater craft of such remarkable size and power as these six giants. As will be seen later, however, their fighting value was greatly overrated. A list of all Japanese warships complete or building at this period will be found in the Appendix, to which the reader is referred for details. The active *personnel* of the Navy included 7,500 officers and 70,000 men. The proportion of officers to men, it will be observed, was abnormally high—about one to nine; whereas in the U.S. Navy it was only one to seventeen. This disparity was due to the Japanese practice of carrying on board each vessel at all times the full complement of officers, both staff and specialist, who would be required in war. In the same way, the crews were invariably kept at 90 to 95 per cent. of the full war establishment. Though this system naturally added to the cost of main-

taining the fleet in time of peace, it conduced to a high
state of preparedness for war. So far as the first-line
fleet was concerned, it lived always on a footing of instant
readiness for action, and mobilisation was therefore
only the affair of a few hours. Behind this active
personnel stood a reserve of nearly 50,000 officers and
men, who averaged fifteen days' training per year
during the seven years they remained in the first *ban*.
Japanese naval discipline, at one time extremely good,
had tended to deteriorate in recent years, probably
owing to the spread of anti-militarist doctrines among
the class of population from which the seamen were
drawn. Nevertheless, for all-round quality the *personnel*
was equal to that of any other fleet. The officers were
well-educated, painstaking, and absorbed in their
profession; the men were intelligent, and, when properly
led, obedient and devoted to duty. Technical training
was on very sound lines. Although not mechanical by
temperament, the Japanese are imitative to a degree,
and in the Navy, at any rate, they had successfully
mastered the intricacies of modern technique as applied
to warfare at sea. Gunnery and torpedo practice were
well up to the mark. Both in the design and construction of ships, machinery, and equipment they had adopted,
and in some cases improved upon, the best Western
models. In no branch had they made more progress
than in aviation. By the year previous to the war
the naval flying corps had attained a strength of 1,200
pilots and 900 planes, many of which were equal to the
best in service abroad. So well had the domestic aircraft industry developed that an output of 150 machines
a month was easily attainable without special effort.
Prominent among naval planes were the huge Asahi
bombers, carrying a ton-and-a-half of bombs, and
powerful torpedo-planes, each armed with two 23-inch
short torpedoes. The Japanese merchant marine comprised nearly 1,000 steam and motor ships above 1,000
tons, including a fair number of large, high-speed liners.
Many of these were taken over for naval duty as armed
cruisers, auxiliary airplane carriers, and so forth. For

a war with the United States, Japan's strategical position very closely approached the ideal. The nearest American fortified naval station was at Hawaii, 3,400 miles distant. From the Kuriles in the north to Formosa in the south an almost continuous rampart of insular bases guarded Japan from assault. Most of the waters that lapped the eastern shores of Asia were dominated by her : the Okhotsk Sea, the Sea of Japan, the Yellow and East China Seas. And now her conquest of the Philippines had extended this control to the South China Sea. Her vital lines of communication with the Asiatic mainland were therefore perfectly secure so long as her fleet remained in being. Furthermore, in the Bonins and the ex-German islands north of the Equator she had a cluster of actual or potential naval bases which lay athwart the direct route of shipping from the Eastern Pacific. Only from the north-east did it seem possible for a hostile fleet to approach her shores without passing within range of some Japanese torpedo base. Most of her insular outposts had been strongly fortified years beforehand. Under the terms of the mandate she was prohibited from making military use of her ex-German territories in the Pacific, but this ruling naturally ceased to have weight with her when war became imminent. Anticipating a possible American attempt to seize one or more of these islands as an advanced base, Japan had taken steps during February and March, 1931, to safeguard them from a *coup de main*. Guns were mounted at the most important islands, as at Yap, Jaluit (in the Marshall Group), and Saipan (in the Marianas); but reliance was placed mainly on aircraft and submarines to keep enemy ships at a distance. While it was manifest that sea-power was destined to play the chief *rôle* in the struggle now developing, military strength on land was by no means a factor to be overlooked. Upon the Japanese army devolved the important task of ensuring the safety of those reservoirs on the Continent from which Japan obtained the major part of her imported food and raw materials. If these were to fail she could not continue the war.

It was therefore of paramount importance that the claims she had staked out in China should be adequately protected from interference, the more so as the Chinese would gladly have seized the chance of revenging themselves for past injuries by denying Japan the commodities she required, had they been in a position to do so. China's attitude in the war had yet to be defined, but that she would be at best a malevolent neutral was fully understood at Tokyo. Moreover, if Japan were to suffer reverses, nothing was more likely than that China would take up arms against her, a contingency the more to be dreaded in view of the growing strength and efficiency of the Chinese military forces, to which allusion has been made in a previous chapter. It was clear, then, that a considerable portion of Japan's army would be tied down to garrison duty in Manchuria and Mongolia, from which provinces she derived most of her Continental supplies. In fact, as the war proceeded and the attitude of China became more menacing, it was found expedient to keep no fewer than six divisions at various centres in Chinese territory. All the arts of Japanese diplomacy were employed to cultivate the goodwill of Russia, with whom relations had been none too cordial during the preceding decade. On the outbreak of war the Moscow Government proclaimed its neutrality; but, here again, Japan saw a doubtful friend who might be translated into an open foe if the fortune of war should go against her. So long as she remained at her full strength, Japan could afford to brave the covert enmity of her Continental neighbours, whom, in the heyday of her power, she had never scrupled to exploit and oppress. But engaged as she now was in a life-and-death struggle, the dread of active intervention by China or Russia, or both, was ever-present in the minds of her strategists, and profoundly influenced their military decisions. It needed the acid test of war to reveal the full consequences of the high-handed policy which Japan had pursued for so many years. When adversity overtook her she found herself encompassed with enemies, eager to strike a deadly blow at her from the rear. Nor was it only in China that she had a vulnerable flank to guard. Early in the war serious disorders took place in Korea. The independence party raised the standard of revolt in April, 1931, achieving so much initial success that an army of three divisions had to be hastily dispatched from Japan. The revolt was quelled after severe fighting, but the temper of the Koreans was such that it was deemed unwise to withdraw a single regiment. Another source of danger lay in Formosa, where the inhabitants had always been restive under Japanese rule. Here, also, the garrison had to be heavily reinforced. Altogether therefore, not less than eleven divisions—or 70 per cent. of the army's peace establishment—were practically immobilised. But even after these deductions the military power of Japan remained exceedingly formidable. With the calling up of the first-line reserves, the strength of the army available for active operations was raised to 800,000 effectives. At the back of these were second-line reserves to the number of 1,400,000 men, the majority of whom had undergone training. Since the world war of 1914–18, the equipment of the army had been vastly improved. Its artillery, train, and special services were organised on up-to-date lines, and furnished with material of the latest pattern. The tank corps, inaugurated ten years before, had now reached a strength of 120 heavy and light battle tanks. The military aviation service had some 800 planes ready for service. Thus, if the course of the war compelled Japan to do any extensive fighting on land, she was in a position to give a good account of herself. It only remains to be added that no effort had been spared to make the coastline of Japan Proper impregnable to assault from the sea. Strong forts armed with heavy ordnance guarded all the principal harbours and strategic channels. Besides these stationary defences there was a network of railroads which enabled large masses of troops to be rapidly concentrated at any point along the coast where attack threatened.

Having now examined as briefly as possible the

armed forces at the disposal of Japan, together with
the salient features of her strategic situation, it is time
to glance at the corresponding factors on the side of
the United States.

Until a few years previous to the war with Spain
the United States Navy had been treated as though
its sole function were coast defence. As late as 1890
it was proposed to expend most of the money available
for shipbuilding on a number of new monitors, powerful
enough as floating batteries, but quite unfitted to cruise
and fight on the high seas. Eventually, however,
these ships were abandoned in favour of sea-going
ironclads, which formed the nucleus of the first American
battle fleet. With the acquisition of Spain's colonies
in the Pacific, the naval commitments of the United
States were largely increased. It was no longer simply
a question of providing for the defence of the home
coasts : protection had now to be extended to American
territory situated thousands of miles away in the Pacific
Ocean. How to make the Philippines reasonably safe
from foreign aggression was a strategical problem of the
first magnitude, and one with which the American
people, it must be confessed, showed no desire to grapple.
To do so would have involved an expenditure on armaments out of proportion to the economic value of the
new colonies. In any case, it would have meant not
only a large increase in the navy, but the erection of
costly local defences as well. Whether the taking of
both these measures would have solved the problem
is a debatable point. American naval officers always
doubted the possibility of making the Philippines safe
by means of ships and fortifications alone. In their
judgment it could only be done by keeping permanently
in the islands a military force equal to that which any
prospective enemy could send to attack them, and this
was a course that public opinion in the United States
would never have countenanced. The alternative was
to develop, either in the Philippines or some adjacent
island, a well-equipped and strongly defended base
which would enable a powerful American fleet to

maintain itself in the Western Pacific; for the presence of such a fleet, or the certainty of its eventual arrival, would be likely to act as a deterrent to schemes of invasion.   For many years, therefore, the development of Cavite, in Manila Bay, or better still, of Guam—an island in the Mariana group, 1,500 miles east of Manila —had been urged as essential by American strategists, who from time to time put forward specific plans to this end.   But all to no purpose.   The nation either did not appreciate the facts of the case, or was indifferent to the fate of these remote possessions, which it had acquired more or less adventitiously.   As a consequence Cavite remained a third-class base with no facilities for the care and replenishment of a modern battle fleet, while Guam continued to serve merely as a fuel station without means of protection.   This negative policy prevailed till 1920, when Congress at length appropriated funds for strengthening the defences of Guam and otherwise improving the port of Apra as a fleet anchorage.   There is every reason to believe that this represented only the initial stage of a plan which aimed ultimately at converting the island into a first-class naval base.   But it was nipped in the bud by the Five Power Treaty signed at Washington in 1922 which disallowed the establishment of new fortifications or naval bases in a specified area that included the Philippines and Guam, and forbade any increase in existing facilities for the repair and maintenance of naval forces and of the coast defences of those islands. The effect of this restriction was practically to bar the American Fleet from the Western Pacific in time of war, for modern battleships can only operate in waters where there are secure bases within easy reach.   Their range of action, governed by fuel endurance, is strictly limited, and especially in war time, when fast steaming is the rule and the consumption of oil or coal is abnormally heavy.   Honolulu, situated 2,100 miles from San Francisco, was the only insular base in the Pacific having the necessary plant for dealing with the requirements of a large naval force.   Pivoting on this base, the fleet could cruise to any point not above 1,500 or 2,000 miles distant. If it went further afield it would risk finding itself short of fuel for the homeward voyage, and under war conditions any reduction in speed for the purpose of economising fuel might be attended with fatal consequences, for ships steaming at low speed are easy targets for submarine attack. Obviously, therefore, a fleet working from Honolulu would be quite unable to extend protection either to Guam or the Philippines, since these places lay respectively 3,325 and 4,800 miles to the westward.

On the outbreak of war the United States Navy possessed eighteen battleships, varying from 21,825 to 32,600 tons; twenty-two light cruisers, more than 300 destroyers, and 125 submarines, with five large airplane carriers. Its *personnel* numbered approximately 115,000 of all grades, including Marines. The short-service system had always been the bane of the American Navy. To turn out a thoroughly efficient man-of-war's man in less than six years is admittedly impossible, yet the majority of American bluejackets served only for four years, and re-enlistment for a second term was exceptional. This involved a heavy turn-over in recruits and discharges each year, with a low average of training and efficiency as the unavoidable conse-quence. Repeated attempts were made to have the minimum period of service fixed at six years, but not until 1929 was this reform sanctioned by Congress. Its beneficial effect had therefore not begun to be felt previous to the coming of war. When the crisis arose about 40 per cent. of the enlisted *personnel* had served less than three years. In these circumstances it would be demonstrably false to assert that the standard of training and discipline was as high in the American Navy as in the Japanese, where the great majority of seamen, being volunteers, had served at least six years. While it may be true that the American recruit was more mentally alert, and showed a greater aptitude for the mechanical details of his work, this advantage could not compensate for the extreme brevity of his training. Knowledge may be acquired rapidly in the hard school of war, but there is no denying the fact that, at the outset, the American Navy was severely handicapped by the inadequate training of its enlisted *personnel*. In 1931 the authorised peace strength of the United States Army was slightly under 150,000. Experience gained during the world war had been turned to good account, and in organisation, training, and equipment the Army could bear comparison with any in the world. The National Guard, or Militia, had an authorised strength of 425,000, but this total was far from complete, and in 1931 failed to reach 200,000. Potentially, the military power of the United States was enormous. In November, 1918, at the close of the world war, 3,600,000 men were under arms, and many classes still remained to be called up. The total number of men registered at that period as liable to serve exceeded 24,000,000. Given the requisite time the United States could create, organise, and equip entirely from its own resources the largest army in the world. Compulsory military service was restored immediately after the outbreak of war with Japan, but since at that time the impending campaign seemed to offer little scope for the employment of land forces, apart from garrison duty, the maximum strength of the Army was provisionally laid down as a million men, although the actual number recruited did not reach this total until several months later. As for the strategic problem now confronting the United States, it may be very simply stated. That Japan would attempt any serious military attack on the American Continent was out of the question. The distance was far too great, and her fleet, outside its own waters, was not sufficiently strong to risk an encounter with the combined naval forces of her enemy. A Japanese invasion of the Pacific Slope was therefore physically impossible, and, despite sensational forecasts to the contrary by certain writers who chose to ignore the rudiments of strategy, it had always been regarded as such by informed naval and military opinion in the

United States. Nor were fears entertained for the safety of Hawaii, for it was unbelievable that Japan would send a military expedition across 3,400 miles of ocean to attack territory which served as the main Pacific base of the American fleet. Both the United States coastline and Hawaii could thus be regarded as immune from serious military attack. But simply to stand on the defensive would not win the war. A decision could be brought about only by defeating the armed forces of the enemy and, then if necessary, by applying the pressure of blockade. To achieve either of these ends it was necessary to have bases in the immediate war zone, namely the Western Pacific. But how were these to be obtained? Therein lay the kernel of the problem. With the loss of the Philippines and Guam there remained no American possession west of Hawaii which was capable of serving as a war base. Midway Island, 1,126 miles to the north-west of Hawaii, was too remote from Japanese waters; while Wake Island, 2,000 miles to the west, was a mere coral atoll without anchorage facilities for large ships. It speedily became evident, therefore, that if a base were to be found at all, it must be sought in Japanese territory. Even here the choice of sites was strictly limited. The Marshall Islands seemed to be disqualified by their distance from the war zone, as also by the fact that ships operating therefrom would have to run the gauntlet of submarines from neighbouring Japanese islands. To Ponape, in the Carolines, which was also considered, much the same objections were held to apply, nor were the hydrographic conditions at that port favourable to its development as a base for big ships. Angaur, in the Pelew group, though well situated as to distance, was at this time rejected on account of its proximity to other Japanese islands, which flanked every direct line of approach thereto. Guam was assumed to be a hostile base, and no other harbour in the Mariana islands had a sufficiently good anchorage. And so, as we shall see in a later chapter, the Bonins came to be selected as the only practicable site for a war base, from which the American fleet could wage a campaign in enemy waters.

Meanwhile, to deal with events in their chronological sequence, we must now turn our attention to Guam. As explained above, this island, the largest of the Mariana group, had never been developed as an important naval base, though its unique advantages from the strategical point of view were obvious. Captured by the American cruiser *Charleston* in 1898, during the war with Spain, it had served thereafter merely as a coaling station for naval vessels and Government transports. Very little had been done to improve the antiquated fortifications left by the Spaniards. Extending about thirty miles from N.N.E. to S.S.W., the island averages six and a half miles in width and has an area of 208 square miles. The northern part is a plateau from 300 to 600 feet above sea level, attaining its highest elevation along the east and west coasts, where steep headlands jut out into the sea. Viewed at a distance, the island appears rather flat, its even outline broken towards the north by the hills of Santa Rosa (870 ft. high), Machinao (610 ft.), the extreme northerly point, and the site of the radio station which had been destroyed in the first bomb attack, and Mataguac (630 ft.). To the southward, however, the country is mountainous, and here there are several lofty peaks, such as Alutum (Mount Reconnaissance), Chachao, and Tinko, all of which are over 1,000 ft. The highest point on the island is Jamullong Manglo, nearly 1,300 ft. above the sea. An abundant supply of fresh water is obtained from a spring near Agaña. There is a belt of open, undulating country between the hills and the sea on the western side; but on the east the coast is steep and rugged, with only one harbour (Port Tarofofo) where vessels can find shelter. This port takes its name from the river Tarofofo, which flows into the harbour. Both sides of the bay are flanked by steep hills. The largest ships can enter here with safety, as there are from eight to six fathoms of water inside. South of Tarofofo there is no other harbour accessible to ships of deep draught, for the reefs which lie off Port Ajayan, the south-eastern extremity of the island, make this last-named bay a place to be avoided in any but the finest weather. Running for several miles to the westward of Ajayan is a reef which encircles Cocos Island and then turns to the north, and beyond this obstruction lies Umata Bay, two miles north of the south-western point of the island. The heavy swell which sets on the shore when the westerly winds are blowing makes this bay a perilous anchorage. There are two ruined forts here, Nuestra Señora de la Soledad at the southern entrance, and Fort San Angelo on the rocky heights at the north. In former times Umata was a fairly large town, but the greater part of it was destroyed in 1849 by an earthquake. Eight miles to the north of Umata is Agate Bay, where ships may lie in safety except during the season of westerly winds; but here the many reefs fronting the beach render landing operations difficult. A few miles further north lies Oroté Peninsula, forming the southern side of Port Apra, the largest and best harbour in the island. It is about three and a half miles wide, and is bounded on the north by Cabras Island and Luminao reef, running more or less parallel with Oroté Peninsula. There is deep water inside, but the port is thickly studded with banks, coral reefs, and islets, which necessitate caution in entering or leaving. An old Spanish masonry citadel, Fort Santa Cruz, stands on a rock at the head of the bay, and there is a second fort, Santiago, at Oroté Point. These forts had never been repaired by the Americans, as they were considered to be too exposed to gunfire from the sea; but an earth-work battery, mounting two modern 6-inch guns, had been thrown up at Oroté Point. A second battery of the same type existed near Sumay towards the eastern end of the Peninsula, and there was a third in the hills above Atantano, overlooking the harbour. The approach to the port was thus commanded by six 6-inch guns, four of which were mounted at an elevation that enabled them to deliver a plunging fire. Agaña Bay, on which Agaña, the capital of the island, is situated, is a long, shallow indentation eight miles to the northeast of Apra. There is practically no shelter for vessels here, as the bay is quite open and exposed to the heavy ocean swell. Its only defences were the old forts of San Rafael and San Agueda, built of stone, and armed at this time with a few light rapid-fire guns. The town of Agaña, which lies midway between the headlands of Adelup and Aperguan, had some six thousand inhabitants and three hundred buildings. Only a few of the latter, such as the Governor's residence, the arsenal, barracks, and jail, are constructed of stone. The streets are paved, and an excellent road connects the town with Apra. From Agaña Bay to Ritidian, the most northerly point in the island, the coast is steep and forbidding, with only one inlet—Tumun Bay. This is partly reef-bound, but there are several channels through the barrier by which boats can pass to the shore, and the beach is favourable for landing. The garrison of Guam consisted of 2,000 United States Marines, most of whom were stationed at Agaña. They also manned the defences at Apra. Besides the guns in the coastal batteries there were a few light field pieces and machine-guns.

CHAPTER VI

MARCH–APRIL, 1931

Captain Harper, Governor of Guam, receives news of fall of Manila —Two steamers arrive from U.S. with war material—Preparations for defence—First attack repulsed with heavy loss—Two submarines the only warships left at Guam—Second Japanese attack proves more formidable—Surrender of the island—Captain Harper's escape

FOR nearly a fortnight after the bomb attack of March 4, which had destroyed the radio station at Machinao, Guam was left undisturbed. Japanese aircraft from Saipan occasionally flew over the island, but without dropping bombs. No attempt was made to engage them, for there were only eight American machines in Guam, and the Governor had determined to hold these in reserve to meet an emergency. On the morning of March 18 the look-out station on Alutum reported smoke on the southern horizon, whereupon a plane was sent up to scout. The new comers proved to be the destroyers *Dent, Lamberton,* and *Rizal* (the last-named fitted as a minelayer), which had broken out from Manila Bay before the capitulation. When still some ten miles west of Oroté Point the flotilla was observed to be zigzagging, putting on speed, and making a smoke screen. A few minutes later the leading boat opened fire, and depth charges began to explode. It was evident to the watchers ashore that a hostile submarine was attempting to attack; but if so, it seemed to have failed, for the three boats came on at high speed. Then, just as the second boat in the line (the *Dent*) was drawing abreast of Oroté Point, a column of water shot up from her starboard side, followed by the dull boom of an explosion. A torpedo, striking amidships, had broken her back, causing her to sink quickly; while two more torpedoes from the unseen enemy narrowly missed the *Rizal.* When this vessel and the *Lamberton* reached their moorings off Cabras Island their commanders at once came ashore to report to the Governor, Captain Harper, U.S.N., who now heard for the first time the tragic tidings from the Philippines. Manila was still holding out when the destroyers left, but it was known then that surrender was only a matter of days, if not hours. That Guam would be attacked in its turn at any moment was patent to all, and with such scanty means of defence as it possessed there seemed little hope of making an effective resistance. The submarines which had left Manila at the same time as the destroyers had not yet arrived, nor with their low speed were they likely to reach Apra for two or three days. At 1 p.m. on March 18 the look-out station on Alutum again reported smoke on the horizon, this time to the westward, and again an airplane went up to reconnoitre. Two large steamers of cargo build were found to be heading for Apra, and were soon identified as the naval transports *Newport News* and *Beaufort,* which had left San Francisco in February bound for Manila, with a consignment of artillery, mines, and other war material. As the *Beaufort's* speed was not above eight knots and the two ships kept together, their voyage had been a long one. On March 9, when still 700 miles to the east of the Philippines, they met a German steamer, which gave them news of the destruction of the American squadron off Manila. This intelligence decided them to retrace their course, since by continuing on to the Philippines they would almost certainly fall into enemy hands. Their intention was to return to Honolulu, but coal was running short, and at dusk on the 13th they sighted what was taken to be a Japanese submarine. This they contrived to evade, but on the following day another suspicious vessel was observed hull down to eastward. It therefore looked as if the homeward route was barred. Guam was now the only refuge within reach of the hunted ships. The *Newport News,* which had a long-range radio installation, repeatedly called up the island without getting any response. This silence indicated that something was amiss; it might even mean that Guam was already occupied by the Japanese. Still, there was nothing for it but to take the risk of entering a trap, for the bunkers of the two ships were rapidly emptying, and in a few days' time would be exhausted. So a course was shaped for the island, it having been decided that both ships should be scuttled at the first sign of danger. But no untoward incident occurred, and in the forenoon of March 18 the coast line of Guam was sighted. Warned by the airplane which had come out to meet them that Japanese submarines were in the neighbourhood, both ships began to zigzag and work up to their best speed. They were soon met by the destroyer *Lamberton*, which circled round them at high speed and put down a depth charge barrage. Thanks to this escort they got safely into Apra, where the work of discharging their valuable cargo was begun with feverish energy. By sunset on the 19th there had been put ashore twelve 7-inch and eight 6-inch guns on caterpillar mounts, with their tractors; fifteen field guns, ten 3-inch anti-aircraft guns, fifty heavy and light machine-guns, and a large quantity of ammunition. Twenty motor trucks were also landed from the *Beaufort*. The 7-inch weapons were of a specially powerful type. They had been removed from old battleships during the world war and adapted for land service. Each gun had a length of twenty-five feet, and discharged a 153-pounder shell containing 24 pounds of T.N.T. From its caterpillar mount it could be fired at an elevation of 40 degrees, which gave the shell an extreme range of nearly fourteen miles. With each gun was a 120-horse-power gasoline tractor, which could take it up steep hills or over the roughest open country. By reason of their great mobility and long range these guns were ideal for coast defence against all but the heaviest warships. Had there been two or three batteries of them in the Philippines when the Japanese invasion took place, that operation might have ended differently, and would in any case have cost the enemy

G

much heavier casualties.   As lecturer at the Naval War College Captain Harper, now Governor and Commandant of Guam, had gained a reputation by his ingenious if somewhat unconventional views on strategy and tactics. He was now to have an opportunity of putting certain of these theories into effect.   Since being appointed to the governorship two years previously, he had devoted much thought to the problem of defending the island.   Had batteries of heavy long-range guns been mounted at strategic points Guam would have been almost impregnable, for the configuration of the ground lent itself admirably to artillery defence against approaching ships, and good landing places were few in number.   But the building of such batteries had been neglected prior to the Washington Conference, and after that event the erection of fortifications on the island was interdicted by treaty. Failing these, mobile guns of heavy calibre would suffice, in Captain Harper's opinion, to keep hostile ships at a respectful distance.   Nothing, therefore, could have been more timely or welcome than the arrival of the two transports with their cargo of big guns.   His study of the defence problem had led him to conclude that an enemy bent on invading Guam would probably select Port Tarofofo on the east and Port Apra or Tumun Bay on the west as landing places, owing to the favourable conditions to be met with there.   Alternative but less likely points of attack were Umata Bay, Agate Bay, and Agaña, all on the west coast.   There were not enough heavy guns to command the approach to each of these places, but there would probably be time, after the enemy had made his intentions clear, to rush several of the 7-inch tractor guns to the danger zone.   Most of the marines on the island had been trained in the use of these weapons during their service in the United States.   Gun crews were hastily organised and the guns themselves formed into batteries of three pieces each, with the same number of motor trucks attached to each battery for carrying the *personnel* and ammunition. For the field pieces and the anti-aircraft guns teams of carabao were provided.   The weak point in the defence, and one that could not be remedied, was the shortage of airplanes. If the invading force were strong in aircraft there would be little chance of putting up a successful resistance, for the guns and their crews would then be exposed to heavy bombing, and with only two thousand men all told there was no margin for severe casualties. Early on March 20 a hundred mines taken out of the *Beaufort* were laid across the entrance to Port Apra by the destroyer *Rizal*. It was intended to sow other mines off Tarofofo and Tumun Bay, but before this could be done the attack had developed. It was heralded by four Japanese planes which approached from the north-west at 11 a.m. on the 20th and flew over the island at a height of 6,000 ft. Expecting a visitation of this kind, Captain Harper had camouflaged all his big guns with tarpaulins and tree branches, which made it impossible to detect them from the air. Striking the island at Urano Point in the north, the enemy planes flew southward along the coast, passing over Agaña at a very low altitude. Here they dropped several bombs, which destroyed many of the ramshackle native houses and caused some casualties among the civilian inhabitants. Unaware of the existence of anti-aircraft guns—for Japanese spies had correctly reported that no weapons of this kind were in Guam just before the war—the planes now came down as low as 2,000 ft. to make a close inspection of the batteries at Apra. The chance was too good to be missed. Six of the newly-landed " sky guns " were at Apra, and at the word of command they came smartly into action. Despite the inexperience of the gunners in this sort of work, the shooting was very accurate. Two of the enemy planes were brought down almost immediately; and a third was disabled and had to descend on the sea. Only one machine escaped injury. At 11.30 a.m. the look-out station on Alutum reported masses of smoke in the north-west. Captain Harper immediately sent up one of his few planes, as it was essential to gain intelligence of the enemy's strength and course at the earliest moment possible; but the pilot of the machine was ordered to keep out of range of attack, and not to get into a fight with hostile planes unless absolutely forced to do so. His report, which came in by radiophone, was to this effect : " Enemy fleet now steering almost due east. There are four armoured cruisers, four scouts, about sixteen destroyers, and what appears to be a plane carrier; also fifteen steamships which are probably transports. Scouts are ahead, cruisers next, and destroyers forming screen round them and transports. Am being fired at by anti-aircraft guns and chased by planes." The air scout was now recalled, and in a few minutes was seen making for Apra at low elevation, with four enemy planes in hot pursuit. He was obviously trying to draw them over the anti-aircraft battery, and succeeded so well that two of the pursuers were brought down before they were aware of the danger. The other two, being well in the rear, turned tail and got away before the ground gunners found their range. At this time, 12.15 p.m., the enemy fleet was in sight from Mount Alutum. It was seen to have split into two sections, one of which was steering north-east, apparently intending to round Point Ritidian and come down the eastern side of the island, while the other was heading due south on a course that indicated some point on the west coast as its objective. There was no longer any doubt that landings were to be attempted simultaneously on both coasts, and it only remained to discover at which points. At 1.20 p.m. two of the armoured cruisers, identified as the *Tokiwa* and *Asama*, stood in towards Apra and opened a heavy fire on the harbour and the batteries. In both these ships, as became known later, the forward 8-inch turret had been replaced by a pair of 12-inch howitzers behind armoured shields. The fire of the cruisers was controlled by Japanese spotting planes. These flew at too great a height to be effectively engaged by the American anti-aircraft guns ; moreover if the latter had revealed their position by opening fire they would at once have become the target of the heavy guns of the fleet, and must soon have been destroyed. The batteries at Oroté Point and Sumay came in for a severe shelling, but amidst a tempest of bursting projectiles the handful of Marines continued to work their guns with such effect that several hits were scored on the two Japanese cruisers, and the *Tokiwa*, with her howitzers disabled by a shell bursting fairly between them, was compelled to haul out of range. In less than twenty minutes, however, both batteries were silenced; three out of the four guns had been dismounted, and the men who had fought them so gallantly lay dead or wounded. The third battery— that above Atantano—was of more recent construction, and its site was evidently not known to the enemy so precisely as the other two, for it survived the bombardment for another half-hour until a chance shell touched off some spare ammunition, causing an explosion that laid low most of the *personnel*. All this time the marines in charge of the heavy mobile guns had been chafing to support their comrades, but Captain Harper's orders were peremptory : not a shot was to be fired until he gave the word. At his camouflaged observation post on Mount Tinkio he received word that the second detachment of Japanese ships was steaming past Taguan Point on a course parallel with the coast. A few minutes later came news that the armoured cruisers *Kasuga* and *Nisshin* were bombarding Port Tarofofo with 10-in. and 8-in. shells. This intelligence confirmed him in his belief that the landings were timed to take place concurrently at Apra and Tarofofo. But so long as the Japanese aircraft were overhead it was impossible to move a single gun without exposing it to almost instant destruction, either by bombs from the enemy planes or by the fire of the ships. Command of the air was absolutely essential to the execution of the Governor's scheme of defence, and how to obtain this was a problem which had been occupying his mind from the first appearance of the invading force. So far as he could see, there was but one airplane carrier with the Japanese fleet, which ship, the *Matsushima*, was in clear view as she cruised some twelve miles off Apra, with an escort of three destroyers. If she could be sunk, or even badly damaged, her planes would be rendered homeless and must soon withdraw from action, either to descend on the sea to be picked up by other ships, or, if their fuel lasted out, to fly to Saipan, the nearest friendly territory. It was therefore worth while taking a big risk to deal with the *Matsushima*, and having reached this conclusion Captain Harper ordered his eight planes to attack her. Four of these machines were scouts or fighters; the remaining four were medium bombers, each able to carry two 600-pounder bombs.   Hitherto they had been held in reserve at Dededo, in the northern part of the island, an improvised aerodrome whose position was partly camouflaged by farm buildings.   On receiving the Governor's orders all eight machines started on what the pilots and observers well knew to be a forlorn hope. Their instructions were to ignore everything but the *Matsushima;* the fighting planes were, if necessary, to sacrifice themselves in order to give the bombers a safe passage to the objective.   Just before the engines started up Lieutenant Jay, commanding the squadron, received a personal message from the Governor : " If you sink the airplane carrier we may save Guam.   Everything depends on how your attack pans out.   Go to it, and good luck ! "   The eight machines had not climbed 2,000 feet before they were observed by Japanese planes, which at once started in pursuit.   But the Americans had a good start, and their pursuers, not knowing what the objective was, lost time in following directly after them, instead of heading out to sea to intercept them before they could reach the aircraft carrier.   This ship was quickly identified by her curious build, with a single funnel placed over on the starboard side and her decks alive with planes.   As the American machines hove in sight two or three planes rose from the deck to engage them, thus masking the fire of the ship's own guns, which did not come into action until it was too late.   Flying well ahead of the bombers the first two American fighters poured a stream of machine-gun bullets into a Japanese machine that rose to meet them, and sent it down out of control.   A second enemy was accounted for in the same way, and then the bombing planes were on the

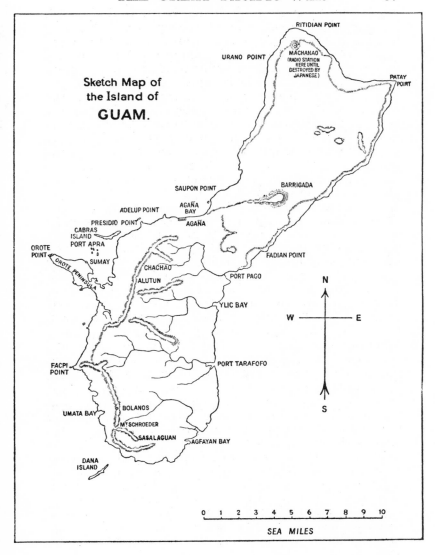

Sketch Map of
the Island of
GUAM.

RITIDIAN POINT

URANO POINT

MACHANAO
(RADIO STATION
HERE UNTIL
DESTROYED BY
JAPANESE)

PATAY
POINT

SAUPON POINT

BARRIGADA

AGAÑA
BAY

ADELUP POINT

PRESIDIO POINT

AGAÑA

CABRAS
ISLAND

PORT APRA

OROTE
POINT

SUMAY

FADIAN POINT

OROTE PENINSULA

CHACHAO

ALUTUN

PORT PAGO

N

YLIC BAY

W ——————— E

S

FACPI
POINT

PORT TARAFOFO

UMATA BAY

BOLANOS

MT SCHROEDER

SASALAGUAN

AGFAYAN BAY

DANA
ISLAND

0 1 2 3 4 5 6 7 8 9 10

SEA MILES

target. The broad deck of the *Matsushima* offered a splendid mark, into which the opening salvo of bombs crashed with unerring aim, dropped as they were at the point-blank range of 500 ft. So violent was the explosion that one of the American bombing machines, caught in the blast, was capsized, and before the pilot could regain control it fell headlong into the sea. The two remaining bombers were at this moment being fired on by Japanese pursuit planes, and their aim was therefore less accurate; but two more 600-pound bombs struck the deck, and a third, hitting the hull of the ship obliquely, detonated exactly on the water-line, where it blew an enormous hole in the side. To the anxious watchers on shore it soon became evident that the audacious attack had succeeded, for the *Matsushima*, vomiting fire and smoke, gradually assumed a heavy list, and as the heel increased more than one airplane was seen to slide from her deck into the water. She had stopped dead shortly after the first explosions. A large bomb had disabled her engines, and others, passing clean through the flying deck, had exploded with frightful effect in the lower compartments of the ship. It is probable that other severe leaks had been started, in addition to the great hole torn betwixt wind and water, since this alone would hardly have caused the vessel to founder, as she did, in ten minutes. Due to the confusion into which the enemy was thrown by this sudden blow, four of the American machines made good their escape and returned to the aerodrome at Dededo, practically undamaged; but the other four had paid the price of a great achievement, and they and their gallant occupants were now lying fathoms deep in the Pacific. The four survivors, three of which were fighting planes, remained on the ground only long enough to take in fresh ammunition, and were then up again with orders to drive off the Japanese spotting planes. At 3 o'clock the one surviving enemy machine was heading north, apparently for Saipan, pursued by bursting shell from the anti-aircraft guns at Agaña, while the wreckage of the last American plane lay smouldering on Mount Barrigada. The Guam air force had ceased to exist, but it had not sacrificed itself in vain. That the Japanese failed to appreciate the significance of the desperate attack on their aircraft-carrier was demonstrated by their subsequent procedure. Looking at the matter in the light of after knowledge, it may seem strange that they did not suspect that the defenders of the island had another card which could only be played when the factor of air observation had been eliminated. On the other hand, it has to be remembered that their knowledge of the defences was based on reports which had been compiled by spies shortly before the outbreak of war. They could not possibly have known of the subsequent arrival of the two transports and the landing of so many pieces of heavy mobile artillery. At 3.15 p.m., the warships off Apra having now ceased fire, several destroyers stood in towards the harbour, cutting a path through the mine-field with their paravane sweeps. They offered an excellent mark as they moved at low speed, threading their way through the reefs and shoals at the entrance, but not a shot was fired at them. The *Lamberton* and the *Rizal* were at this time lying near Santa Cruz Island; but both were on their beam ends, their decks were deserted, and to the enemy it must have seemed that these vessels had either been wrecked by the bombardment or scuttled by their crews. Encouraged by the absolute silence prevailing ashore, which was doubtless taken as proof that the last semblance of opposition had been crushed, nine transports now began to move in, their decks crowded with troops, their boats slung out-board, and destroyers going alongside to assist in the disembarkation. Eight miles out at sea lay the armoured cruiser *Kasuga*, while the *Tokiwa* and *Asama* were much closer inshore. The transports did not actually enter the harbour, but they approached to within a mile of the Catalan Bank before heaving to. Then the first contingent of troops went over the side and entered the boats, which made for the harbour in tow of the motor pinnaces and destroyers. The disembarkation was well under way and the first boatloads

were within less than half a mile of the shore before
Captain Harper played his trump card. Suddenly there
came the dull boom of a great gun from among the hills
behind Apra, followed an instant later by regular salvos
from other guns, so well placed as to be invisible from
the sea.   The first shell pitched into the water just ahead
of the leading transport, which lay broadside on to the
shore, offering an easy target to skilled gunners at a
range of barely four miles.   Heavy explosions were now
observed on board this ship and her consorts as the
7-inch projectiles got home.   The field guns on the
island had also come into action, spraying the crowded
boats with shrapnel and blowing a good half of them
to matchwood in the first few minutes.   Three of the
transports were ablaze and others had suffered severely
before the Japanese recovered from their surprise.   Then
their destroyers gallantly steamed in to shield the
remaining boats, firing heavily but blindly at the hidden
batteries ashore, and the large warships further out
reopened with every gun that would bear.   But not for a
moment did the hail of projectiles cease to scourge the
transports, which had now been transformed into
slaughter pens.   Three of them, all badly damaged,
succeeded in withdrawing from effective range, but the
remaining six were in a hopeless plight.   One sank as a
destroyer was towing her out, and shortly afterwards the
destroyer herself lay helpless on the water with her
engines wrecked by a shell.   The armoured cruiser
Tokiwa was so badly hit that she steamed out of action,
the *Asama* had her forward funnel blown over the
side, and a few hits were even made on the *Kasuga*.
By 4.30 p.m. the landing attempt at Apra had been
utterly defeated.   What remained of the enemy's ships
had hauled out of range, and boats from the *Lamberton*
and *Rizal* were outside the harbour, picking up a few half-
drowned Japanese soldiers.   The carnage on board the
transports and in the boats had been frightful.   Not less
than five thousand men had perished, and each of the
ships still afloat had the greater part of its contingent
disabled by wounds.   At Port Tarofofo, on the other

side of the island, events had meanwhile been taking much the same course, though at this point the American artillery was less numerous and only three transports were actually sunk, the others making good their escape in a more or less damaged condition. But it was here that the Japanese Navy suffered its first serious loss. The armoured cruiser *Nisshin*, having incautiously approached to within three miles of the shore before the American guns were unmasked, came under so tremendous a fire that she was disabled in five minutes, and before the destroyers which came rushing to her assistance could pass a towing hawser she blew up and sank. At Tarofofo, as at Apra, the Japanese warships had reopened fire with all guns as soon as the cannonade from the island began. At both places clouds of brown smoke rising from the woods and hills seemed to denote the presence of American guns, and these positions were accordingly swept with projectiles of every calibre. And yet not a single gun was touched, nor were there more than a dozen casualties among the American gun crews. The smoke which had drawn the enemy's fire came, not from the guns, but from small charges of a smoke-producing compound which were touched off periodically at various points well away from the batteries, each burst of smoke being timed to coincide with a discharge from the guns. By this means the Japanese observers were completely deceived, and their ships expended an enormous quantity of shell with practically no result. Both sections of the invading fleet were well out to sea before darkness fell, and it looked as if the attack had been definitely abandoned; but the garrison stood to its guns throughout the night, for there was a bare possibility that the Japanese would try to land on some other part of the coast under cover of darkness. But when the sun rose on the 21st the sea was empty of ships; only a faint haze on the northwest horizon marked the whereabouts of the discomfited enemy, who was, in fact, returning to Formosa at the best speed of which his sorely damaged remaining transports were capable. Guam was safe—for the time being, but its elated defenders well knew that a fresh attack, this time in overpowering force, was merely a question of days. Nor was there any real foundation for the hope, which a few of them cherished, that the United States fleet would arrive from the east before the next Japanese assault took place. Since the island had no longer any means of communicating with the outer world, the American naval authorities necessarily remained ignorant of the situation at Guam, though they assumed it to be already in Japanese possession. In fact the Tokyo wireless bulletin of March 20 had announced—somewhat prematurely, as it turned out— that "the fortress of Guam has fallen to a combined attack by the Imperial military and naval forces." Captain Harper employed the respite which had been granted him by marking out new gun positions, building emplacements and trenches and improving the roads over which the tractor batteries were likely to pass. He knew, however, that there was not the least hope of repeating his former success. This time the enemy would come well provided with aircraft, and these would infallibly locate the position of the guns as soon as they opened fire. On March 22 five American submarines reached Apra, three more coming in the next day. Unfortunately most of them had expended all their torpedoes, and there were none of these weapons in reserve at Guam. As submarines without torpedoes were useless for defence purposes, Captain Harper ordered six of the boats, after replenishing their oil tanks, to proceed to Honolulu, together with the destroyers *Lamberton* and *Rizal* and the transport *Newport News*. Only two submarines, *S 23* and *S 50*, were retained at Guam. Damage to her machinery caused by a stray shell in the first attack prevented the *Beaufort* from sailing. It may be mentioned here that all the other vessels made the voyage to Honolulu without mishap. Not until April 3 did the second Japanese attack develop. At an early hour that morning enemy aircraft appeared over the island in great strength, and soon afterwards a squadron of transports and naval vessels, including six battleships and cruisers, was seen approaching. Profiting by the severe lesson they had had on the previous occasion, the Japanese now adopted different tactics. No preparatory bombardment took place, but four of the transports headed towards the harbour with the apparent intention of coming right inside, to land their troops on the beach at Sumay. To counter this bold stroke it was absolutely necessary for the defenders to open fire, reluctant as they were to reveal the position of their guns while enemy airplanes were swarming overhead; but any further delay would enable the invaders to gain a foothold ashore, and that would be the beginning of the end. So Captain Harper passed word to the hidden guns, which at once came into action against the transports. But scarcely had the first flashes betrayed the battery positions when a dozen Japanese planes came swooping down, regardless of anti-aircraft fire, to drop their bombs with deadly aim. A few minutes later the warships lying off the island opened a terrific bombardment with gas and high-explosive shell, the whereabouts of the American batteries having been reported to them by the airmen. It was no longer a case of blindfold shooting. Thanks to the spotting aircraft, almost every salvo took effect on or near the batteries, and in a very short time half the guns had been silenced. Being without gas masks, the men were completely exposed to the fumes from asphyxiating shell. In more than one battery the entire *personnel* was *hors de combat ;* in others, guns and men had been destroyed by the big high-explosive projectiles. More Japanese transports now headed for the harbour, to be received this time with a desultory fire that did little harm to them, though it drew upon the defenders another annihilating blast of steel and gas from the Japanese squadron. At 11.30 a.m. the troops from the leading transports entered their boats and were towed inshore. By noon several thousand men had been landed, and were steadily advancing over the densely-wooded heights of Oroté toward Apra. The landing had been effected with small loss, for practically all the American guns on the western side of the island had been silenced, and only a few hundred members of the garrison had escaped injury. Here and there a handful of marines stood their ground and opened fire with machine-guns as soon as the Japanese troops became visible, but whenever this happened an airplane dived down and released a gas bomb which either disabled the defenders or forced them to retreat. When it appeared certain that no landing would be attempted on the east coast Captain Harper had ordered the 7-inch guns in the hills near Tarofofo to reinforce the western batteries, but no sooner had they left their camouflaged positions than they were attacked by aircraft, and eventually by ship fire as well. Not one of these guns got within reach of Apra. In some cases the tractor was damaged by a bomb or shell, making it impossible to drag the gun any further; in others, the entire crew of tractor and gun were killed. Seeing that further progress was impossible, the officer in command, Lieutenant Oliver, resolved to destroy the guns lest they should fall intact into enemy hands; and this task was successfully performed, in spite of the Japanese airmen, who planed down to machine-gun the demolition party. At dusk on April 3 the entire southern half of the island was occupied by enemy troops. The remnant of the garrison had retreated to the north, but their position was hopeless. Only by keeping to the shelter of the woods were they able to escape the bombs and bullets of the ubiquitous Japanese planes. That night Captain Harper held a council of war with his three surviving officers. Further effective resistance was impossible, and repugnant as was the thought of surrender it was the only alternative to a useless sacrifice of the remaining men, who had fought so gallantly against tremendous odds. In the morning, therefore, the little party—not more than a hundred all told—came into the open and laid down their arms in full sight of the first Japanese airplane that appeared. Observing what had happened, this machine at once turned and flew back to headquarters. Two hours later a company of Japanese infantry reached the spot and escorted the captives to

Agaña, where General Awakara, in command of the invading force, had already established himself in the Governor's residence. He received Captain Harper with marked courtesy, congratulating him on his gallant defence and assuring him that his men would be well treated. Fate, however, had willed that Captain Harper's captivity should be of short duration. On April 6 he and two other officers were sent on board the destroyer *Hagi*, which was to convey them to Japan. This vessel had not proceeded twenty miles on her voyage before she was struck by a torpedo from the American submarine *S 50*, which caused her to founder in a few minutes. While her victim was in the act of sinking, *S 50* rose to the surface a short distance away, whereupon Captain Harper swam to within hailing distance and announced his identity. He was promptly picked up, together with Lieutenant Schreiner, but although a lengthy search was made the third American officer could not be found, having evidently met his death in the water. As Japanese aircraft were then approaching the scene, the *S 50* had to dive. This submarine remained in the vicinity of Guam for some days longer, hoping to catch one of the larger Japanese warships. No opportunity presented itself, however, and as fuel was running low the *S 50* eventually made her way to Honolulu. Her consort, the *S 23*, did not reach that place, nor was she ever heard of again, and since the enemy made no claim to have sunk her it was surmised that she had been lost either by some accident or through striking a mine off one of the neighbouring Japanese islands.

CHAPTER VII

Survey of strategical situation after fall of Guam—Economic position
   of the United States superior to that of Japan—Japanese operations against American seaborne trade

WHEN the fall of Guam occurred, on April 4, the war
had been in progress just one month. Events in this
opening period had vindicated the judgment of those
American strategists who had all along warned their
countrymen that the remote islands of the Western
Pacific could not, in existing circumstances, be held
against a hostile Japan, and must inevitably be for-
feited soon after the outbreak of war. But although
these grave reverses had been foreseen by the initiated,
and discounted in advance, their moral effect both in
the United States and abroad was nevertheless very
marked. Since at this time nothing was known of the
heavy price which Japan had been compelled to pay for
her initial successes, it was widely assumed that her
losses were trivial, nor did the official Japanese bulletins
seek to correct this impression. Not until the submarine *S 50*, with Captain Harper on board, reached
Honolulu did the world learn the truth about the heroic
defence of Guam. His story of the smashing repulse
of the first attack, together with the submarine and
destroyer officers' accounts of the casualties inflicted
on the invaders of the Philippines, were hailed with
enthusiasm in America, for at least these proved that
the enemy was not invincible, as not a few people,
disheartened by successive misfortunes on sea and land,
were beginning to believe. At the same time, there
was no gainsaying the formidable nature of the task

which now confronted the United States. It was clear
that the military power of Japan was enormous. Her
Navy and Army were obviously in a high state of
efficiency, and her sailors and soldiers appeared to be
fighting with all their traditional prowess. Behind
them, too, stood a united nation, for a truce had been
called to the political feuds which only a few weeks
before had threatened to plunge Japan into civil war.
The call to arms had evoked an instant response from
all classes. Steps had been taken by the authorities to
forestall the pacifist campaign which the Socialists were
expected to launch, but these measures proved superfluous. With a few unimportant exceptions the leaders
of the party gave their unqualified support to the
Government. The cause of national unity was further
promoted by the announcement of an amnesty to
political prisoners. How far matters had progressed
in this direction was shown by the publication late in
March of the famous " National Manifesto," setting
forth at great length the reasons which had constrained
Japan to defend herself against " the unprovoked and
intolerable aggression of the United States." To this
document were appended the signatures of a hundred
Japanese prominent in every walk of life, including
half-a-dozen leading members of the Socialist Party.
For the time being, at least, the hosts of Nippon had
closed their ranks, presenting an unbroken front to the
blast of war. It seemed, moreover, as if Japan held
every winning card in the game of strategy now developing. Too remote herself to be attacked, she had yet
been able to deliver telling blows against her opponent.
In the space of a few weeks she had achieved her
primary objective by wresting the Philippine archipelago and the island of Guam from American hands,
leaving her foe without a single base, either actual or
potential, adjacent to the theatre of operations. What
would her next move be? Would she rest content with
her initial gains, and, strong in the knowledge of her
impregnable position, calmly await the counter-attack,
assuming this to be possible across 4,000 miles of sea;

H

or would her martial ardour, fortified by motives of policy, lead her to carry the war further afield, even as far, perhaps, as Hawaii or the United States itself? The consensus of American opinion inclined towards the latter theory, for which indeed there seemed to be substantial grounds. It was hardly credible that Japanese statesmen should deceive themselves as to the eventual issue of a protracted war with so redoubtable an opponent, nor could they be under the illusion that the blows already administered were severe enough to compel the United States to sue for peace. Much more would have to be done before this desirable result was attained, and meanwhile everything pointed to the necessity for swift action. Month by month the military power of America would increase in progressive ratio. Given sufficient time she could build up a fleet of overwhelming size, raise an army millions strong, and, above all, mobilise her matchless financial resources for an offensive that Japanese credit could never hope to resist. From the Japanese viewpoint, therefore, time was the essence of the problem. But granting the will to prosecute a bold offensive, where and in what manner could this be done? The very remoteness which made Japan herself so difficult to assail made it equally impossible for her to aim a mortal thrust at the enemy's heart. In the present war the factor of distance dominated the whole scheme of operations, and whichever side succeeded best in converting that factor to its own advantage might count with tolerable certainty on a fortunate decision. Command of the sea was thus a condition precedent to the delivery of any blow of sufficient weight to turn the scale, but such command would have to be effective over an area the immensity of which had never been paralleled in former wars. In this case each of the belligerents could claim an indisputable supremacy, not merely within its local waters, but over a generous sector of the contiguous ocean. With a powerful battle fleet pivoted on Hawaii, the United States was master of the situation so far as the Eastern Pacific was concerned. From this central

position, aided by light naval forces working from bases
in the Aleutian Islands (off the Alaskan coast) and from
Tutuila (Samoa), the fleet could exercise control over
all lines of approach from the westward, and so long
as it remained " in being " there was not the remotest
possibility of an attempt by Japan to invade Hawaii,
still less the United States.   On the other hand, it was
impossible to guarantee complete immunity from raiding
attacks by enemy ships acting alone or in small flying
squadrons, but the military effect of such raids could
in no case be serious.   Japan, on her part, had no reason
to fear an immediate attack in force.   She had eliminated this possibility by her prompt seizure of the only
bases of which an American fleet, advancing into the
Western Pacific, might have made use.   Her control of
these waters was at least as absolute as that enjoyed
by the United States over the eastern sector.   If her
battle fleet was numerically small, she had an abundance
of light craft with which to patrol the outer cordon of
her defences.   She had, moreover, a number of advanced
bases at the disposal of these craft.   Within a radius
of two thousand miles from Japan Proper she now
possessed such admirable *points d'appui* as the Philippines, the Mariana, and the Bonin Islands, while further
to the east lay the Caroline and Marshall Islands, where
emergency bases for submarines and other small vessels
could be improvised with ease.   Very early in the
war, measures were taken to guard the approach from
the north-east by stationing two light cruisers, a submarine flotilla, and a flight of aircraft at a convenient
harbour in Sakhalin (Karafuto).   Japan, in short, held
all the keys of the Western Pacific, and it seemed
impossible that any hostile force could venture into
that area without courting destruction.   Such was the
position on either side of the Pacific.   Between the two
guarded zones lay, as it were, a neutral belt of water
roughly one thousand miles in width and more than
four thousand miles in length stretching from the
Aleutian Islands in the north to Samoa in the south.
Ships of large fuel capacity belonging to either belligerent

were free to traverse this belt, but if they did so they at once became exposed to attack by a superior concentration of force.   Major fleet operations can only be conducted from a well-equipped base, and then only against an objective that in point of distance is well within the steaming endurance of the smallest ship accompanying the fleet.   All the larger vessels of the two navies carried sufficient fuel for a voyage across the Pacific.   There is, however, a world of difference between steaming endurance in peace and in war.   A vessel engaged in a peace-time cruise can jog along at " economical speed," which may be from one-half to one-third of its maximum speed, and thus make the most of its fuel supply.   In war this leisurely mode of travel becomes impossible.   Ships moving at slow speed on a straight course offer an inviting mark for submarine attack.   Consequently, in waters where enemy submarines are active it is essential to maintain a fairly high rate of speed and to make frequent changes of course, a form of progress known as zigzagging.   In these circumstances the consumption of fuel is very heavy.   Authentic figures of warship steaming endurance are rarely published, but it is a safe surmise that the battleships and cruisers of both navies were limited *under war conditions* to a continuous voyage of 4,000 miles.   This meant that they dare not venture more than 2,000 miles away from their nearest base.   The collective radius of either fleet was still further circumscribed by the presence of its destroyers, the fuel capacity of which was much smaller than that of the big ships.   It was possible, of course, to re-fuel these boats at sea, but to do this the vessels concerned had to reduce their speed, so that the process entailed the risk of submarine attack.   Yet for the battleships to have put to sea without their escort of destroyers would have been madness.   A survey of all these considerations made it clear that neither the American nor the Japanese fleet could operate beyond a distance of more than a thousand miles or so from its bases.   This, as we have seen, ruled out the possibility of direct oversea attacks in force. If Japan wished to deal heavy blows at her enemy she had first to secure a base within easy reach of the objective, and how was such a base to be secured? Conversely, the United States could not wage offensive warfare until base facilities in the Western Pacific had been acquired. Having regard to these patent truths, it is not to be wondered at that many observers prophesied that the Pacific campaign would speedily end in stalemate. Peace must soon be negotiated, they said, because of the physical impossibility of deciding the issue by combat. This view was widely held in the United States, where a section of the Press was already urging the Government to make overtures for peace, on the ground that nothing was to be gained by prolonging a struggle so obviously futile. The peace movement received considerable impetus when the economic effects of the war began to make themselves felt. In the ten years preceding the war, American commerce with the Far East had undergone a rapid expansion, and in 1930 it represented an appreciable percentage of the total foreign trade of the United States. With the outbreak of hostilities this profitable traffic came suddenly to a standstill. The ports of Eastern Asia could no longer be reached by American shipping, and while American goods might still be conveyed to the Chinese market in neutral bottoms, it was only too evident that other countries would make a determined effort to capture for themselves the lucrative trade from which their erstwhile American rivals were now excluded. This was a serious prospect for the United States, which in recent years had become more and more dependent on Asia as a market for her surplus commodities. As far back as 1921 a well-known American economist had emphasised the vital importance of developing trade in this quarter. New markets, he showed, must be found to replace those of Europe, whose effective purchasing power had been reduced by the consequences of the world war of 1914–18. " American manufacturers must export greater quantities of their products than at present, in order to keep running at full capacity the plants which have been enlarged to meet the demands of the last seven years and to continue to employ all American workmen at wages that will enable them to maintain unimpaired the American standard of living, of which we are so justly proud. The Far East offers the great possibilities of an unexploited field." His advice had not fallen on deaf ears. In the race for commercial supremacy in China the United States had gained a definite lead. American capital had been lavishly invested in Chinese industries, some of the richest concessions there were in American hands, and the economic relationship of the two countries was growing ever closer. Now, however, the fruits of ten years of strenuous work were threatened with ruin. Although this danger may have been imperfectly realised by the American people at large, events soon occurred to remind them that the apparent deadlock in the main naval sphere did not extend over the entire Pacific.

American trade with the Far East at this time was largely conducted under neutral flags, and could not therefore be entirely dislocated by the war with Japan. All merchant vessels flying the Stars and Stripes within the sphere of Japanese naval operations were either seized, captured, or driven into neutral ports, such as Shanghai and Hong Kong, within the first two weeks of the war; but their total number was inconsiderable, and it could not be said that their loss or immobilisation had any appreciable effect upon the course of the conflict. Altogether, eleven ships fell into Japanese hands in this way, apart from those taken in the Philippine campaign and intercepted on the high seas during subsequent operations, their hulls and cargoes representing a total value of about $2,500,000. A good deal of unfavourable comment was aroused by the action of the Japanese in taking possession of an American steamer at Yingkow, the port of Niuchwang, in Manchuria, which was regarded by Japan as one of her dependencies. An attempt was also made to appropriate an American ship at Chifu, in the Chinese province of

Shantung, on the opposite side of the Gulf of Pechihli; but here the local port authorities, backed up by secret orders from Peking, assumed an attitude of passive resistance, at which the Chinese are adepts. Much acrimonious correspondence passed between Tokyo and Peking, as a result of which China invoked the intervention of the League of Nations (to which both countries were subscribers); and after some weeks had passed Japan unwillingly yielded in face of a growing volume of neutral disapproval of her arbitrary action. Incidentally the League of Nations, which for some time had ceased to be taken very seriously by the world in general, was able to make a certain amount of capital out of its success in this dispute. China was not slow to digest the lesson thus taught, and henceforth utilised every opportunity of setting neutral interests in opposition to those of Japan.

The most valuable of the interned U.S. steamers had taken refuge in the British port of Hong Kong. In order that they might not thereby be deterred from attempting escape, the Japanese Navy Department issued strict orders that no cruisers were to venture too near the port. But the American Consul at Hong Kong, being a shrewd man with some knowledge of Eastern mentality, advised that the experiment be tried of sending out alone the slowest and oldest ship, instead of all American shipping in the port making a general dash to sea. The vessel chosen was the *Borneo*, of 2,000 tons gross, which had been employed in the local trade between Hong Kong, the Philippines, and North Borneo ports, and was then in ballast. The Consul pointed out, with reason, that if she should succeed in getting through the South China Sea and out of the war zone without being intercepted, the remaining larger and faster steamers ought to stand an even better chance of eluding capture. As was invariably found to be the case, the Japanese intelligence service, so far as Eastern affairs were concerned, proved efficient. Prompt information of the *Borneo's* movements must have been furnished, for she had not long quitted territorial waters when a Japanese submarine appeared, and ordered her by semaphore to heave-to, enforcing the command by a shot across the steamer's bows when she pretended not to understand. Her radio apparatus, if any were fitted, does not seem to have been in working order, but the sound of gunfire brought a British destroyer on the scene. Her report of the *Borneo's* capture caused the masters of the other American ships at Hong Kong to congratulate themselves on having taken the advice of the Consul in awaiting the success of their consort's venture before quitting harbour themselves. For some weeks after the outbreak of war Japanese cruisers were busily engaged in searching neutral bottoms for American owned goods which might be deemed contraband of war, but it was not long before means were found to evade this inquisition, neutral shippers and consignees being employed on an elaborate scale. Despite innocent-looking bills of lading and manifests, these methods were sometimes revealed through espionage. The Japanese, however, very soon found it expedient to refrain from detaining goods in cases where the clearest proof of enemy ownership was not to be had, since it became abundantly clear as the war proceeded that they could not afford to take the risk of offending powerful neutrals.

As we saw in a previous chapter, Japan had not scrupled to make the affair of the *Nikko Maru* an excuse for employing her submarines as commerce destroyers. Proof of their activities was soon forth-coming. In spite of orders having been sent out to all U.S. merchantmen when war became imminent, warning them to give the danger zone a wide berth, several suffered in the early days from the attentions of Japanese surface and submarine raiders. But if the Japanese had borrowed a leaf from the German war book by utilising submarines to harry enemy shipping, they did their work with a scrupulous regard for the law of nations that stood in refreshing contrast to the brutal methods of the German U-boat commanders. What happened at the capture of the freight steamer *Orient* on April 28 may be recorded as a typical instance of Japanese procedure. The *Orient*, on passage from Sydney to San Francisco, was intercepted by the Japanese submarine *Ro. 51* in mid-Pacific, some 150 miles north-west of Washington Island. When first sighted the submarine lay about two miles ahead. She fired a blank charge as a signal to heave-to, whereupon the American ship put on speed, altered course, and endeavoured to shroud herself in a pall of smoke. But the superior speed of the submarine foiled this manœuvre. Two shots were fired across the bows of the *Orient*, and it was not until the chase had continued for some time that the submarine began shooting in earnest. Even then only unfused 12 lb. shell were used. One of these hit the steamer's funnel, upon which her master stopped his engines and ordered the boats to be cleared. The submarine now approached to within a few hundred yards, keeping her guns trained on the steamer, and sent off a boarding party. His papers having been impounded, Captain Sandstrom was informed that an armed guard would be placed on board, and that he must navigate his ship to Jaluit, in the Marshall Archipelago, which was serving at this time as one of the Japanese advanced bases. He was required to sign a document putting him on his honour to attempt no escape, the alternative being the destruction of his ship and the casting of himself and his crew adrift in open boats. After some hesitation he gave the required pledge, an action for which he was subsequently abused by many critics in America. A few days later, in the same locality, another submarine held up the U.S.S. *Bath*, a fleet auxiliary carrying cargo, on her way from Honolulu to Tutuila. On this occasion the victim, though in no condition to offer effective resistance (she was only armed with two machine guns), made a resolute effort to escape, and was only brought to a halt when her engines were wrecked by a shell. Five members of the crew were killed and several others wounded. The injured men were taken on board the submarine, and after receiving medical treatment were transferred with the rest of the crew to a British steamer which had put in an appearance during the chase.   The *Bath*, her engines being found to be beyond repair, was scuttled.

Finally, on April 30, occurred the affair of the *Pershing*, in which the Japanese behaved with a remarkable degree of chivalry, the underlying motive for which was not immediately appreciated.   The *Pershing*, a Government transport recently renamed on being taken over from the Shipping Board, had sailed from Honolulu on the previous day, bound for San Francisco.   She had on board upwards of 200 officers belonging to the Army and the Coast Artillery Corps, the majority of whom had been recalled for instructional duties in connection with the training of the new armies which were being enrolled in the States.   There were besides a number of officers and men invalided home, and some score of officers' wives, with their children.   It had not been considered necessary to provide an escort for the voyage to San Francisco, since there had been no reason to suspect the presence of enemy vessels on this route, though as a matter of precaution all the approaches had been patrolled by flying boats since the outbreak of war.   So the transport sailed alone with no premonition of danger.   Shortly after dawn on April 30 the radio station at Pearl Harbour, Hawaii, picked up a signal from the ship which read : " We are being chased by Japanese submarine ; enemy gaining fast and firing on us."   No further message came through, and it is easy to imagine the consternation that prevailed at Honolulu when the alarming news became known.   As a Government transport the *Pershing* would be legitimate prey for the enemy, and the gravest fears were entertained for the safety of those on board. Two large seaplanes were ordered to rush to the rescue, and destroyers were also dispatched, but there was little hope of their arriving in time to avert disaster. An hour later suspense was ended by the receipt of a further message to this effect :   " Ship released and proceeding on voyage."   Relief at this welcome intelligence was mingled with astonishment and incredulity that the Japanese should have permitted such a valuable prize to go free. But the transport duly reached San Francisco, with a remarkable story to tell, which is here reproduced in the captain's own words : " Fourteen hours out of Honolulu the look-out sighted a submarine on the starboard bow. It was a very large craft, and at first everybody took it for one of our own, for it seemed impossible that an enemy ship should be cruising so far from Japanese waters. But we were quickly undeceived when the stranger sent a big shell screaming over our bridge. As our best speed was 15 knots and the submarine was doing at least 18, escape seemed hopeless. However, I turned away, ordered full steam, and held on until a shell burst only a few feet away from our bows, throwing a deluge of water on to the forecastle. At this, knowing we must be hit by the next shot and being anxious for the safety of my passengers, I judged it best to stop. As the submarine came up rapidly we saw that she was at least 300 feet long, with two heavy guns mounted on deck. An officer and four armed sailors boarded us and made me show my papers. I was then ordered to muster everybody, passengers and crew, on deck, and was told by the officer : ' This ship is to be sunk. You have enough boats to take all these people, and I will let them go on condition that all the men sign an undertaking not to serve in any military capacity while the war lasts.' I pointed out that bad weather was threatening, that in any case the boats would be dangerously overcrowded, and that we had upwards of 40 women and children with us. He then said : ' Very well, perhaps my captain may let the ship proceed if the men give their parole not to serve in the war.' I communicated this to Colonel Warner, who said he would under no consideration give his parole, and he forbade the others to do so. Hearing this, the Japanese officer, who had so far been polite though visibly impatient, grew angry, and went back to the submarine for further orders. Returning in a few minutes, he said : ' The colonel and five officers of highest rank will be taken prisoners of war, but we have decided to let your ship go.' Knowing resistance to be out of the question, Colonel Warner, with Majors Henderson, Hoffmann, and Green, and Captains Longman and Seibold, stepped forward and said they were willing to go. They were given time to take a small amount of personal baggage, and were then rowed across to the enemy vessel in one of our boats. When last seen they were standing on the deck of the submarine, waving farewell to us. Meanwhile the boarding party, having stripped our radio gear and confiscated all cameras on board, left the ship, and we continued our voyage.'' It transpired later that the second message received at Honolulu, announcing the release of the transport, had been dispatched by the commander of the Japanese submarine—another act of courtesy rare in the annals of war, and one which was highly appreciated by those whose anxiety it relieved. The submarine, with her captives on board, returned to Japan a month later.

With regard to this incident, it has been suggested, probably with justice, that the humane methods practised by the Japanese in their war on commerce were calculated to yield better results in the long run than a policy of ruthlessness. A study of history is believed to have convinced the Japanese Naval Staff that belligerents employing such methods not only avoided giving any offence to neutrals, but encouraged a readiness on the part of pursued vessels to surrender at the first summons. That it would have been folly for Japan to have conducted her operations on any other lines is a proposition the truth of which is self-evident from an examination of the consequences attending the " sink at sight " methods favoured by the Germans in the world war of 1914–18.

But no amount of courtesy on the part of the Japanese could assuage American anger at the damage which they were inflicting upon shipping and overseas trade. Though the tale of losses was, comparatively speaking, insignificant, the American papers loudly demanded to know what the Navy was doing. " Why," inquired one San Francisco journal, "are enemy warships free to come and go as they list, sinking our shipping right and left, and making even the passage between Hawaii and the mainland unsafe for our transports? Apparently there is nothing to prevent them from sailing right into San Francisco harbour. Have the American people been spending vast sums each year on the upkeep of a Navy, only to be told when war comes that it cannot do its job?" And much more to the like effect. The truth was, of course, that the Navy was singularly ill-equipped for the task that lay before it. For the protection of American sea-borne trade a large force of cruisers was required, and no such force was available. There were barely enough cruisers to form the scouting division of the battle fleet, whose claims were rightly given precedence over all others. No modern ships could be spared for commerce protection, but the Navy Department so far yielded to newspaper clamour as to furbish up the old armoured cruisers *Charlotte* and *Huntington*, which had been laid up since many years, and commission them for service on the Hawaii–Pacific Coast route. These ships had to be manned with "green" crews, for the mobilisation of the effective fleet had already strained *personnel* resources to breaking point, and at least a year would elapse before the men who had swarmed to the naval recruiting stations at the outbreak of war would be sufficiently trained for duty afloat. For the moment, therefore, American shipping had to be left pretty much to its own devices. Practically no help could be rendered by the Navy. Preparations were made for arming all ocean-going merchantmen out of the reserve of artillery which had been kept in store ever since the world war, but here again the shortage of trained gunners was severely felt. In the absence of suitable escort vessels it was useless to institute any system of convoy, even had the volume of American trade in the Pacific justified such procedure. The Panama Canal being closed, shipping was for the time being practically restricted to coastwise movements, except for the route to Hawaii and Samoa.

CHAPTER VIII

APRIL–MAY, 1931

Events in China and Korea—Friction between Japan and Russia—
Importance of Japanese trade with Europe not realised by U.S.
Government—Mines laid by Japanese off Hawaii—Another mine-
field discovered near San Diego—Distribution of American warships at end of May—Anxiety caused by shortage of trained
personnel

HAVING surveyed the situation that developed in the
United States during the opening stages of the war,
it will be appropriate to bring under review the trend
of events in the Far East in the same period.   Thanks
to the rigorous Japanese censorship—which extended
far beyond the confines of Japan, being particularly
efficacious in those provinces of China that were under
Japanese control—news from the Asiatic side was meagre
and unreliable.   Judging from the bulletins emanating
from Tokyo, the teeming millions of China had made
Japan's cause their own, hailing her as their champion
against the white interlopers who had sought to bring
the peoples of the East under their domination.   So
friendly was popular sentiment in China, the bulletins
avowed, that the Japanese garrisons in Manchuria
were being reduced, and large reinforcements had thus
become available for the main army of operations.
Neither in Korea nor Formosa, it was added, had any
symptoms of unrest appeared.   Both colonies were
giving proofs of unswerving loyalty to Japan, who was
thus left free to devote all her energies to the defeat
of her arrogant foe.   As for the Japanese people, " their
martial fervour remains undiminished," the world was
assured.   " ' Victory at all costs ' is the slogan heard
on every hand."   While there was for the moment no

means of checking these statements as to the morale of the Japanese masses, it soon became known through other channels that the attitude of China had been grossly misrepresented by the Tokyo bulletins. So far from espousing the Japanese cause, the central government at Peking was already adopting a policy that bade fair to cause serious embarrassment to Japan. One of its first actions was to place an embargo on the export not only of arms and munitions, but of raw materials susceptible of conversion into munitions of war. Within this category were placed coal, iron ore, and other minerals that were going to Japan in enormous quantities. Had the embargo been effective it must speedily have crippled Japan's war effort and compelled her to discontinue the struggle, but since the central Government's writ did not run in the provinces under Japanese control— which were precisely those richest in mineral resources— the edict could not be enforced. Nevertheless, the fact that it had been issued afforded clear proof of China's latent hostility to her powerful neighbour. When the embargo was ignored, Peking addressed a Note to the Powers, charging Japan with violation of Chinese neutrality and reserving the right to take counter-measures. And so, even at this early stage, Japan had to reckon with the possibility of serious trouble in a quarter where she had interests of vital importance. As we have seen, so far from reducing her garrisons there, she had found it expedient to reinforce them. Nor was the ill-will of China limited to diplomatic protests, for it was well known that Chinese emissaries with ample funds at their disposal were behind the insurgents in Korea, where the whole country seemed to be ripe for revolt. Tokyo had a further cause for anxiety in the attitude of Russia, whose Government was already displaying a tendency to fish in troubled waters. Of the many controversial issues between Japan and Russia, that of Sakhalin had become most acute. For ten years the northern, or Russian, half of this island had been held by the Japanese, who had gone there in April, 1920, as a reprisal for the massacre of seven hundred of their nationals by Bolshevik partisans at Nikolaievsk. The subsequent discovery of rich oilfields in the territory thus seized made Japan very loath to part with it, and all Russia's efforts to recover her property had proved abortive. The agreement signed in January, 1925, which aimed at composing these differences, had but a brief duration, being denounced by Russia two years later on the ground of alleged Japanese violation. Now, however, Japan's preoccupation with the war gave the Soviet rulers the opportunity for which they had been waiting. Barely a month after the outbreak of hostilities a Note was addressed to Tokyo, demanding not only the immediate and complete evacuation of Northern Sakhalin, but a recognition of Russian rights over the Chinese Eastern Railway in Manchuria, to which Japan had hitherto refused so much as to listen. It will be recalled that in 1924, during one of the chronic civil wars which had been the curse of China ever since the revolution of 1912, the Russians had contrived to regain their former dominating influence in the management of the Chinese Eastern Railway as the price of their support of Chang Tso-lin, the Manchurian Tu-chun, in his victorious campaign against his rival, Wu Pei-fu. Though this control remained effective locally, the retrocession of the railroad had never been recognised *de jure* by any power other than China. Although not an ultimatum, the Note from Moscow was couched in somewhat peremptory terms, and arriving at a time when persistent reports of big military concentrations on the Manchurian frontier were current, it alarmed the Japanese Government more than they cared to admit. Their interest lay in keeping Russia neutral at almost any price, yet this, it appeared, would necessitate bitter sacrifices entailing more than a mere loss of prestige. By restoring Northern Sakhalin to its former owners, Japan would lose what had become one of her principal reservoirs of oil. As it was, the stocks of this precious fuel were none too large, and the naval authorities were already making anxious search for new sources of supply, which, of course, were strictly limited. Research work had for some time been in progress at the Fushun colliery, in Southern Manchuria, in the hope of producing fresh reserves of crude oil by means of dry distillation from shale. High hopes had been founded on this source; but after lengthy experiments had been carried out at considerable expense, it was found that only meagre supplies of oil of inferior quality could be obtained, at a cost out of proportion to their value. Boring for oil in Formosa, though less disappointing, did not yield petroleum in quantities adequate to the needs of the country in war time. The only other source which promised well was a new area which Japanese experts had located in the island of Mindanao, in the Southern Philippines. The chief objection to this oilfield was its distance from a convenient port, as it was situated very near the centre of the island, which has an area of close on 37,000 square miles. As a natural consequence, the Chief of the Naval Staff entered a weighty protest against any hasty acceptance of the Russian demands, emphasising that Japan's renunciation of the Sakhalin oilfields would be likely to lose her the war. Yet it was only too clear that the ultimate retrocession of this otherwise unimportant territory was but one, and that not the greatest, of the sacrifices which Japan would be called upon to make if she wished to assure the neutrality of her formidable neighbour. To provoke Russian enmity at this juncture was clearly madness. None knew better than the statesmen of Japan that the Imperialist traditions of the Tsarist régime had survived the revolution of 1917, and that Russia still turned covetous eyes on the rich lands of Manchuria and Mongolia, which she was only too eager to bring under her sway should circumstances afford her the opportunity. Sooner or later, as most Japanese believed, another war would have to be fought with Russia for the control of China. Since 1904, when Japan had risked her very existence by challenging the mighty colossus of the North because she regarded the extirpation of Muscovite influence in Manchuria as vital to the future safety of

I

the Empire, her own stake in China had become immeasurably greater—so great, indeed, that it was now one of the main sources of her national strength and prosperity. Ostensibly, at least, the present war was being waged to resist American encroachment on this preserve. But although Russia was recognised as a potential enemy, this was certainly not the time to provoke a clash with her. It was of the first importance that she should be placated until the present struggle had been brought to a conclusion. The Naval Staff was accordingly informed by the Foreign Office that negotiations for the return of Northern Sakhalin were about to be set in train, but that every effort would be made to prolong them. As for the Russian claims in regard to the Chinese Eastern Railway—which involved nothing less than the control of this line from the western Manchurian frontier to the Ussuri railway at Nikolsk—these were at once accepted " in principle " by Japan, who suggested the holding of a conference at Chita to settle the details. Doubtless she hoped that before the proceedings had committed her to any definite pledge, a fortunate turn in the tide of war would enable her to drop the mask of conciliation and show a defiant front to Russia. Such, then, were the grave political embarrassments with which Japan had to contend almost at the beginning of her duel with the United States. Already she was finding it needful to walk warily in her dealings with China and Russia, and it was fairly obvious that nothing but a succession of brilliant strokes against her immediate antagonist would clear the political horizon of the ominous clouds that were gathering.

The effect upon Japanese trade of the cessation of intercourse with the United States was not long in making itself felt, and at the outset some important industries were threatened with semi-paralysis from this cause. Before the war Japan probably imported nearly half her supplies of raw cotton (an indispensable material for the manufacture of munitions) from the States, and this shortage had now to be made good from other sources, often at greatly enhanced prices. A similar situation existed to some extent with regard to iron and steel, to say nothing of petroleum. All these products were of inestimable value in war time. Two of Japan's principal exports, silk and cotton goods, were also seriously threatened, since not only had the United States been one of her best customers for these, but the sudden shortage in the supply of raw cotton, accentuated by the commandeering of stocks for munition purposes, forced many industrial undertakings to work short time. Such a contingency had been foretold in pre-war days by certain Japanese publicists, despite the unpopularity of such predictions, but for some time it looked as though they had under-estimated the effect upon Japanese trade of a war with her trans-Pacific neighbour.

However, after the first few months the inexorable laws of demand and supply asserted themselves, and trade found its way by devious channels through the artificial obstacles imposed by a state of war. Neutrals largely benefited, as each of the warring nations had good reason to know by the high prices they were compelled to pay for many necessaries of life. It is to be doubted whether they realised that no small proportion of these necessaries came from the enemy in the first place, though purporting to be of neutral origin.

To repair the immediate deficiencies in raw materials, and at the same time build up a reserve of munitions equal to any conceivable demand, all available Japanese tonnage was quickly thrown into the trade with China, Australia, India, South Africa, and Europe, which for some considerable while was not interfered with by America's armed forces at sea. But American superiority in the field of finance soon began to tell, and Japan found that not only had she to pay exorbitant and ever-rising prices for many of her most pressing needs, but in some markets supplies were practically unobtainable, having been cornered by her opponent. Matters would have been much worse for Japan had not her Government, apprehending some such *impasse*, promptly closed a number of huge forward contracts for such vital products as rice, cotton, wool, copper, iron, oil, etc.

Even as it was, the Japanese public did not take kindly to intermittent scarcity combined with soaring prices; and though something was done to check profiteering by means of a system of Government control, it was soon apparent that more energetic steps would have to be adopted if the morale of the nation were to be preserved.

Neither combatant, it must be realised, was in an advantageous position to make any sustained attack upon the commerce of the other, owing to the immense distance separating them and the mutual lack of bases.

It is true that at the outbreak of war the United States maintained in the Mediterranean a squadron, comprising the modern cruiser *Trenton* and a number of destroyers; but on the outbreak of war this force was recalled to home waters, in accordance with prearranged plans for fleet mobilisation. Not until much later does it seem to have occurred to anyone in authority that it would have been a far sounder policy to have retained and reinforced this squadron with the object of interrupting the very important Japanese trade with Europe. The principal Japanese steamship line, the Nippon Yusen Kaisha, had the bulk of its large fleet of 100 vessels engaged on regular voyages between Japan and European ports, a number that was greatly augmented when the cessation of trade with the United States released a vast supply of fresh tonnage. It is now plain that serious interference with her Occidental traffic would have forced Japan into taking such action as would inevitably have led to an earlier decision. But seaborne trade not being a matter of vital concern to the United States, American strategists were slow to perceive that to Japan (no longer a self-supporting country, especially in time of war) it constituted one of her main arteries, which it should have been her adversary's first aim to sever. Only when disaster in other quarters had compelled a change in the naval strategy of the conflict, was a more correct appreciation of the needs of the situation brought home to those Americans who had hitherto failed to grasp it.

Comparatively few vessels of the Japanese mercantile marine fell into American hands at the outbreak of war, and even these were unimportant in size and value. There is no doubt that early warning must have been given of the imminence of hostilities, a fact of which the blocking of the Panama Canal by the *Akashi Maru* affords further proof.

At the same time, however, a few people in Washington did evince a clearer perception of the difficulties confronting Japan. More than one member of the War Cabinet, it has since been affirmed, foresaw that Japan would eventually find herself assailed either by Russia or China, perhaps by both, and would then be compelled to make peace and restitution to the United States in order to free her hands for defence against these new enemies. This view no doubt appealed to some minds because, if it were sound, it did away with the uncomfortable necessity for a more vigorous prosecution of the war. According to their arguments, it would suffice for America to stand on the defensive, taking only such measures as were necessary to protect her coastline and her floating trade, but without incurring the costs and hazards of operations in the war zone overseas. In other words, she should restrict her combatant energies to the minimum consistent with defence in the narrowest sense of the term, and, for the rest, wait upon the march of events in the Far East, which would, they suggested, soon compel Japan to put forward peace proposals. This specious reasoning, however, failed to impress the majority of American strategists, nor did it escape criticism in the Press, a section of which emphasised the folly of gambling on optimistic expectations which might at any moment be falsified. That Japan should have gone to war without first insuring herself against an attack in flank seemed quite incredible to thoughtful Americans, who remembered with what careful judgment she had selected the right moment for breaking off relations with Russia in 1904. At this time, be it remembered, the world was in ignorance of the domestic motives which had impelled Prince Kawamura and his colleagues to precipitate the war. Whether they had foreseen or fully estimated the dangers of complications with Russia and China must always remain in doubt; but it is clear from reports of the conference at Tokyo on the fateful 5th of January that they were prepared if necessary to take immense risks rather than allow their country to drift into revolution.

While these discussions were going on at Washington, alarming news came from the Pacific. In pursuance of their policy of taking the initiative, and with the object of maintaining the morale of the populace, the Japanese had determined that the war must be carried to the enemy's coasts. Their first move in this direction was the laying of a series of mine-fields, the earliest of which were planted off the Hawaiian capital, Honolulu, in the island of Oahu, and Pearl Harbour, the naval station some few miles from it. This work appears to have been carried out by a 7000-ton Japanese submarine, of the type described in a previous chapter, and its first effect was to sink the United States Shipping Board steamer, *Dewey*, of 5630 tons gross, immediately after she had sailed from Honolulu on May 20. The local naval authorities acted promptly, suspending all departures and warning expected arrivals by radio, pending an investigation of the mine-field's extent. Thanks to good organisation and favourable weather, both groups of mines were located and swept up within a week, without further loss than the sinking of one auxiliary mine-sweeper. The United States Navy was favoured by fortune on this occasion, since a considerable concentration of force had now been effected at Pearl Harbour, and the enemy's mine-field might easily have revealed its existence by the sinking of some important warship.

The next spot where mines were discovered was to the southward of Gammon Shoal, just outside the entrance to San Diego Bay. Here again matters might well have been more serious. A flotilla of destroyers ran into this mine-field on leaving port for exercises on the morning of May 25, the consequent casualties involving the loss of the *Yarborough* and *Thompson,* and the temporary disablement of the *Ballard, Laub* and *Aaron Ward.* Energetic measures resulted in the removal of the remaining mines without further loss. There is still considerable doubt as to the agency employed in this instance. Since no actual proof can be found of Japanese mine-laying submarines operating so far afield, the most probable explanation is that the mines had been laid by Japanese fishing craft, many of which before the war had followed their avocation off the Mexican coast of Lower California. This view was held by the naval authorities at San Diego, who thereupon established a patrol in Lower Californian waters to guard against a repetition of the incident. These measures threw a severe strain on American resources in the way of patrol vessels, in spite of the fact that a large number of auxiliary craft had been taken up for the purpose.

Before closing this chapter it is as well to set out the distribution of the United States Fleet as it was left after the closing of the Panama Canal. There is no question but that the Japanese were kept well informed of such matters at this early period, as an effective censorship did not yet exist, and there was consequently a serious leakage of news through the American Press.

Excluding the Asiatic squadron, which, with the exception of 2 destroyers, 7 submarines, and some unimportant units in Chinese rivers, had been practically wiped out when the Japanese descended on the Philippines, the following ships were in the Pacific :—

12 Battleships : *West Virginia, Maryland, Colorado, California, Tennessee, New Mexico, Idaho, Mississippi, Pennsylvania, Arizona, Oklahoma, Nevada.*
13 Modern Cruisers : *Minneapolis, Portland, Kansas City, Indianapolis, Omaha, Milwaukee, Cincinnati, Raleigh, Detroit, Richmond, Concord, Marblehead, Memphis.*
(Three more cruisers of the new 10,000 ton type were completing, but not ready for sea.)

7 Older Cruisers : *Charlotte, Huntington, Huron, Seattle, Charleston, Salem, New Orleans.*

2 Aircraft Carriers : *Saratoga, Langley.*

113 Destroyers (First Line), all of " flush deck " type.

41 Submarines, including 6 of " V " type, 16 of " S " type, and 19 of " R " type.

15 Patrol Vessels of " Eagle " type.

2 Mine-layers : *Aroostook, Baltimore.*

12 Mine-sweepers of " Bird " class.

4 Destroyer Tenders : *Altair, Rigel, Melville, Buffalo.*

2 Submarine Tenders : *Holland, Canopus.*

2 Repair Ships : *Medusa, Prometheus.*

14 Miscellaneous Auxiliaries, including Oilers, Colliers, Supply Ships, Hospital Ships, etc.

Very soon after the blocking of the Panama Canal there had been concentrated at Pearl Harbour, Hawaii, the whole of the twelve battleships, organised in three divisions of four ships each ; eight of the modern cruisers, in two divisions of four ; the old cruiser *Seattle*, as Administrative flagship for the fleet ; thirty-six destroyers in six divisions of six boats each, with the modern cruiser *Concord* as flagship and the tenders *Altair, Rigel* and *Melville* attached ; six submarines of " V " type and twelve of " S " type, with the tender *Holland ;* six of the minesweepers, and about a dozen auxiliaries. The remaining strength of the U.S. Navy in the Pacific was distributed between San Diego, Mare Island, and Bremerton, the largest number being at the first-named base, where the auxiliary *Procyon* served as flagship.

In the Atlantic were the following ships, mostly of older types :

6 Battleships : *New York, Texas, Arkansas, Wyoming, Utah, Florida.*

1 Modern Cruiser : *Trenton.*
   (Several cruisers of the new 10,000 ton type were completing, but were not immediately ready for sea.)

9 Older Cruisers : *Pittsburgh, Pueblo, St. Louis,*

Rochester, Birmingham, Chester, Olympia, Chattanooga, Des Moines.

2 Aircraft Carriers : *Lexington, Wright.*

160 Destroyers, all of First Line (a few Second Line Destroyers still existed, but were pronounced unfit for active service).

70 Submarines of various types, none being fit for long-distance cruising with the Battle Fleet.

6 Patrol Vessels, mostly armed yachts, several more of which were acquired later.

4 Destroyer Tenders : *Dobbin, Whitney, Denebola, Bridgeport.*

5 Submarine Tenders : *Bushnell, Fulton, Beaver, Camden, Savannah.*

2 Mine-layers : *Shawmut, San Francisco.*

30 Mine-sweepers of " Bird " class.

1 Repair Ship : *Vestal.*

32 Miscellaneous Auxiliaries, including Oilers, Colliers, Supply Ships, Hospital Ships, etc.

Great difficulty was found in manning destroyers and other vessels brought forward from reserve at the outbreak of war, and in view of the situation created by the closing of the Panama Canal, 50 per cent. of the complements of the Scouting Fleet in the Atlantic were transported overland to complete the crews of the undermanned Pacific fleet. The strength of the Scouting fleet was made up with new recruits, of which large numbers were being drafted to sea by the Navy Recruiting Bureau. A fair number of these had served before, but the majority were new to naval life, and even those with previous experience were necessarily ignorant of the latest improvements in gunnery and other branches.

Without exaggeration it may safely be said that in the earlier stages of the war the shortage of trained *personnel* gave American admirals more cause for anxiety than the manœuvres of the enemy.

CHAPTER IX

JUNE–JULY, 1931

Japanese submarine attacks on U.S. Pacific coast—Air raids in California—Japanese aircraft-carrier makes good her retreat— U.S. Government finds popular demand for energetic measures too strong to resist—New ships ordered—The Scouting fleet to proceed to Pacific *via* Cape Horn

THE next Japanese move was decidedly sensational. On June 17, or approximately three weeks after the discovery of the mine-field referred to in the preceding chapter, a freight train heavily laden with stores for the fleet at San Diego was derailed 45 miles south of Santa Ana. While the ensuing confusion was at its height, shells began to explode amid the wreckage. These came from a Japanese ocean-going submarine, *I 54*, lying a mile off shore. After setting some of the cars on fire and causing numerous casualties, the vessel dived and was not seen again. It was then discovered that a considerable section of the line had been torn up. This outrage was at first attributed to enemy agents on shore, but it was later suggested, with a greater element of probability, that the submarine may have landed a party at night to damage the line, which at this point runs very near and in full view of the sea. Certainly the submarine must have been in communication with the land, since she was evidently waiting in a half-submerged condition for the train to pass. Destroyers sent to hunt for her could find no traces of her presence in the vicinity. As a matter of fact, she had proceeded further north, to reappear that same evening off the coast near Los Angeles. A large Standard Oil tanker, the *J. A. Moffett Junior*, was torpedoed in

Santa Monica Bay, and had to be beached in a sinking condition, eventually becoming a total loss. Before the facts could be fully ascertained, the submarine had made a third raid, this time off the Golden Gate, where she succeeded in sinking four ships without interference. Exasperated by this further exhibition of audacity on the part of the enemy, the naval authorities ordered all available patrol vessels and aircraft to the scene of the latest attacks; but the Japanese commander had evidently calculated with accuracy the length of time in which he would be able to operate undisturbed, for the patrols found only the floating wreckage of his victims. No lives were lost, the crews of all ships intercepted being allowed time to take to their boats.

It is now known that submarine *I 54* did not operate alone; she had been accompanied most of the way to the Pacific Coast by the auxiliary aircraft carrier *Hakata* and the oiler *Tsurugizaki*. But at the time no suspicion of this fact appears to have been entertained, and the only quarry sought was the submarine, which was a vessel of close on 2000 tons, mounting a pair of 5·5-inch guns. She also carried a seaplane of small size and special design.

After lying in concealment for two days to allow the hunt to die down a little, *I 54* continued her northerly course as far as the mouth of the Columbia River. Here a similar programme was enacted, two ships being sunk, while Aberdeen, South Bend, and other coastal towns in Washington found themselves under fire from the sea. Although the damage caused was insignificant, these daring attacks set the whole Pacific slope in an uproar. The wildest rumours found ready credence. An immense flotilla of gigantic submarines had crossed the Pacific with orders to lay waste the entire coastline, declared one Los Angeles journal. No place could be considered safe, for a city lying beyond the range of gunfire might be attacked by aircraft, with which the submarines were well provided (here the newspaper was nearer to the truth than was at the time realised). Several of the coast town authorities telegraphed to

Washington, demanding that warships be permanently stationed at their ports. One enterprising mayor would not be content with less than a squadron of battle-ships ! There were, of course, no ships available for such duty, and even if there had been, the Navy Depart-ment could not have so allocated them without deranging all its war plans. A similar agitation had arisen in 1898, when the supposed approach of the Spanish fleet under Admiral Cervera so alarmed certain cities of the Atlantic seaboard that some ancient monitors, of no value for war, were assigned to various harbours for guard duty. But in view of the pressing demands now made upon them, the authorities can hardly be blamed for having ordered every spare airplane to the Oregon coast, leaving California denuded of aircraft. Nothing could have suited the Japanese better, for their main line of attack was now unmasked by the almost simultaneous bombing on June 22 of San Francisco, Oakland, and Los Angeles by squadrons of airplanes, flying so high as to be almost invisible to the naked eye when first perceived. At San Francisco the citizens, hearing gunfire from the few anti-aircraft guns in position (which, it may be mentioned, were all outranged), flocked into the streets in their thousands to learn what was passing, nor could all the efforts of the police prevent dense crowds from gathering in the main thoroughfares. Hardly had it dawned upon them that an air attack was impending when several loud detonations were heard close at hand, and a terrible stampede for shelter at once ensued, many unfortunate people being trampled to death. As bombs continued to fall and explode with devastating violence, it became painfully apparent that a serious attack was in progress, not merely a lone-hand raid by a small machine flown off from a submarine. In the absence of all local airplanes in Oregon and Washington, the enemy had everything in his favour, and utilised the opportunity to distribute his entire load of bombs upon the unfortunate inhabitants of San Francisco and Oakland. The greater number of these missiles appear to have been filled with high explosive, and their effects upon life and property were most disastrous, hospitals being filled to overflowing with victims who had been struck down by bomb fragments or falling masonry, or crushed beneath the feet of panic-stricken fugitives. Some of the bombs were undoubtedly incendiary, but at San Francisco, thanks to an efficient fire-fighting service, these proved comparatively ineffective, only one serious conflagration being caused. This was confined to the shipping quarter facing Goat Island, and was responsible for a vast amount of damage to warehouses and wharves. Altogether, the loss of life and property caused by this lightning raid on the San Francisco district was very severe.

At Los Angeles, though only nine airplanes were engaged as compared with eleven at San Francisco and Oakland, the damage was, if anything, more extensive, as many fires were started. These took long to subdue, several oil reservoirs being involved. The motion picture industry was seriously affected by the destruction of several important studios. Exaggerated estimates of the number of attacking aircraft were prevalent locally at the time, but it is now known that only twenty were engaged. The American planes which had been sent north in search of submarines were hastily recalled to California, only to find that no certain indication existed as to the quarter in which the raiding machines were to be sought, these having flown straight in from the sea and departed in the same direction. The fact that the submarine *I 54* had retreated northward after her first appearance on the Californian coast caused many to urge that attention be concentrated in that area, on the theory that the attacking force might have been launched from some secret base in one of the numerous islands fringing the coast of British Columbia. Some time elapsed before the riddle was partially solved, and even then there were few facts to go upon. Not until the end of the war was the whole truth revealed. It appears that the *Hakata*, originally a large fast passenger steamer, had been hastily fitted out at Yokosuka as an auxiliary aircraft carrier, with stowage capacity for twenty large seaplanes, each able to carry half a ton of bombs. These machines were stowed in the holds with their wings folded. The ship herself, elaborately disguised as a British freighter of the Blue Funnel Line, mounted an armament of four 6-inch guns concealed behind dummy deck houses. She sailed from Jaluit on May 31, in company with the oil tanker *Tsurugizaki*, and for the greater part of their voyage across the Pacific the vessels had the ocean to themselves. Not until they had reached a point 400 miles north-east of Hawaii, to which the two steamers had given a wide berth, was another ship sighted. This was a British merchantman bound from Vancouver to Australia, whose radio operator was puzzled to know why his greetings to the passing vessels met with no intelligible response, but he thought little of the matter at the time. At dusk on June 16 the two Japanese ships had crept to within 200 miles of the American coast without being challenged or even sighted by a patrol. Here they separated, the *Hakata* steering a southerly course parallel with the coast, while her smaller consort (which was also disguised as a British ship) proceeded at low speed toward the north, as if making for a Canadian port, but actually heading for a rendezvous which had been arranged beforehand. At midday on the 22nd the *Hakata* was 20 miles to the south-east of Point Reyes, and therefore about 70 miles west of the Golden Gate. Here she was sighted by an American armed yacht on patrol duty, manned by naval reservists, but on hoisting the number of the British ship she was impersonating and giving her destination as Valparaiso, she was allowed to proceed. Had the yacht approached near enough for verbal conversation the ruse might have been detected, in spite of the fact that the officers of the *Hakata* are said to have been selected for their knowledge of the English language; but in that case the yacht herself would no doubt have been blown out of the water by the heavier armament of the disguised ship. As it was, the *Hakata* was able to pass on without arousing suspicion. An hour later, no sail being then in sight, she was hove-to, while the airplanes were brought up from the holds, their wings assembled, and a supply of bombs placed in the traps. They were then lowered to the water, and, with engines started up, flew off to carry death and destruction to the Californian cities. While they were away the *Hakata* had to cruise in the vicinity with steam enough for full speed, awaiting the return of her flock. This was the most perilous phase of the whole adventure, for the alarm might be given at any moment, and all patrol craft within call would then be on the alert. However, nothing occurred until a call was received by radio-phone from one of the returning airplanes, asking for the position of the ship. Just after this four other machines were sighted, and twenty minutes later all but one of the planes had been accounted for. Eventually eighteen were picked up and hoisted inboard. Of the remaining two, one was wrecked by a faulty landing on the water and the other failed to return, though the ship remained in the neigh-bourhood for another hour at imminent peril to herself. Owing probably to engine trouble, this machine must have come down in the sea, as its wreck was driven ashore near Santa Barbara some days later. Hope of its return having been abandoned, the *Hakata* set off at high speed for the rendezvous with her consort. Some time after darkness had set in the beam of a searchlight was concentrated on her from a ship about a mile distant, and several shots were fired. She held on her course without attempting to return the fire, the target being practically invisible. Her opponent was the U.S. Coastguard cruising cutter *Haida*, a vessel of 1780 tons displacement and 16 knots maximum speed, armed with two 5-inch guns. She was normally stationed at Port Townsend, Wash., but had been attached to the Naval service in view of the urgent demand for patrol craft of every description. Contact with the *Hakata* was soon lost, and it remained doubtful whether her refusal to stop when fired on was any positive proof of her being an enemy—until a Japanese official announcement revealed the facts. All that the naval authorities could do was to broadcast a general warning for a sharp look-out to be kept for a suspicious vessel, of which only a very general description could be furnished by the *Haida's* people. The obsolete cruiser *Charlotte*, which, as already mentioned, was employed on escort work between San Francisco and Honolulu, and was then within 500 miles of Hawaii, was the only ship in a position to take advantage of the news. Having obtained permission by radio to allow her convoy to proceed on its voyage without her, she stood off to the north-west at her best speed. Originally 22 knots, this had decreased, owing to the age of her boilers and long disuse, to a doubtful 19 knots, which she maintained with difficulty for nearly twelve hours, when speed had to be reduced. The cruiser kept on for a further twelve hours at a reduced speed averaging under 17 knots, but there was still no sign of the quarry. It seemed useless to continue the hunt, so a course was set for Honolulu. The *Charlotte* had, in fact, never been within 250 miles of the *Hakata*, which on leaving the Californian coast had steered almost due north for some time, this being judged to be the direction in which American warships were least likely to be encountered. Contact with the *Tsurugizaki* was made on the 24th, and on the following day, the weather being propitious, the *Hakata's* bunkers were replenished with oil from the tanker. Thereafter the two vessels proceeded on their homeward voyage, still keeping well to the northward, and finally reached Yokosuka without misadventure.

The submarine *I 54* was less fortunate. After her raid upon Oregon shipping she continued her voyage northward, and broke surface again in sight of several steamers off Cape Flattery on June 23, the day after the air raids upon San Francisco and Los Angeles—no doubt with the object of diverting attention from the retreating aircraft carrier. Unluckily for the submarine, the American destroyers *Rathburne* and *Shirk*, which with others had been undergoing an extensive refit at Bremerton Navy Yard, were proceeding down the Strait of Juan de Fuca to reinforce the coast patrols when they received intelligence by radio of the submarine's latest appearance. The senior officer, Lieutenant-Commander Maynard, of the *Shirk*, calculating that only a very few miles separated him from the reported position of the enemy craft, ordered his consort to follow him at full speed to the spot, where he surprised *I 54* in the act of holding up a large Shipping Board steamer, the *West Jappa*. The small airplane carried by the submarine was out of action; and the towering hull of the freighter, which was in ballast, appears to have hidden the approaching destroyers from the Japanese until they were quite near, but the submarine had time to discharge a couple of torpedoes into the *West Jappa* before submerging. Numerous depth charges were dropped in the vicinity, and though no direct hit was claimed by the destroyers it is now practically certain that some fatal injury was thus inflicted upon *I 54*, for she was never seen again by friend or foe. At the time, however, there was no means of knowing this, and it was even doubtful whether only one submarine had been engaged in these repeated attacks upon American shipping. On the assumption that other boats were off the coast, the naval authorities continued to take every precaution, all merchantmen being held up in port for some days while aircraft and patrol vessels made an exhaustive search of the locality, until it became evident that the danger was past. There is no doubt that the diversion caused by *I 54* was of material assistance to the *Hakata* by enabling her to avoid observation, so much attention being concentrated on the area around Cape Flattery that more distant waters were neglected.

The whole enterprise had been well planned and skilfully conducted. It was acclaimed with tremendous enthusiasm in Japan, where highly coloured versions of what had been accomplished were served out to the newspapers. But measured by its military results, it was questionable if the expedition had been worth the effort it had cost. Doubtless its main purpose was so to terrorise the inhabitants of the Pacific slope as to compel the naval authorities to modify their plans in deference to popular agitation. It certainly threw the

K

whole coast into a ferment, and demands for local protection became so insistent that the Government could no longer afford to ignore them entirely. Twelve destroyers were recalled from Hawaii to reinforce the coastal patrol, and additional yachts and merchant steamers were taken over and hurriedly equipped for the same purpose. The War Department was induced to send two batteries of railroad artillery, operated by the Coast Artillery Corps, to the Los Angeles area, where the proximity of the railway to the sea would give these guns —7-inch high-velocity pieces—a wide range of action. Two large naval dirigibles and two of the Army's smaller airships, together with twenty airplanes, were told off to maintain a night and day watch along the seaboard, while anti-aircraft batteries were mounted at San Francisco, Los Angeles, and other cities within reach of attack from the sea. By diverting so much of America's man power and material to passive defence, which contributed nothing to the effective prosecution of the war, the Japanese could claim to have reaped a certain amount of indirect military advantage from their dramatic *coup*. But there was no possibility of repeating their exploits in the face of the improvements now made in the defence organisation, while the general effect in districts remote from the Pacific coast was to stimulate the war spirit and harden the American nation's resolve to see the thing through. Thus again it was proved that a policy of intimidation can only be expected to succeed where it is backed by overwhelming force, which in this case was lacking. At the same time, the results of these daring coastal raids could not be surveyed with any feeling of satisfaction by the United States. The enemy had impudently invaded American territorial waters, holding up the traffic of the principal Pacific ports and heavily bombarding California's biggest cities, and yet by adroit tactics had contrived to withdraw his forces almost intact. At the time the only loss that could be proved was that of the airplane whose wreck had been found near Santa Barbara; and it was not until many months afterwards that the failure of submarine *I 54* to return to a Japanese port became known.

Not since the Civil War had an American Government to face such a storm of criticism and vituperation as now broke upon them.   If they had not yielded to the tremendous pressure that was brought to bear from all quarters, but especially from districts immediately affected by the raids, the President and his Cabinet would have been superhuman.   As it was, in addition to the local measures detailed above, they were forced to broadcast an undertaking that, in view of the delay in repairing the Panama Canal, all available forces should be concentrated around the stricken area without waiting until this means of communication was restored. The Japanese, who appear to have been informed of what was happening, could therefore congratulate themselves upon having to a large extent achieved their object in forcing their enemy into premature action.   But, paradoxical as it may sound, there is little doubt that the ultimate effect of the raids by submarines and aircraft was more advantageous to the American cause than to the Japanese.   Immediately on the outbreak of war Congress had voted an emergency appropriation of $250,000,000 for increasing the Navy, and the nation assumed as a matter of course that numerous ships of every type had been laid down immediately.   But, in fact, no such action had been taken.   The voices of those who predicted a speedy ending to the war were still powerful in the councils of Washington.   Even in the naval administration there were men of high position who disputed the need for an intensive programme of shipbuilding, believing as they did that the campaign would be over long before the new ships went afloat. It is now known that both the Secretary of the Navy and the Chief of Operations were of this opinion, and it was due to their influence that the new construction ordered in the first two months of the war was limited to four cruisers, twenty destroyers, a few submarines, and two airplane carriers.   But the raids on the West Coast showed the enemy to be bolder and more enterprising than had been suspected. Nor could they be reconciled with the theory that Japan desired and would soon make overtures for an early peace by negotiation. If such was her aim she would hardly have done the one thing calculated to excite belligerent sentiments in the United States. It looked, indeed, as if she were bent on exasperating American opinion by every means in her power, a policy that seemed to indicate a resolve on her part to press conclusions to the bitter end. Instead of proffering an olive branch, she had flung down a gauntlet of steel. The reaction on American opinion, Governmental as well as popular, was immediate and decisive. Since all the omens pointed to a prolonged struggle, the nation in grim earnest set about arming itself for the fray. Compulsory service had been introduced at the start, but since there appeared to be no prospect of large military operations developing, the number of men called to the colours had not as yet exceeded 150,000. Now, however, the whole scheme of Army expansion was recast on a far greater scale. In less than a week after the San Francisco raid the strength of the Army, already fixed provisionally at 1,000,000, was sensibly nearer that figure, and the industrial resources of the country were in process of mobilisation for the equipment of this vast force. At the same time a great programme of naval construction was framed, the principal items of which were four battle-cruisers, twenty-five cruisers, 100 destroyers, fifty submarines, and six airplane carriers, besides numerous mine-sweepers and other auxiliary craft. Since this amount of tonnage was far beyond the capacity of existing shipyards in the Union, the Government financed extensions to the great shipbuilding yards on either coast and the laying-down of new plant for standardised production. To relieve the strain on home industry, large orders for ship material, heavy castings, guns, mounts, and munitions of every description were placed in Europe, the value of these foreign contracts alone amounting to $250,000,000. High prices had to be paid, because Japan was already in the market for similar supplies, and the European manufacturers were thus in a position to dictate their own terms. This was the first time in thirty years that the United States had gone abroad for its naval supplies, but the circumstances were such as to leave no alternative. While we need not review the emergency building programme in detail, some brief explanatory remarks may be offered. In deciding to include four battle cruisers of the largest dimensions, the naval authorities were influenced by rumours of corresponding activity in Japan, where, it was said, three or four capital ships of unexampled power had been placed on the stocks during February. Their displacement was reported to be close upon 50,000 tons and their battery as consisting of 18-inch guns. To match these monster ships the American type was designed on a basis of 52,000 tons, with a speed of 35 knots, and an armament of eight 18-inch guns. The contract called for delivery in twenty months, though there was little chance of this schedule being observed. In size and battery the twenty-five cruisers were of uniform type—namely, 10,000 tons and nine 8-inch guns; but whereas fifteen were to have steam turbine machinery, the remaining ten were to be equipped with oil motors. This involved a reduction in speed, for despite the progress it had made in recent years, the internal-combustion engine had not yet succeeded in rivalling the steam turbine as a prime mover for large ships of the highest speed. Each of the ten motor cruisers was to be fitted with three engines developing together 60,000 brake horse-power, which would propel it at a maximum velocity of 28 knots. This was 7 knots less than the speed of the steam-driven ships, but, on the other hand, there would be a gain of 30 to 40 per cent. in cruising endurance, which was a point of prime importance in the case of ships destined to operate over the enormous expanse of the Pacific Ocean. Of the destroyers it need only be said that a certain number were fitted with oil motors for cruising, while relying on their turbines for great speed. The submarines were divided into several classes, but the majority averaged 1700 tons and were designed for a wide radius of action. As

many of the above vessels as possible were laid down as
soon as the drawings could be prepared, but however
strenuously the shipyards might labour, it would be a
long while before the first vessels were ready to commission, and in the meantime the Navy had to do the
best it could with the inadequate means at its disposal.
As a first step it had become necessary, in fulfilment of
the President's pledge, to dispatch nearly one-third
of the United States Navy a distance of 14,000 miles
round South America, practically a two months' voyage.
Transports and supply ships had to be found and
assembled, repairs in hand at Atlantic Navy Yards
accelerated, and a complete schedule for the voyage
prepared by the Operations Bureau. This could not be
done in a moment, and it was only by publishing far
too many details of the preparations made and of ships'
movements that the popular clamour for energetic naval
action could be allayed. It says much for the energy
and resourcefulness of the Navy Department and Atlantic
Navy Yard staffs that by July 10 the following fleet
had been assembled in Hampton Roads, whence it was
dispatched southward with orders to effect a junction
with the Pacific Base Force at San Diego :

  6 Battleships : *New York, Texas, Arkansas, Wyoming,*
      Utah, Florida.
  6 Cruisers : *Trenton, Pittsburgh, Pueblo, St. Louis,*
      Birmingham, Chester.
  2 Aircraft Carriers : *Lexington, Wright.*
100 Destroyers, all of " flush deck " type.
  2 Mine-layers : *Shawmut, San Francisco.*
 20 Mine-sweepers of " Bird " class.
  3 Destroyer Tenders : *Dobbin, Whitney, Denebola.*
  1 Repair Ship : *Vestal.*
 40 Miscellaneous Auxiliaries, including Oilers, Colliers,
      Supply Ships, Hospital Ships, and Transports.

No submarines accompanied the fleet, as practically all
those available were of obsolescent types, which it was
feared might occasion delay through mechanical break-

downs. It will be noted that there was a distinct shortage of long-range scouting vessels, the only fast modern cruiser being the *Trenton*, which served as flagship of the Destroyer flotilla. The whole force was under the command of Admiral E. C. Templeton, whose flag was flown in the *Texas*.

The larger ships were ordered to conform to a programme which involved their calling at the following ports :

San Juan (Porto Rico), distant from Hampton Roads				1280 miles.
Pernambuco (Brazil), a further distance of				2500 ,,
Montevideo (Uruguay)	,,	,,	,,	2100 ,,
Punta Arenas (Chile)	,,	,,	,,	1410 ,,
Valparaiso (Chile)	,,	,,	,,	1274 ,,
Panama	,,	,,	,,	2800 ,,

The total distance, including the run to San Diego, was practically 14,000 miles. Some of the smaller vessels, with lower fuel capacity, called also at other ports, such as Port of Spain (Trinidad), Para and Rio de Janeiro in Brazil, and Callao (Peru). On the whole the progress of the fleet down the East coast of South America was uneventful, though, owing to so many of the ships having been hastily commissioned after long periods of lying-up, various machinery and other defects were encountered, which in some cases involved putting into the nearest port and following the fleet independently after the necessary repairs had been effected. Advantage was taken during the voyage to exercise the fleet in tactical evolutions, while continuous training of the crews, who included an unusually large proportion of " green " recruits, was carried on.

CHAPTER X

Two Japanese submarines await U.S. Scouting fleet in Magellan Straits
—Attack partially frustrated—American vessels sunk and damaged
—Fate of Japanese submarines—Scouting fleet arrives at its
destination—Tactical observations

WITH their usual enterprise the Japanese, in the expectation that American warships would use the Cape Horn route, had prepared an ambush there. Two submarines had been lying in concealment for an uncertain period in the Beagle Channel, a remote Strait separating Tierra del Fuego from Navarin and Hoste Islands. Some 120 miles in length, with an average breadth of about two miles, this channel is almost perfectly straight for the greater part of its course, which runs nearly due east and west. Bounded on either shore by mountains and cliffs, it is one of the most remarkable features of this wild region. Here was an ideal hiding place for submarines, for the Strait is seldom visited by ships, and has near its middle an independent exit, known as Ponsonby Sound, leading southward to the open sea near Cape Horn. The exact spot in which the submarines (*I 58* and *I 53*) established their temporary base is uncertain, as there are many small coves on both sides of the Beagle Channel. It is known, however, that they occasionally shifted from Chilean to Argentine waters and back again, with the object of confusing the issue should awkward questions arise in connection with their infringement of neutrality. It should be noted that the boundary between Chile and Argentina, after cutting across Tierra del Fuego from north to south, turns somewhat abruptly to the east-

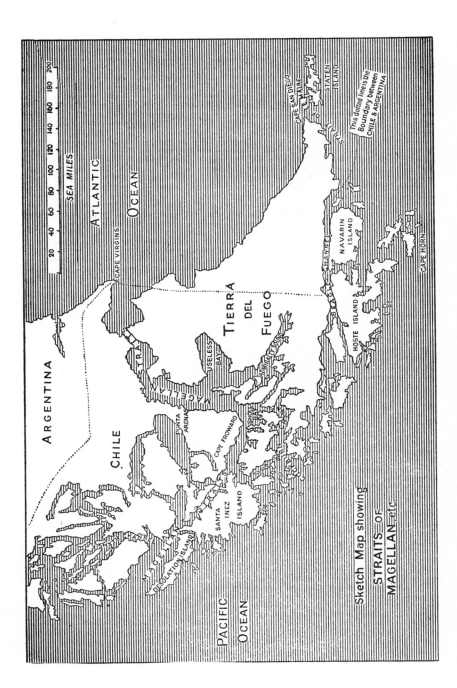

Sketch Map showing
STRAITS OF MAGELLAN etc.

This dotted line is the Boundary between CHILE & ARGENTINA

ward on reaching the Beagle Channel, and thence runs in a line with its course, so that all the islands to the south of Tierra del Fuego are Chilean territory.

On August 7 the American fleet passed Cape Virgins and entered the Straits of Magellan. Reference to the accompanying sketch map will elucidate the events that followed. For about the first hundred miles of their course from the Atlantic the shores of the Straits are comparatively level, but from a point a little beyond the second " Narrows " they become rugged and hilly, until both sides are hedged with mountains, densely wooded, and often snow-capped. Here and there the landscape is diversified by the appearance of a glacier, though at certain seasons mist and rain render it difficult to pick out anything distinctly. The scenery when visible is magnificent, and the shore can be approached closely in most parts, the water, though remarkably clear, being very deep right up to the base of the cliffs. A conspicuous feature of the heights when closely approached is the gigantic tree fuchsia, which flourishes everywhere.

Just within the second " Narrows," on the northern shore, is situated the southernmost town of the Republic of Chile—Punta Arenas (Sandy Point). This isolated port is well furnished with piers, quays, cranes, and all the normal accessories of a coaling station, but there are no docks. It is practically the only settlement of any size on the Straits, which elsewhere are but very sparsely populated, the climate being damp in summer and severe in winter.

It will be noticed from the map that innumerable channels, bays, and inlets open off the Straits between Punta Arenas and the Pacific, offering a fine choice of routes, but also providing many opportunities for an ambush. Of the several alternative courses which can be followed to reach the Pacific from Punta Arenas, the three principal ones are :

(a) Straight out into the Pacific through Cockburn Channel.

(*b*) To the termination of the Magellan Straits Proper, passing into the Pacific by the channel leading between Queen Charlotte Island to the north and Desolation Island to the south.

(*c*) Right through the continuation of the Straits known as Smyth Channel, this being the route followed by the majority of merchant steamers.

In its passage through the Straits the fleet preserved the same general formation as throughout its voyage. Under this arrangement destroyers and mine-sweepers took the lead, followed by the heavy ships, each division of which was accompanied by more light craft. The aircraft carriers *Wright* and *Lexington* were stationed in the van and rear respectively, and the various auxiliaries distributed between the several divisions of the fleet. Owing to the slowness of certain auxiliary craft, the necessity for economising fuel, and the mistiness of the weather at this time of year—which in these southern latitudes is winter—the speed of the fleet was never more than 10 knots, and at times fell below that figure. The target offered by such a long procession of ships (numbering at this stage 170 units) was therefore a tempting one, but, on the other hand, it must be remembered that low visibility has its disadvantages for an attacking submarine.

Two days earlier the Japanese boats, *I 58* and *I 53*, had taken their station at a point of vantage near Sholl Bay, where the Cockburn Channel leads out from the Magellan Straits into the Pacific. Here they were in a position to deliver an attack upon the American fleet irrespective of the route it might elect to follow. They had been kept closely advised of the fleet's movements by the Japanese Vice-Consul at Punta Arenas, whose fast motor launch was busily engaged in maintaining communication with the submarines during their vigil. Apparently it was considered too dangerous to employ radio signals for this purpose, lest the suspicions of the Chilean authorities should be aroused.

At Punta Arenas the fleet made a stay of twenty-four hours, in order to refill bunkers from the accompanying colliers and oilers, as well as from ships which had been specially chartered to deliver fuel at this stage of the voyage. Provisional arrangements were also entered into for the engagement of local pilots in case it should be decided to follow the route through Smyth Channel.

Reference must now be made to a factor which was to prove of considerable importance. The cruiser *Trenton*, a vessel of 7500 tons displacement and over 33 knots speed, had been temporarily detached from the fleet on reaching the entrance to the Straits. She had proceeded southward through the Strait of Le Maire and round Cape Horn, where she encountered heavy weather which was scarcely felt by the fleet in the shelter of the Straits. Her orders were to rejoin the flag by way of Cockburn Channel, the Admiral proposing to decide, according to the nature of her report on weather conditions in the Pacific, whether or not to take the somewhat longer and more exposed route *via* Cockburn Channel and the open sea. In pursuance of these instructions the *Trenton* passed eastward through Cockburn Channel and in due course reached Sholl Bay, where she awaited the arrival of the fleet from Punta Arenas.

In this spot the mist, which had been drifting across the Straits in scattered patches, seems to have perceptibly thickened on the morning of August 9. After a couple of hours, as it showed no signs of clearing, Captain Soames of the *Trenton* ordered one of his two airplanes to go aloft and report whether the fleet was in sight. Owing to damage to aerials sustained in the heavy weather of the preceding day, the *Trenton's* radio apparatus does not appear to have been in a condition to despatch messages at this juncture.

In the meantime, the sudden appearance of the cruiser from an unexpected direction had seriously perturbed the commanders of the two lurking submarines. They could not understand what object the

Trenton could have in remaining at this spot in particular, and began to suspect that their existence might somehow have become known to the American Admiral. If this were so, he might not intend to take his fleet further until he was satisfied that the route was clear.

In such a contingency as this they found it difficult to decide on the right course to pursue, since it does not appear to have been covered by their instructions. Like other men of action under similar circumstances, they could not reconcile it with their sense of duty to remain inactive, but they hesitated to forsake the carefully chosen point of vantage which they occupied at the mouth of Sholl Bay. As a compromise, they divided forces, *I 53* remaining to watch the *Trenton* at Sholl Bay, while *I 58* proceeded up the Straits towards Punta Arenas to ascertain the whereabouts of the United States Fleet.

Shortly afterwards a seaplane ascended from the deck of the *Trenton*, and rising to a height sufficient to keep above the low-lying mist banks, flew away to the northward. Close to Cape Froward she came over a comparatively clear patch of water, where her observer, Lieutenant Murton, who had undergone a special course of instruction in anti-submarine operations, discerned the track of *I 58* proceeding in the same direction as the airplane. After directing the pilot's attention to the phenomenon, and confirming its existence by circling over the spot once or twice, speed was increased to over 150 miles an hour, and contact with the approaching fleet was quickly obtained. The alarming intelligence of the hostile submarine's presence was at once communicated to Admiral Templeton, by whose direction the entire fleet, with the exception of the destroyers and the light cruisers *Birmingham* and *Chester*, turned sixteen points and retraced their course in the direction of Punta Arenas, which they had left an hour earlier. Unfortunately, in the course of this evolution the collier *Ajax*, whose steering gear had been giving trouble for some days previously, failed to answer her helm, and fell aboard the battleship *Utah* in the parallel column. In a vain attempt to avoid ramming the *Ajax*, the *Utah* reversed her engines with such suddenness that her next astern, the battleship *Florida*—which failed to perceive what had happened owing to the poor visibility—did not stop her engines in time, and struck the *Utah's* starboard quarter with great violence, opening a large rent on the water-line. For a couple of minutes the three ships remained locked together, much damage being done to upperworks before they drew clear; and it was only by skilful manœuvring on the part of the other ships in the Third Squadron that further collisions were avoided. Of the three vessels involved, the unlucky *Ajax* was in the worst case. She had been badly holed in the engine-room, and it soon became apparent that it would be impossible to save her, as her list became more and more pronounced. All hands were taken off, and she sank inside half an hour, the steep cliffs with deep water alongside rendering it impossible to beach her. The damage to the *Utah*, though less severe, might also have proved fatal had it occurred in bad weather or far from port; as it was, her powerful pumping installation was fully taxed to control the inrush of water from the flooded compartments, the shock of the collision, in spite of her stout construction, having started the bulkheads in the vicinity of the leak. She was able to reach Punta Arenas under her own steam, and with the assistance of harbour tugs was berthed alongside the quay at a spot where the water was sufficiently shallow to prevent her becoming completely submerged. Here it may be remarked that the skilled *personnel* of the repair ship *Vestal*, with the aid of local contractors and salvage plant, were able to prepare and fit a temporary patch which enabled the battleship eventually to complete her voyage.

The *Florida*, though leaking slightly forward, had not damaged her bows to an extent affecting her seaworthiness, and she was able to remain with the fleet.

Had the Japanese submarine been at hand when the

collision occurred she could scarcely have hoped for a more favourable opportunity of delivering an attack; but she was too far distant, and indeed was soon sufficiently occupied with the problem of her own safety. The destroyer flotillas, numbering ninety boats (six having remained with the *Utah*), and led by the *Birmingham* and *Chester*, were not long in locating *I 58*, to whose lair they were guided by the *Trenton's* plane and other aircraft sent up by the fleet. Numerous depth charges were dropped without immediate effect, but in a hunt by such a swarm of swift vessels the odds were heavily against the submarine, which sealed her doom by steering an underwater course which took her into Useless Bay. Here she was sighted by seaplanes, and her retreat being cut off by the pursuing destroyers, she was forced to the surface in a crippled condition, after depth charges had been dropped all around her. The concentrated gunfire of the destroyers quickly completed her destruction, and her shattered hull sank without having exhibited any sign of surrender. So far as could be ascertained, she discharged two torpedoes in the course of the hunt, neither of which took effect. When the report of her destruction reached Tokyo it was embodied in a much magnified account of her exploits by the vernacular Press, which credited the sinking of the *Ajax* and damaging of the *Utah* and *Florida* to her torpedoes. Doubtless Japanese official circles were better informed, but colour was given to these and other exaggerated reports by the posthumous promotion and decoration of the officers and men who were lost in the submarine.

In the meantime the *Trenton,* in obedience to instructions by radio, had rejoined the destroyer flotillas, without any suspicion that another Japanese submarine was in hiding near her rendezvous at Sholl Bay. The rest of the day was occupied in re-forming the fleet and making arrangements for the safety and repair of the *Utah.* Next morning the voyage was resumed, the fleet steaming in practically the same order as before, with the *Trenton* in the van division. Admiral Templeton had determined, in spite of the *Trenton's* unfavourable report on the weather in the Pacific, to proceed *via* Cockburn Channel, his decision being strengthened by the knowledge that the shorter route through the Straits afforded many more opportunities for submarine attack. The fleet had passed Cape Froward, and was bearing up to enter the Cockburn Channel, when two torpedoes exploded in rapid succession, the first striking the transport *Mount Evans* in the starboard column of the Second Squadron, the second the oiler *Trinity*, in the port column.   There is no doubt both were intended for the battleships of the centre column, as the track of the second torpedo was seen from the battleship *Arkansas*, and barely avoided by prompt use of the helm.

In accordance with orders already circulated in readiness for such an emergency, all ships began zigzagging, at the same time increasing speed to their utmost capacity, while the destroyers, interposing themselves between the major vessels and the quarter from which the torpedoes had appeared to come, commenced to search for the source of this fresh attack, assisted by aircraft as before.

One of the first to proceed to the assistance of the two stricken vessels was the *Trenton*, which had been rear ship in the First Squadron.   As she slowed up on approaching the *Trinity*, her long broadside of 550 feet was probably the best target within reach of *I 53*, for the great cruiser was immediately struck by two torpedoes amidships, and had to run for Sholl Bay.   But her stokehold fires were extinguished by the rising water before she could be beached, and the nearest destroyers had a busy time rescuing her crew as she settled down. The sinking of this cruiser was the crowning achievement of the Japanese submarines, which were unable to attempt any further *coup*.   For some hours the surrounding area was searched by aircraft and destroyers, but it was still very misty, and no trace could be found of the submarine, which was probably lying quietly on the bed of the Straits, as microphones gave no clue to her movements.

Meanwhile the *Mount Evans* had foundered; but the *Trinity*, taken in tow by a couple of mine-sweepers, eventually struggled into Punta Arenas, badly down by the head. This Chilean port reaped quite a harvest in the way of repair work and other business as a result of the American fleet's misadventures.

Determined to stamp out the submarine menace in the Straits, Admiral Templeton ordered four divisions of destroyers, with the *Birmingham*, to remain in those waters and continue the hunt, while the remainder of the fleet proceeded up the Chilean coast, keeping well away from the land until they reached Valparaiso. The strongest representations were made by the U.S. Minister at Santiago as to the misuse of Chilean territorial waters by the Japanese. The local authorities, with whom this had been a tender subject ever since the Germans had taken similar liberties in 1914–15, willingly responded by sending a number of warships south with orders to deal stringently with any Japanese submarine or other belligerent vessel found committing a breach of neutrality. The first result of this policy was that the Japanese Vice-Consul at Punta Arenas was restricted from using his motor launch except for harbour purposes, and this measure, no doubt, contributed to the ultimate rounding up of *I 53*. Ten days later she was surprised in a remote inlet of the Straits, near the southern end of Santa Inez Island, by a couple of Chilean destroyers, and forced to surrender under threat of being fired upon. She was in no condition to submerge, as she had been aground a short time previously, and had badly strained her hull and damaged her hydroplanes. Under escort of the Chilean destroyers, and with an armed guard on board, she was taken to Talcahuano, and there interned. This inglorious end to her operations so preyed upon the mind of her commanding officer, Lieut.-Commander Yamioka, that he committed hara-kiri some days afterwards, in spite of the fact that he had been notified

L

through the Japanese Minister that his conduct in sinking two American ships and crippling a third was regarded with approbation by his superiors.

A good deal could be written about the operations of the American flotilla detailed to search the Straits. Before *I 53* was found they had explored the labyrinth of channels which the sea has made in the South American mainland and through the innumerable islands adjacent to it between the fiftieth parallel and Cape Horn. Each division of six destroyers was assigned a definite area, which they covered in as short a time as possible, according to the number of possible hiding places which it contained. Those inlets where the water was comparatively shallow were left untouched, since it was obvious that no submarine could find safety in them.

The remainder of the fleet's voyage to Panama and San Diego was comparatively uneventful, the main portion reaching the latter port on September 9. After their long voyage several ships required to be overhauled and to have sundry defects made good, and to relieve the strain upon the resources of San Diego some units were ordered to Mare Island and Bremerton for repair. Altogether it was nearly a month before everything had been dealt with, and even then the *Utah's* repairs were still outstanding. As the Panama Canal was reopened at the end of September, the only positive gain from the voyage was the training in seamanship which it imparted to the raw crews of Admiral Templeton's fleet.

The effects of the Magellan Straits affair upon the two countries concerned differed somewhat. In Japan, the carefully edited accounts given by the newspapers intensified the enthusiasm evoked by the raids upon the American seaboard, and the suicide of Lieut.-Commander Yamioka excited this to fever heat. Together with Lieut.-Commander Kuroi, of *I 58*, he was made the object of a display of hero-worship, which the Government were not slow to turn to account.

In the United States, on the other hand, the public

regarded the incident with less complacency. Some were inclined to criticise the arrangements made by the Navy Department and by Admiral Templeton, while others refused to hear a word against the Admiral, contending that he had shown skill and ability in extricating his command from what might have been a serious disaster. On the whole, however, the result was to strengthen the hands of the Government in instituting a limited censorship over details published in the newspapers of naval movements. It was pointed out with justice that the frequent reports of the progress of the voyage which had appeared in print must have been of material assistance to the Japanese in making arrangements to intercept the fleet in the Magellan Straits.

From the purely objective standpoint it is difficult to avoid the conclusion that the Japanese deserved better luck. They had taken every precaution to ensure that their ambush should be laid at the right moment and in the most favourable place without arousing any suspicion of their intention, and only the fortuitous circumstances that led to *I 58* being spotted from the air prevented the two submarines from delivering their attack together, without any previous warning. Lieut.-Commander Yamioka of *I 53* certainly handled his boat with the greatest skill. His ultimate internment was not surprising, and was probably foreseen by the Japanese Naval Staff, from the remarks on the subject appearing in their official history. As regards the actual setting of the ambush, it may be suggested that more than two submarines might have been employed; but in view of all the conditions it is reasonable to conclude that two was the ideal number. Any force in excess of that would have increased out of all proportion the risks of premature detection, quite apart from the question of the number of suitable craft which the Japanese had at their disposal.

So far as the American arrangements were concerned, the Navy Department cannot be absolved from blame, in that they should at least have considered the possibility of the enemy attempting something of the kind, and either framed plans for dealing with it, or allowed Admiral Templeton more discretion in laying down the route to be followed. By his instructions he was bound to call at Punta Arenas, and it is to his credit that he gave what proved an all-important order to the *Trenton* to proceed round the Horn and rendezvous at Sholl Bay, and so saved his command from what probably would have been a serious reverse.

CHAPTER XI

OCTOBER–DECEMBER, 1931

U.S. Government determines to assume the offensive—Admiral
Morrison advocates expedition to the Bonins—Reconnaissance
carried out by submarines—Topography of the Bonin group—
Composition of force to be employed—Admiral Dallinger's misgivings

THE course of the war, so far, had been singularly
indecisive, and it is doubtful whether the net results
could be viewed with any greater satisfaction in Tokyo
than in Washington. Japan, it is true, had swept the
American flag from the Western Pacific, besides dealing
some painful if superficial blows at the coastline of her
enemy. But now it looked as though she had shot her
bolt. The possibilities of direct attack, limited from
the first, were apparently exhausted. Before attempting
any serious military action, she would have to destroy
or immobilise the American fleet, which was still intact,
and certain to grow stronger as time went on. In pre-
war days imaginative Japanese writers had drawn lurid
pen-pictures of the invasion of Hawaii by the all-conquer-
ing legions of Nippon; some, indeed, had gone so far as
to predict the landing of whole army corps in California
itself. Nor was it only in Japan that such fantastic
notions found expression. Many years previously one
Homer Lea, an American military critic, had written a
book to prove how easily Washington, Oregon and
California could be invaded and overrun by armies
from Japan. But although a few papers in the West
endeavoured to revive the invasion bogey, the more
sober organs of the Press poured ridicule on these fears.
How, they asked, was Japan to transport troops across

4,500 miles of water in the teeth of a superior American fleet? No nation, and least of all Japan, whose rulers were deeply versed in the science of war, would dream of sending its armies to certain destruction. Equal risk would attend an expedition to Hawaii, where, as everyone knew, the bulk of the American Navy was stationed, in readiness for instant action. "As well talk of an American invasion of Japan," scoffed the San Francisco *Argonaut*, "as of the Japanese invading our shores." Yet, had the *Argonaut* but known it, projects not far removed from an invasion of Japan were even then under discussion in Washington. Disillusioned by now as to the prospects of an early peace, the executive authorities were beginning to cast about for means of ending the strategic deadlock which had developed. They were in the mood to consider any scheme that promised to give a decisive turn to the conflict, the blighting influence of which had begun to make itself felt throughout the country. Business of every description was suffering, the financial barometer was unsteady, and the stock markets exhibited symptoms of panic at every fresh rumour. Pacifists of the militant breed were openly preaching their seditious doctrines, which appealed to the less orderly elements of the public. Unrest was in the air, and although it was too soon to speak of positive danger to the social system, there were not wanting alarmists who painted the future in gloomy colours. In view of the immense sums already appropriated for army and navy expansion, the theory that defensive warfare could be waged at small cost had ceased to be convincing. Would it not eventually prove cheaper in every sense, asked members of the Cabinet, to abandon the passive strategy which had thus far been pursued, and prepare to take the offensive on a grand scale? With the full weight of the national resources behind it, a stunning blow might be aimed at the enemy, breaking that will to win which had been nourished by more or less facile triumphs, and forcing him to his knees. Admitting the hazards of such an operation, were they more to be dreaded than the ultimate effects of a war that might drag on interminably with no promise of final success? Hitherto no clear-cut purpose had inspired the efforts that were being made to reinforce the fighting services. In the absence of a definite objective, neither army nor navy chiefs knew precisely what to ask for, and from this uncertainty, waste of money and overlapping of effort inevitably resulted.

What the situation demanded was a clearly-defined plan of campaign which would ensure the closest and most fruitful co-operation between all arms. Once such a plan was evolved, it would be a simple matter to provide the material required for its execution. As things stood at present, the Army was competing against the Navy for war munitions of every description, which both Departments were ordering in prodigious quantities, though apparently without any clear idea of how they were to be used. The War Department, for example, had placed a contract for fifty railroad mounts for guns of the heaviest calibre, intended to reinforce the mobile railroad batteries of the Coast Artillery Corps. Guns of this type would be effective enough against hostile battleships, but for any other purpose they were needlessly powerful, and there was scarcely one chance in a thousand that they would ever fire a shot at the Japanese battle fleet. Early in June a conference was held at the White House to bring the whole military situation under review. At this meeting, which was attended by all the principal members of the Cabinet and high officials of the Army and Navy, Admiral Morrison, the Chief of Naval Operations, submitted a plan of which the details had been worked out by the staff of his Bureau. Nothing less was proposed than a descent on the Bonins, a group of Japanese islands lying some 500 miles to the south-east of Yokohama, and their seizure as a base for the American fleet. This project had not been developed on the spur of the moment. It was one among several Pacific war plans which the Bureau of Operations had studied in collaboration with the War College and the General Board of the Navy, long before hostilities were in sight. This particular

scheme, however, had failed to win the approval of
more than a few senior officers of the Navy. The
majority regarded it as unsound and dangerous.
Experienced military officers were equally dubious.
But no argument availed to shake Admiral Morrison's
faith in the merits of the plan. For every criticism he
was ready with a plausible answer, and though he did
not convince the professional strategists, who roundly
condemned the project as foolhardy and impracticable,
his eloquence finally won over the Cabinet. Still, the
first condition of success in every great enterprise—
unanimity of purpose and mutual confidence among the
leaders—was wanting. Once the decision was taken,
however, all concerned in the plan worked loyally to
carry it through to a fortunate issue. As so many
conflicting versions have since appeared in print, it may
be as well to give a brief summary of what was intended.
Starting from the assumption that a base within reasonable distance of the hostile coast must be obtained before
a systematic offensive could begin, Admiral Morrison
had arrived by a process of elimination at two possible
objectives, either of which would serve the end in view.
One was Guam; the other, Port Lloyd, in the Bonin
Islands. For some reasons Guam was to be preferred.
While on the one hand its remoteness from Japan would
render a close blockade of the enemy's coast impossible,
on the other, possession of this island would enable the
American fleet to deploy at full strength in those waters
where Japan had hitherto enjoyed an absolute supremacy. Nothing would be so likely to force her into
accepting a decisive fleet action as the prospect of seeing
American naval power firmly entrenched once more
in the Western Pacific. From Guam, also, American
cruisers would be in a position to cut across the steamer
routes from Europe, holding up those supplies of war
material without which Japan could not long sustain the
struggle. Even her communications with the Chinese
mainland would be exposed to attack by long-range
submarines penetrating into the Yellow Sea and the
Sea of Japan. Finally, the island would be invaluable

as a stepping-stone to the conquest of the Philippines, should the march of events justify such a move. But the difficulties in the way of recovering Guam by direct assault were held by Admiral Morrison to be insurmountable, a belief in which most naval officers heartily concurred. In the first place, as it was precisely the quarter in which the enemy might expect to be attacked, he would undoubtedly have taken precautions against surprise. A sufficient period had now elapsed since the fall of Guam to permit of its defences being strengthened, and the intelligence service reported Japanese submarines and air scouts to be particularly active in the neighbourhood of the Mariana Islands. Probably, therefore, the approach of an expeditionary force would be detected in ample time for a warm reception to be prepared for it. For these reasons, and others that need not be gone into, the idea of making an attempt against Guam was given up. It was then that Admiral Morrison recommended the Bonins as a more promising objective. As he himself admitted, the plan was an exceptionally bold one, but its very audacity held out the best promise of success. Japan, he argued, would never anticipate so daring an operation as the seizure of islands that lay within a day's steaming of her great naval arsenals. Fortifications were known to exist at Port Lloyd, but they were not believed to be powerful. In any case, surprise was the keynote of the scheme. Though the battle fleet would have to cover the voyage of the expedition at long range, it was not expected to pit itself against the defences of the island. Resistance was to be overcome by an intensive gas attack carried out by airplanes. These were to sweep in from seaward and drench the position with a flood of the gas recently produced at the Edgewood factory and known as " 847," which rendered its victims unconscious in a few seconds, and against which every known type of mask had proved impotent. Following the delivery of this attack the transports, carrying some 20,000 picked men, with artillery and stores, were to enter the harbour at Port Lloyd, the ships being equipped with special gear for

rapid unloading.   The invaders would have with them
fifty guns of 7-inch and 155 mm. calibre, high-velocity
weapons ranging up to 18,000 yards.   Futhermore, it
was probable that the suddenness of the gas offensive
would overwhelm the Japanese garrison before they had
time to dismantle their guns, in which case the coastal
batteries might be captured intact.   The arrival of the
Japanese main fleet from its base at Yokosuka, only 500
miles away, was not only expected but hoped for.   On
reaching the Bonins it would find the principal island
already in American occupation and bristling with long-
range guns.   These it would have to silence before
attempting to eject the intruders, and experience at the
taking of Guam had taught the Japanese to be wary
of exposing even their heaviest ships to the fire of well-
concealed artillery ashore.   In the meantime the American fleet, operating from its advanced base at Midway,
with Wake Island as an intermediate port of call for
the small craft and submarines, would be held in readiness to approach the Bonins and fall upon the Japanese
fleet at a moment when the latter had expended much
of its ammunition against the forts and perhaps had
several ships damaged by their fire.   An action fought
under such conditions might easily result in a smashing
victory, and so end the war at a blow.   In any case, the
loss of the Bonins and their conversion into a strong
base from which the United States could develop a
powerful offensive against Japan's home coast must
sooner or later compel her to fight a fleet action, and this,
after all, was one of the chief objects to be striven for.
Such, in broad outline, was Admiral Morrison's plan, the
fate of which we are about to relate.   Obviously, the
first step was to determine the whereabouts of the Japanese main fleet, which had been heard of at the Bonins
during April, though it was not believed to have
remained there longer than a few days.   The seemingly
impossible task of reconnoitring the islands was performed by a submarine division consisting of six boats
of the " S " class, reinforced for the occasion by *V 1*.
Temporary headquarters were established at Wake

Island, situated about 1500 miles to the eastward of
Port Lloyd. It is merely a coral atoll, enclosing a
shallow lagoon, to which loaded boats and motor
launches could gain access by a channel blasted through
the coral reefs. Beyond affording a lee under which
vessels might lie-to and refuel, the island—or rather
group of islands, for there are three of them—is destitute
of anchorage facilities. An American naval officer who
visited the place some years before the war wrote that
" the total land area is about 2600 acres, much of which
lies at 10 to 15 feet above sea level. The group is about
$4\frac{1}{2}$ miles long by $1\frac{1}{2}$ miles wide, with its major axis lying
north-west and south-east, and as the prevailing winds
range from east to north-east, a lee is usually found."
On October 23 the *V 1* (Commander Groves) accompanied by two " S " boats, sailed from Wake on a
reconnoitring cruise to the Bonins. All three vessels
were carrying their maximum load of fuel. On the
evening of October 28 the *V 1*, having left her consorts
300 miles to the eastward, sighted Peel Island (Chichi
Shima), the main island of the group, which she proceeded
to reconnoitre. The utmost caution had to be exercised,
not only on account of the submarine's own safety, but
to avoid giving alarm to the Japanese, for the success
of the whole enterprise depended on their remaining in
complete ignorance of the objective. Had they known
that the Bonins were being watched their suspicions
would have been aroused. The *V 1* remained off the
islands for three days, without seeing anything to indicate the presence of a large fleet. During the hours
of daylight the submarine spent most of her time on the
bed of the sea, her favourite refuge being Walker Bay,
some miles to the north of Port Lloyd. The water here
was less than 100 ft. deep, and the bottom, though somewhat hard and uneven, afforded a fairly good resting
place. At intervals throughout the day Commander
Groves brought his boat up to periscope level—though
without breaking surface—and took a survey of the
position. Occasionally a vessel was heard passing
overhead, and once at least the unmistakable throb of

a destroyer's screws was audible close at hand.   Shortly before dusk the submarine would leave her lair in the green depths and head out to sea, coming to the surface when some 15 miles from land to re-charge the electric batteries and enable the officers and men to get some much-needed fresh air and exercise on deck.   There was always a danger that the noise of the charging engine might be heard by a Japanese patrol, but this risk had to be accepted.   When the batteries were charged Commander Groves would again close the land, this time proceeding on the surface, though ready at the first hint of danger to make a sudden dive.   At midnight on October 29 he ventured within a mile of the entrance to Port Lloyd (Futami Ko), but again without seeing or hearing anything to suggest that a considerable naval force was lying in the harbour.   On the following night he cruised round the islands with the same negative result.   At length, on November 2, he brought his visit to a close and headed back for Wake Island.   Three hundred miles east of the Bonins he was met by sub-marines *S 28*, *S 40*, and *R 23*, which carried a full relief complement for the *V 1*.   Commander Groves and his men having transferred to the *S 40*, their places were taken by Lieut.-Commander Bryant and the new crew, while *V 1* refilled her fuel tanks from the *R 23*.   This boat had been converted into a submersible tanker by the removal of her engines and all other equipment, and had been brought to the rendezvous in tow of *S 28*. Thanks to this ingenious arrangement, the *V 1* was back at her post near the Bonins in less than forty-eight hours after leaving it.   As time went on the inshore patrol was reinforced by *V 3*, and so organised that the islands were kept almost continually under observation.   It speaks well for the skill and discretion with which this extremely difficult work was accomplished that the Japanese never, from first to last, suspected the presence of enemy submarines.   The only incident of importance that occurred during a vigil lasting for months was the arrival at Port Lloyd on December 4 of the Japanese main fleet.   The *V 3*, on patrol at the time, sighted them 30 miles north-west of Ototo Shima, and stayed on the surface long enough to identify the big battle-ships. She then dived, and remained below for the rest of the day, compelled to keep her electro-motors running because the sea was too deep for her to rest on the bottom, and fervently hoping that the hydrophones in the Japanese ships would not betray her presence. She made no attempt to attack the oncoming fleet, since for obvious reasons the submarines of the Bonin patrol had stringent orders never to molest enemy ships. On this occasion the fleet spent only one day at Port Lloyd, which was fortunate for the V 3, seeing that she was due to pick up her relief, the V 1, at the distant rendezvous on December 7, and her non-arrival would have thrown the patrol organisation out of gear. On the other hand, it was of the first importance that the length of the enemy fleet's sojourn in the islands should be noted. On December 5 it again put to sea, and that same day the American submarine watched from a respectful distance the Japanese battleships carrying out gun practice. These periodical cruises to and from the Bonins were evidently made for training purposes only, and did not appear to have any strategical significance. Nevertheless, they introduced a further element of uncertainty into Admiral Morrison's project, for if the would-be invaders were to find Japanese battleships awaiting them, nothing could avert disaster. To guard against this risk it would be necessary for the sailing of the expedition to be held back until the enemy's fleet was known to have returned to Yokosuka after one of its visits, and this in turn made it doubly essential to carry on the submarine patrol with undiminished vigilance. Preparations for the great enterprise had all this time been going forward actively. The scene of operations was unfamiliar to American naval officers, few of whom had ever visited the Bonins. First sighted by the Spanish explorer Villalobos in 1543, they were re-dis-covered fifty years later by a Japanese navigator, Ogasawara Sadayori. From early in the nineteenth century American whalers used occasionally to touch at the islands, and in June, 1853, Commodore Perry paid a call with the U.S. warships *Susquehanna* and *Saratoga*. In 1861 a party of Japanese colonists, headed by a Government commissioner, landed in Peel Island, but they seem to have found the territory inhospitable, for their stay was brief. Oddly enough, the first white resident of the Bonins was an American, Nathaniel Savory, who was born at Bedford, Mass. In the course of his roving career he came to Peel Island in 1830, there married a native woman from the Mariana group, and settled down. Surrounded by numerous children he lived on the island for many years, dying in 1874 at the ripe age of eighty. Previous to 1875 Japan had evinced little interest in the Bonins. In that year, however, she learned of a British design to annex the territory, and proceeded to forestall it by dispatching a commissioner. Landing at Port Lloyd on November 26, this official took possession in the name of the Emperor of Japan. The Bonins—or Ogasawara Islands, as they are officially designated, after their second discoverer—are of volcanic origin. The largest of the group are Peel Island (Chichi Shima), Bailey Island (Haha Shima), and Buckland Island (Ani Shima), the principal harbour being Port Lloyd (Futami Ko) in Peel Island. Here are situated the Government buildings, the observatory, the garrison headquarters, and the cable station, for the trans-Pacific cable from Hawaii crosses the island. The harbour, which is simply an immense volcanic crater, is small, but easy of access and fairly well sheltered. In many places the cliffs rise almost sheer from the beach, and deep water is found everywhere save right inshore. While nothing authentic was known of the fortifications at this place, it was believed that the armament was confined to heavy rapid-fire guns, mounted in concrete emplacements on the heights overlooking Port Lloyd and Fitton Bay, the last-named being a small harbour on the southeast side of the island. The great depth of water in this area made mine-laying difficult, and the impunity with which American submarines had approached almost to the mouth of the harbour was held to be proof that no mine-fields existed. As a measure of precaution, however, all ships taking part in the expedition were to be equipped with paravanes. For the transport of the invading force twenty-five steamers had been taken over, the slowest of them having a speed of 12 knots. Those in which guns and other heavy materials were to be carried were fitted with powerful derricks, and had large ports, provided with strong hinged gangways, or " brows," cut in their sides. Trials made at Puget Sound, where many of the transports were fitted out, showed that 7-inch guns could be brought up from the holds and passed down the gangways to the quay in a very short space of time. Among the impedimenta carried were eighty airplanes, mainly of the combat type. These, it was estimated, could be unloaded, assembled, and made ready for flight within a few hours from the time of landing. The army of invasion, under the command of General Dykeman, was made up of a complete Army Division, with certain additions, and included the following units :—

2 brigades of Infantry.
3 regiments of Field Artillery.
1 regiment of Heavy Tractor Artillery.
1 company Signal Corps.
1 Gas Battalion.
1 regiment of Engineers.
1 Medical regiment.
Various other units, including an Air Detachment, Motor Transport and Ammunition Units.

This force numbered in all about 22,000 men. Having regard to the restricted harbour area at Port Lloyd and the limited quayage available, it was arranged that a flotilla of motor lighters should assist in the unloading of ships for which there was no room at the wharf. A great many of these lighters had been ordered, with the idea that each transport should tow one or two on the last leg of the voyage, from Wake Island to the objective.

The naval escort over this stage was to be furnished by
the new cruiser *Minneapolis*, of 10,000 tons, with a
battery of 8-inch guns; the cruisers *Concord* and *Marblehead;* and 30 destroyers, with the tenders *Buffalo* and
Melville. This force was under the command of Rear-
Admiral Doyle. The initial gas bombardment of Port
Lloyd was to be carried out by 100 seaplanes from the
carriers *Saratoga, Langley, Houston,* and *Shafter,* the last
two being large steamers improvised for the purpose.
Admiral Dallinger's battle fleet was under orders to
assemble at Midway, whence it would make a sweeping
movement in the direction of Wake Island, remaining
within radio call of the expedition. Oilers and store-
ships would follow, in readiness to replenish the fleet
at Wake Island should circumstances render this
necessary. All these movements, of course, were co-
ordinated by a schedule drawn up by a board of naval
and military officers. Allowance was made for every
contingency that could be foreseen. If the attack on
Peel Island brought out the Japanese main body from
Yokosuka, the American battle fleet was to steam to the
Bonins at full speed and engage the enemy. Admiral
Dallinger's ships, it is true, would arrive there with
much of their fuel consumed, but if the Japanese fleet
were destroyed, or even badly mauled, this would be
a matter of small moment; for with the Bonins securely
held by the invading force, tankers and supply ships
could proceed there in comparative safety. The draw-
back to this plan was that no dock was available in the
islands, and severely damaged ships would thus be
without means of repair. On the other hand, if battle
were fairly joined, the American preponderance in
gun-power ought to ensure a swift and complete victory.
Subject to favourable reports from the submarine
patrol off the Bonins, the expedition was timed to leave
Honolulu on December 20, and Midway six days later.
Wake Island should be reached on or about January 2,
and Port Lloyd by the 8th. Towards the end of
November the troops selected for the enterprise were
all gathered at Hawaii, and as many of the transports

were then ready, it was possible to put the officers and men through a special course of disembarkation drill. As the Japanese fleet had last visited the Bonins on December 4–5, there was small likelihood of its reappearing there for at least two months in the ordinary course of events; and in any case the American submarines on guard might be trusted to give timely warning if it again approached the islands while the expedition was *en route*. After weighing all these considerations, the Naval Staff decided to adhere to the original schedule, and the transport fleet, with its naval escort, was ordered to sail from Honolulu on December 20. At 4 p.m. on that date the twenty-five steamers, crowded with troops, passed out of the roadstead and were joined at sea by the warships. No chances were taken, for enemy submarines had already been active in Hawaiian waters, and had even sown mines off Pearl Harbour, as related in an earlier chapter. The fleet was accordingly preceded by mine-sweepers for a distance of ten miles, while the destroyers acted as a screen against submarine attack, this duty being performed by them throughout the voyage. At Midway, which was reached without incident on December 26, the greater part of the battle fleet was found at anchor in Seward Roads. By this time the troops, having gained their " sea legs," were in high spirits and full of confidence in the success of their great adventure. Among the senior officers, however, optimism was less in evidence. Admiral Dallinger himself entertained serious misgivings, to which he had previously given expression in a memorandum to the Navy Department. The whole plan, he pointed out, ran directly counter to the first principles of naval strategy. Mahan, Colomb, and other authoritative historians of sea power had all demonstrated by numerous precedents the importance of gaining command of the sea before embarking on military expeditions against hostile territory. Yet in this instance no such command had been gained. As a bait to entice the enemy's fleet the expedition might justify itself, but the risks were—in the Admiral's words—" appalling,"

M

and he did not hesitate to describe the scheme as "verging closely on a reckless gamble." These criticisms, however, had failed to convince the Cabinet; and finding their decision immutable Admiral Dallinger turned with a heavy heart to do his share in achieving what he, at least, firmly believed to be the impossible.

CHAPTER XII

DECEMBER, 1931–JANUARY, 1932

Expedition suffers severe damage in a gale—Arrangements for junction of squadrons dislocated—Japanese take the alarm—Expedition retreats, but is brought to action by Japanese—Both sides suffer heavily—Return of remnant of expedition

AFTER a twenty-four hours' stay at Midway, where the final arrangements were concerted, the expedition left on December 27 for the second stage of its voyage— the 1034-mile run to Wake Island. The battle fleet sailed a day later, steering a course more to the north- ward. The weather, up to this date, had been propitious, but on the night of December 29 a violent S.W. gale broke. Huge waves swept over the transports, causing much damage to boats and deck gear, while the look-out men, blinded by flying spray, could no longer see the dim stern lights that marked the position of the ships, this being the only illumination permitted now that the expedition was nearing enemy waters. At 1 a.m. on the 30th, when the storm was at its height, the transport *Marquette* was rammed by her next astern, the *Arlington,* which struck her a violent blow on the port quarter, tearing a great rent in her side and putting the steering gear out of action. Instantly the damaged ship began to fill, her plight being rendered hopeless by the moun- tainous seas which broke over her as she lost way and became unmanageable. Searchlight signals apprised the rest of the scattered convoy of the disaster, but it was little they could do to help their ill-starred consort. As the 1200 troops on board the *Marquette* tried to muster on deck, scores were swept to their doom by the waves that washed over the waterlogged vessel. No boats

could live in such a sea, and of the few that were
lowered, none survived for more than a minute. By
now, however, destroyers were on the scene. With
splendid gallantry the commanders of the *Somers*,
Worden, and *Bancroft* brought their craft alongside the
sinking ship, disregarding the imminent peril of being
dashed against her hull. Seeing help near at hand,
most of the soldiers threw themselves into the water,
and though many were engulfed, 530 were picked
up by the destroyers. Half-an-hour after the collision
the *Marquette* gave a last lurch and foundered by
the stern. Including members of the crew, upwards
of 900 lives were lost. Nor did this complete the full
tale of the disaster, for at 1.30 a.m. the *Arlington*
reported herself to be making water fast and unable to
steer. Her bows had been stove in when she ran into the
Marquette, and a large section of plating below the water-
line wrenched away by a great sea that struck her as she
was drawing clear of the former ship. With the forward
bulkhead showing signs of collapse she dared not steam
ahead; one of the forward compartments was flooded,
the forecastle was nearly awash, and the propellers were
lifting out of the water. Had the sea been calm she
might have remained afloat, but in view of the weather
then prevailing it was clear she was doomed. There was
nothing for it but to abandon the ship, but before launching his boats on that tempestuous sea, Captain Starkey
requested the destroyers to pump oil on the raging waters,
and by this expedient several boatloads of men contrived to reach the warships. Others jumped overboard
and were picked up, while more were saved by lifelines.
The *Arlington* sank at 3 a.m., taking down with her about
150 men. By noon on the following day, when the sea
had become less rough, the shipwrecked troops saved by
the destroyers were put on board other transports, and
the voyage was resumed, though the tragedy of the night
cast a gloom over the whole expedition. Apart from the
heavy loss of life, a quantity of munitions and other
essential stores had gone down in the two ships. Several
vessels had sustained such injury to derricks and other

gear as would prevent them from discharging rapidly.
Worse still was the loss of the lighters, which it had been
necessary to cast adrift when the storm began. Four
were recovered, but the others had vanished. As these
craft were to have been the means of getting a great
part of the artillery and heavy stores ashore at Port
Lloyd, their absence would inevitably lead to delay, and
might therefore have serious consequences. On re-
viewing the position, Admiral Doyle felt grave doubts
as to the wisdom of going on with the enterprise. As
senior naval officer it lay in his discretion to break off
the voyage and turn back, but this he was loath to do,
knowing the immensity of the issues at stake. Whatever decision he came to must be reached on his own
responsibility, for his orders expressly enjoined him not
to send radio signals after leaving Wake Island until the
landing had been accomplished, or unless Japanese
warships appeared. He was thus debarred from communicating with the Commander-in-Chief of the battle
fleet, or with any other authority competent to instruct
him. At length, after conferring with General Dykeman,
who entered a strong protest against turning back, he
made up his mind to proceed. Whether he erred in
taking this course is a question which has since provoked
endless discussion. Since Admiral Doyle did not himself survive the expedition, we are left in doubt as to
the considerations which led him to form his resolve.
It can only be said that the facts, so far as they are
known, fully warranted his reluctance to abandon the
voyage. The sinking of two transports, with the loss
of nearly 1100 troops and valuable war stores, was
admittedly a heavy blow, but it could hardly be said to
have so weakened the force as to rule out all chance of
success. Much more serious from the strictly practical
point of view was the loss of the motor lighters and the
extensive damage to cargo-handling gear, for these
factors were to have played a supremely important *rôle*
in the actual landing. But Admiral Doyle had good
grounds for believing that the invading army, together
with its equipment, could still be thrown on shore before

the Japanese fleet had time to intervene, always assuming the preliminary gas offensive to have done its work. If enemy battleships were not at sea, the only naval forces likely to be encountered would be torpedo-craft and submarines, or, at the very worst, light cruisers, and to deal with these Admiral Doyle had his three cruisers and numerous destroyers. In view of these circumstances, impartial historians will acquit him of having acted rashly in deciding to proceed with the venture. Owing to the delay caused by the storm and the sinking of the two transports, the morning of January 8, 1932, found the flotilla still some 250 miles to the eastward of the Bonins. Here it was to have been joined by the airplane-carrier squadron, under Captain Miller, but when the rendezvous was reached no trace of these ships could be discerned. The expedition, it was true, was forty-eight hours behind time, but it was scarcely conceivable that Captain Miller had failed to allow for the possibility of delay. Admiral Doyle assumed, therefore, that his colleague was in the vicinity, and dispatched four destroyers to look for him. Airplanes from the *Minneapolis* and the *Concord* were also flown off to join in the search. But, in fact, Captain Miller's squadron was still at a considerable distance from the rendezvous. He, too, had met with heavy weather some ten days before, and the *Shafter* had sustained such damage to her rudder and one of the screws as practically to disable her. An attempt was made to repair the injury to the rudder, but without success, and there was nothing for it but to take the vessel in tow. As her starboard propeller was still in action she was able, with the assistance of the *Saratoga's* towing spring, to maintain a speed of 14 knots, but since this was some knots less than the collective speed of the squadron, its voyage was seriously retarded. Perceiving that he would be several days late in arriving at the rendezvous, Captain Miller detached his only escort cruiser, the *Cincinnati* (Captain Edwards) to try to establish contact with the expeditionary force and explain the situation. His destroyers he kept with him, for the squadron was now within the radius of submarine attack and, with a partially disabled ship on his hands, he could afford to take no chances. Shortly after dawn on January 8 the *Cincinnati* observed a periscope less than a thousand yards ahead, and almost simultaneously two torpedoes were seen approaching. These were easily avoided by a touch of the helm, but before the cruiser could open fire the enemy had disappeared. Five minutes later a second submarine was observed on the surface, too far off for torpedo attack. Several shots were fired at her, but she dived before the range could be found. Fearing lest the airplane carriers should run into an ambush, Captain Edwards flashed a message to Captain Miller, giving the position in which the submarines had been sighted. He used his radio without hesitation, knowing that his presence would in any case be reported to Japanese headquarters by the submarine scouts which had intercepted him. Moreover, since he had been detected comparatively near the Bonins, the enemy would certainly jump to the conclusion that an assault on the islands was impending, and instantly take counter-measures. The entire situation had thus undergone a radical change. Surprise was now out of the question. Not only would the garrison be warned, but, what was far more serious, every Japanese warship within call would soon be rushing toward the islands. Even the battleships, provided they were at Yokosuka, could reach Port Lloyd in twenty-four hours. That a general alarm had been sounded was made clear by the radio activity which now ensued. In the space of a few hours scores of messages were taken in by the *Cincinnati*, but being in Japanese code they could not be read. Nevertheless, their significance was unmistakable. The *Cincinnati's* message reporting enemy submarines had reached Captain Miller at 6.30 a.m. Fully alive to the critical posture of affairs, his whole concern now was for the safety of the transport convoy, of whose whereabouts he was still ignorant. He therefore ordered the *Cincinnati* to continue her search. It was clear, of course, that the projected attack on the Bonins could not now take

place. Consequently, the airplane-carriers were no
longer needed, and it was essential to their safety that
they should be withdrawn as quickly as possible from
what would speedily become a highly dangerous area.
But since a fast and powerful carrier like his flagship, the
Saratoga, with her complement of bombing planes, would
be invaluable for covering the retreat of the transports,
he proposed to join up with the convoy, while the three
other carriers, including the disabled *Shafter*, steamed
eastward until they made contact with the battle fleet.
By this time Admiral Dallinger, the Commander-in-Chief,
had been apprised of the situation, the full gravity of
which was painfully evident to him.   His position was,
roughly, 450 miles to the north-west of Wake, and therefore about 1200 miles from the Bonins.   Although still
unaware of the delay to which the expeditionary force
had been subjected by reason of the storm and the sinking
of two transports, the fact that it had not yet joined the
airplane-carrier squadron showed that a fatal hitch had
occurred in the programme.   If, as he surmised, the transports were now nearing the Bonins, it meant that the
Japanese fleet from Yokosuka could reach them in less
than half the time it would take him to do so, and he
knew that Admiral Doyle's small force could offer no
serious resistance to such an overwhelming attack.   In
face of this appalling danger, no effective action seemed
possible.   But although his worst forebodings seemed to
be confirmed, the Commander-in-Chief was in no doubt
as to what he should do.   His fleet had expended
approximately one-third of its fuel during the voyage
from Midway, so that enough remained for a prolonged
run at high speed, though it was essential to preserve
a margin for the homeward journey.   Still, the safety
of the expeditionary force overrode every other consideration for the time being.   And so, at 8 a.m. on
January 8 the three battle divisions, comprising the
swiftest of the heavy ships, with their attendant cruisers
and destroyers, were driving westward at a speed of 18
knots, steering a course direct for Port Lloyd.
   In the meantime, however, we must revert to the

expeditionary force, which circumstances had placed in extreme jeopardy. When the coming of daylight on January 8 failed to reveal the airplane-carriers which were to have met him, Admiral Doyle, as we have seen, sent out destroyers and air scouts to locate the missing squadron. Pending news of it he deemed it prudent to alter course to the north—from which direction the carriers were expected to come—rather than hold on toward the Bonins. At 7.30 a.m. he intercepted the *Cincinnati's* signal to Captain Miller, reporting enemy submarines, and at once realised all that this portended. The expedition, he saw, must be abandoned forthwith, for the enemy would now be on the alert, and it could only be a question of hours before powerful Japanese forces were converging upon him. Orders were accordingly given for the convoy to retrace its course at the highest speed possible. The destroyers sent out to reconnoitre were recalled. Half-an-hour later came the welcome intelligence from one of the *Minneapolis's* airplanes that the *Cincinnati* was in sight. She arrived by noon, and Admiral Doyle learned from her that the *Saratoga* was racing at full speed to join his flag. By 5 p.m. the convoy was 350 miles to the west of the Bonins, and as every hour reduced the danger of pursuit by the Japanese main fleet, those on board began to breathe more freely. But the evil fortune which had dogged the expedition almost from the start had not yet deserted it. When the general warning was sent out from Yokosuka on January 8, the Japanese main body was at sea, cruising about 300 miles due east of that port. At the same time the " South Seas Squadron," under Rear-Admiral Isomura, was fifty miles north-west of the Mariana Islands, having left Sasebo three days before on a cruise to the south seas. This squadron consisted of the *Chitose* (flag), *Yoshino*, and *Kasagi*—10,000-ton ships of recent construction, armed with 8-in. guns and possessing a speed of 34 knots—besides the smaller cruiser *Ohi*. A message relayed from Port Lloyd was received by Admiral Isomura, instructing him to cut off enemy forces which were believed to be 400 miles east or north-east of the Bonins, and he at once complied by ordering his ships to increase speed to 25 knots.   The Japanese main fleet, being at so great a distance from the scene, had little chance of intervening, but three of its 28-knot battle-cruisers were sent on ahead to join forces, if possible, with Admiral Isomura.   Further to strengthen the pursuit, twelve big flying boats, with a great radius of action, were dispatched from Yokosuka and Kure to Port Lloyd, whence they were to co-operate with Admiral Isomura in locating the American force and bringing it to action.   Finally, a division of submarines from Guam was ordered to cruise to westward of Wake Island, for which the Americans were thought to be heading, and to harass their retreat.   These dispositions naturally were unknown to Admiral Doyle, but he can have been under no illusion as to the peril in which he stood.   The convoy was maintaining a steady 12 knots. The flagship *Minneapolis* steamed ahead, with the *Marblehead* and *Concord* on either flank, while the destroyers formed an anti-submarine guard round the squadron, and the *Cincinnati* brought up the rear.   The big airplane-carrier *Saratoga*, with Captain Miller on board, arrived at 6 p.m., and was ordered to take station abreast of the flagship.   And now for the first time those in the convoy had visual proof of the net that was closing round them.   Heralded by the drone of their powerful engines, two large seaplanes were sighted coming up astern.   They were greeted with a hot fire from the anti-aircraft guns of the *Cincinnati*, while the *Saratoga* sent up pursuit planes to engage them.   One of the Japanese machines, flying over the convoy at a height of 5000 feet, dropped two heavy bombs, but the aim was bad and no ship was hit.   The other machine made for the *Saratoga*, apparently bent on delivering an attack from a low altitude, but before it could release any bombs it was brought down by a shell bursting under it, some of the *débris* falling on the deck of the *Minneapolis*.   The first plane, having discharged its bombs without effect, flew off to the westward, closely pursued by the fighters from the *Saratoga*, which were at least twice as speedy.   In five minutes it was overtaken and brought down, after a brisk action in which one of the American planes also came to grief. Admiral Doyle knew, however, that the two Japanese scouts would have reported his position to the pursuing fleet before launching their attack. Twice during the night other airplanes were heard, but no bombs were dropped. It was now all but certain that the morrow would decide the fate of the expedition. If the next twenty-four hours passed without bringing a superior force of enemy ships on the scene, the convoy would probably be safe, for the Japanese, knowing as they must that the American battle fleet was steaming westward at full speed, would certainly not press the pursuit so far. But with the first glimmer of dawn on the 9th came unmistakable signs of danger. On the southwest horizon smoke was observed, from which soon emerged the dim shapes of four large vessels. Planes sent up to scout signalled the approach of enemy cruisers, which appeared to be of powerful design. It was, indeed, the squadron of Admiral Isomura, who, having found his quarry, was coming up at maximum speed to strike a deadly blow for the cause of Nippon. At first sight the opposing forces did not seem unequally matched. Each contained four cruisers, and although the *Minneapolis* was the only American ship that mounted 8-in. guns— against three Japanese vessels so armed—Admiral Doyle had his thirty destroyers, not to speak of the *Saratoga*, whose planes might well turn the balance in his favour. The enemy had no destroyers, and their only airplanes were those carried on board the cruisers. Had Admiral Doyle been free to handle his fighting ships as a tactical unit, he might, nay probably would, have had the best of the duel. But cumbered as he was with the flock of slow and helpless transports, which must on no account be left unguarded, his freedom of action was necessarily restricted. Line of battle was formed at 7 a.m., the enemy then being 23,000 yards away. The *Minneapolis* and her three smaller consorts, in line ahead, were on the starboard side of the transports, which had been ordered to steer a course to the north-east. Twelve destroyers were told off to guard them, for the danger of submarine attack was ever present. The *Saratoga,* occupying a station between the transports and the battle line, was out of range of gunfire and yet in a favourable position to send her planes either to support Admiral Doyle or repel an attack on the convoy, as circumstances required. The twenty destroyers retained with the squadron were disposed ahead and to starboard of the flagship, ready to attack the enemy's line with torpedoes at the word of command. While these dispositions were being made, more Japanese seaplanes were observed coming up from the west, though at too great a height to be reached by gunfire. They had come from the Bonins, and formed part of the contingent of long-range flying boats which had left Yokosuka and Kure on the previous day. With a cruising endurance of 3000 miles, they were able to keep aloft for two days at a time. " It was from the radio-phone reports of these aircraft that Admiral Isomura obtained that early and precise intelligence of the enemy's formation which enabled him to deliver his attack with telling effect," to quote from the Japanese naval staff history of the war. " On learning the respective positions of the American columns, he at once ordered the *Kasagi* to make a *détour* and sweep down upon the transports from the north, while the Admiral himself, with his three other ships, held the American naval squadron under fire." Observing that one of the Japanese cruisers withdrew from the line and steamed north at high speed, Admiral Doyle —as we know from surviving officers of his staff—realised immediately what was intended. His first instinct was to turn his whole line 16 points and hasten in pursuit, but a moment's reflection showed him the futility of such a procedure. As the three Japanese cruisers, which were now running almost parallel with him but gradually closing the range, held on unswervingly, it was plain that if he turned in pursuit of the *Kasagi* they would themselves steer straight for the transports. The most he could do was to signal the destroyers with the convoy to head off the *Kasagi* at all costs, at the same time ordering the *Saratoga* to launch planes against her. Even as these orders were being issued, the action opened with a salvo from the Japanese flagship, which, with the *Yoshino* and *Ohi*, had now closed to 18,000 yards. But this distance, although nominally within the reach of their 8-inch guns, was too great for effective practice, and for some time the shooting was erratic. Not until the range was down to 16,000 yards did Admiral Doyle give the word to open fire. All his ships opened on the enemy, but the 6-inch projectiles from the *Cincinnati*, *Marblehead*, and *Concord* were seen to be falling short. The third 8-inch salvo from the *Minneapolis* straddled the *Chitose*, and the cannonade from both sides now rose to a crescendo of fury. Admiral Doyle tried repeatedly to close the range in order to bring the 6-inch guns of his other ships into action, but the enemy each time turned away, keeping just inside the 16,000-yard limit at which they reaped the full benefit of their higher-powered artillery. Moreover, they were forging rapidly ahead, for Admiral Doyle dared not let himself be lured too far away from his transports and accordingly had not yet exceeded 20 knots, though his adversaries were doing at least 25. But at this juncture he raised speed to 23, for the Japanese were plainly trying to " cross his T "—that is, to cut across the head of his line and subject it to enfilade fire, a manœuvre that would also open the transports to direct attack. It was to circumvent this design that the American commander put on more speed. As the Japanese had already turned inward four points, the two squadrons were now converging at high velocity, and the range dropped swiftly from 16,000 yards to 12,000, and, for a short interval, even to 9000 yards. This proved the hottest phase of the action. Each side was firing with the utmost rapidity, and hitting had begun in earnest. A well-placed 8-inch salvo from the *Minneapolis* struck the *Chitose* amidships, bringing down her forward funnel and starting a big fire. Two minutes later the *Minneapolis* herself received several hits in succession, one of which wrecked the conning-tower, killing Admiral Doyle on the spot and laying low all its other occupants. Momentarily out of control, the flag-ship yawed badly, presenting her bows to the enemy, who plastered her with bursting shell before she could be swung back into line. It was now 8 a.m. The battle had been in progress a full hour, but it continued to rage with unabated fury. At 8.05 a.m. the *Ohi*, upon which the *Cincinnati* had been concentrating rapid salvos, was seen to be dropping astern in a grievous plight. Her quarterdeck was blazing, dense clouds of steam arose, and few of her guns remained in action. Three more broadsides finished her. Following a terrific explosion amidships, she turned over and went to the bottom at 8.15. But she did not pass unavenged. Already the Japanese preponderance in heavy metal had begun to tell. The *Minneapolis*, with two turrets knocked out and half-a-dozen great gaps yawning in her side, was nearing the limit of her endurance. In the *Marblehead* 8-inch shells had wrecked the entire forward battery, while others, penetrating the sides of the ship, had caused so much water to enter that she had a heavy list to starboard. This not only brought down her speed, but prevented her guns from bearing on the enemy. The *Concord* also had received extensive damage, though she was still able to steam and fight most of her guns, albeit with " scratch " crews, most of the original gun parties having been killed or wounded by heavy splinters which the thin turret and casemate armour failed to keep out. The *Cincinnati*, engaged principally with the lightly-armed *Ohi*—seven 5·5-inch guns—had escaped serious injury, her only bad hit being a shell in the forward boiler room. On the Japanese side, the *Chitose* had one turret disabled, her port engines were wrecked, and fires were raging in several parts of the ship. The *Yoshino* had only superficial damage until she was hit by a torpedo—the only one that found a billet in spite of several attacks by the American destroyers —and even this failed to disable her, exploding as it did a few feet from the bows. At an early stage of the engagement Admiral Doyle had ordered his destroyers to attack. This they proceeded to do with the utmost gallantry, in the teeth of a hurricane fire that took a heavy toll of the flotilla. Five boats were sunk outright or disabled in the first onslaught, and not one of the twenty or thirty torpedoes they discharged scored a hit. In the second attack the *Yoshino* was hit, but again the aggressors were driven off with heavy loss. Of the twenty boats originally with the squadron, only nine were still battle-worthy. It was now 8.45 a.m., and Admiral Isomura made a determined attempt to end the business. Signalling the *Yoshino* to concentrate on the *Minneapolis*, he turned his own big guns on the same target, ordering rapid fire. Under this terrible punishment the American flagship seemed literally to crumple up. Her sides being almost bare of armour, the 250-pounder shell hacked her through and through, whilst repeated detonations had ruptured the armour deck in more than one place, causing fragments to rain down on the machinery. Cascades of water were also pouring below, putting out the furnaces and driving stokers and engineers from their posts. Finally the ship, ceasing to move, lay helpless under the hail of fire and steel that continued to beat upon her. The *Marblehead*, sorely wounded though she was, made a valiant effort to shield the flagship by interposing her own battered hull between the enemy and their prey. But it was too late. The *Minneapolis*, now at her last gasp, made her final plunge at 9.05, destroyers rescuing eighty officers and men from the water. Having disposed of his chief antagonist, the Japanese admiral steamed in to finish off the rest of the American squadron. His two ships were pouring shell into the *Marblehead*, and also hitting the *Concord* freely, when they found themselves assailed in turn by a flight of planes, which rained down gas and phosphorus bombs. The *Chitose* bore the brunt of this attack, and suffered severely, especially from the gas fumes, which disabled every man on deck and soon percolated through into the turrets and lower compartments. Enveloped in a shroud of noxious vapour, shot here and there with livid flame, the big cruiser turned sharply away, seemingly quite out of control, with every gun silent. At this moment the destroyers *Goldsborough* and *Preston*, observing the enemy's plight, dashed forward and fired their tubes at a range of only 500 yards. Most of the torpedoes struck home together, the detonations merging in a single thunderous roar, while tongues of fire leapt as high as the masthead. As the smoke lifted the *Chitose* was seen to be on her beam ends, and two minutes later she capsized and sank. While American destroyers were searching for survivors, the airplanes were fiercely assailing the *Yoshino*, which ship was now in full flight. Although hit several times, with half her crew gassed into insensibility, she contrived to make good her escape. That the American aircraft had only intervened at this belated stage of the fight was due to their previous engagement with the *Kasagi*, the ship, it will be recalled, which had been detached by Admiral Isomura to raid the transport fleet. Probably she would never have got within range of the objective had the *Saratoga* been able to send up her planes promptly, but the huge aircraft carrier had first to endure a determined attack by four Japanese flying boats which bombed her from a low ceiling, inflicting considerable damage. They were soon driven away, but on account of injuries to the flight deck her planes could only be flown off with difficulty, and meanwhile the *Kasagi* was playing havoc among the defenceless transports. On first approaching she was met by the destroyers *Hopewell, Evans, Farragut,* and *Zeilin*, which rushed headlong to the attack; but so well-directed was her fire that the two latter were sunk and the others beaten back, none of their torpedoes making a hit. One of her earliest victims was the destroyer tender *Melville*, blown up by a shell which evidently touched off the war-heads in her torpedo magazine. Other ships sunk by the *Kasagi's* shells were the *Lake Champlain, Spokane Falls,* and *West Point*, while the *Cheyenne Bridge* and three others were more or less badly hit. Just when it seemed as though nothing could save the whole convoy from annihilation, the first planes from the *Saratoga* came swooping down to the rescue. It was no time for caution, and the

American airmen, entirely disregarding the *Kasagi's* anti-aircraft guns, held on until they could be sure of hitting the mark. Their heavy gas bombs, which had been intended for the batteries at Port Lloyd, crashed into the Japanese cruiser, whilst other missiles, each containing 600 pounds of explosive, destroyed her topworks. More than one of the low-flying planes, caught in the blast of its own bombs, fell into the sea; but the rest continued to attack until every bomb had been expended. By then the *Kasagi* was in a hopeless case. Four-fifths of her crew had been stricken down by the gas, and there was no one left to point a gun when the five remaining destroyers of the convoy guard charged forward to administer the death-blow. Three torpedoes sufficed. As the enemy ship lay deep in the water just before foundering, it was noticed that only a score or so of men made any effort to save themselves. Hundreds of their comrades, overcome by gas, went down with the ship, mercifully unconscious of their doom. The action was now over, and it remained to count the cost. Of the four cruisers which had comprised Admiral Isomura's squadron, all but one had been sunk. According to Japanese statements after the war, their loss in personnel in this fight exceeded 1200. On the American side the *Minneapolis* had gone, together with the tender *Melville*. The *Marblehead*, already in a sinking condition, eventually had to be despatched by a torpedo; and the *Concord*, with extensive damage to hull and machinery, was just able to move, but no more. Only the *Cincinnati* had escaped serious hurt. Eight of the destroyers had sunk, and three others were scarcely seaworthy. Upwards of a thousand officers and men had perished in the squadron. Apart from injury to her flight deck, the *Saratoga* was still in battle trim. It was, however, upon the troop-ship convoy that the worst blow had fallen. Here there was a ghastly list of casualties. Including men drowned in the three sunken transports, the loss of life throughout the convoy reached a total of 4000, while thousands more were wounded. Nor was this all. Some of the vessels were so battered by gunfire that they could no

N

longer move, whilst others could steam only with difficulty. And the danger of further attack still existed, for there was no telling what new enemy forces might yet be in pursuit. Had Admiral Isomura's squadron been the vanguard of the enemy's battle fleet? And, if so, how long would it be ere his battleships came up to blow the remnants of the convoy out of the water? These were the ominous questions that were heard in the transports. With only one cruiser, a few destroyers, and the *Saratoga* in condition to fight, no defence worth the name could be offered in the event of a fresh assault. But, in fact, the worst was now over, for the Japanese battle-cruisers had been ordered to abandon the pursuit when radio signals from the American battle fleet were intercepted. At 3 p.m. on the 9th the big dirigible *Chicago*, scouting in advance of the battle fleet, came in sight of the convoy, and after communicating with Captain Miller proceeded to reconnoitre towards the west. Four hours later this airship, then 200 miles to the west, reported that no enemy ships were in sight. It was clear, therefore, that the pursuit was not being pressed. Most fortunately the weather continued to be favourable, since had another gale arisen some of the shattered transports must have been lost. With the few surviving destroyers guarding either flank, and with the disabled ships in tow, the convoy steamed slowly in the direction of Wake Island. During the morning of the 10th it was twice attacked by submarines, the *Concord* receiving the *coup de grâce*, and one torpedo narrowly missing the *Cincinnati*, whilst another hit, but failed to sink, the transport *Garfield*. Driven off by destroyers, the enemy did not renew the attack. At dusk on the following day the 10,000-ton cruisers *Portland*, *Indianapolis*, and *Kansas City* came up. They had been sent ahead by the Commander-in-Chief to guard the convoy over the last stage of the journey. With the coming of these powerful warships there remained only the peril of submarine attack, and even this risk would disappear when contact was made with the destroyers of the battle fleet. Having been kept informed of the progress of events, and knowing that there was no longer any chance of meeting the Japanese main body, Admiral Dallinger had reduced his speed to 12 knots, with a view to saving fuel.   He had also ordered two of the battleship divisions to return to Wake, coming on himself with the flagship, the *Colorado, Maryland,* and *California,* accompanied by two hospital ships.   The convoy was sighted at 4 p.m. on the 13th, and after the worst of the wounded cases had been transferred to the hospital ships, the combined force continued its voyage.   At Wake Island, which was reached on the 15th, tankers and supply ships were found waiting.   Here a stay of two days was made, while the ships were re-fuelled and damaged hulls temporarily repaired.   It was found necessary to scuttle two of the half-disabled transports.   Then, on the 17th, the remaining ships of the orginal convoy sailed for Hawaii, under a strong escort of destroyers.   Honolulu was reached on January 25.   The ill-starred expedition was over, and to this day its survivors still marvel that any one of them lived to tell the tale.

CHAPTER XIII

DECEMBER, 1931–JANUARY, 1932

Admiral Morrison resigns, and is succeeded by Admiral Muller as Chief of Naval Operations—Rear-Admiral Harper becomes Assistant Chief—Admiral Templeton replaces Admiral Dallinger as Commander-in-Chief—Decision to attack Japanese commerce—More warships ordered—Plans for a new expedition—Failure of " stop-the-war " agitation—Japan's troubles in China—Gunboat action on the Yangtsze

THE United States Government, spurred to drastic action by public clamour for a change in the conduct of the war, was not slow in taking to heart the lessons of the disaster to the Bonin expedition.

Admiral Morrison, who had practically staked his reputation on the success of the enterprise, resigned his post as Chief of Naval Operations immediately definite news of its failure was made public. To succeed him the choice of the Secretary of the Navy fell upon Admiral Lincoln B. Muller, an officer whose reputation for sagacity and sound judgment rendered it in the highest degree unlikely that he would advise the Government to embark upon any undertaking which did not offer reasonable prospects of success. For the position of Assistant Chief of Naval Operations (left vacant by the resignation of Rear-Admiral Hubbard), a popular selection was made in the person of Rear-Admiral Joseph Harper, the former Governor and Commandant of Guam, who had only lately been promoted to flag rank. Before the war he had been regarded as an authority on naval strategy, and by his skilful conduct of the defence of Guam he was proved also to be the possessor of tactical abilities of no mean order. A man of strong personality, he exercised considerable influence over all with whom he came in contact, including his Chief. Throughout the period of their association these two fine officers worked together in perfect harmony, with results that proved them to be an absolutely ideal combination. In the campaign that followed, it may reasonably be concluded that Rear-Admiral Harper supplied the driving force and most of the plans, which Admiral Muller tempered by his caution and far-sightedness.

As a further concession to public opinion, Admiral Dallinger was relieved of his command, and given the less considered appointment of President of the Naval Examining and Retiring Boards. Hard though it may seem for a distinguished flag officer to be thus superseded as the result of a disaster which he had foreseen and done his best to avert, the Government no doubt felt that it would be unwise to continue in his command one who had come to be regarded by the public as an unlucky admiral. Such things often happen in war, and it was in keeping with his character that Admiral Dallinger should have loyally accepted the verdict of his superiors without complaint or apparent dissatisfaction, unlike some instances known to history. His successor in the chief command of the United States fleet was Admiral Templeton, who, it will be remembered, had taken the Scouting fleet from Hampton Roads to San Diego by way of the Straits of Magellan. Certain other changes were also made, but these were of less importance, and need not be noticed here.

One of the first matters to occupy the attention of the new Chief of Naval Operations and his Assistant was the problem of attacking the enemy's seaborne commerce, pending the organisation of a new expedition which had already been determined upon. To arrange for immediate interference with the Japanese trade in European waters was by no means an easy task, since all the modern cruisers in the U.S. Navy were in the Pacific, in which area, indeed, they were most needed as scouts for the battle fleet. But there were available several passenger vessels belonging to the United States

Lines, possessing qualities, such as speed and fuel endurance, which made them suitable for conversion into auxiliary cruisers. These ships were the *Leviathan*, of nearly 60,000 tons gross and 23 knots speed, one of the two largest ships in the world; the *George Washington*, of 23,788 tons gross and 18 knots; and the *Mount Vernon*, 18,372 tons and 20 knots. There were also the twelve American-built steamers of 14,100 tons and 17 knots, named after various Presidents; some of these ships had already been utilised as transports for the Pacific, but five were available for use in the campaign against Japanese commerce. They were the *President Cleveland*, *President Jefferson*, *President Madison*, *President Pierce*, and *President Taft*. These eight steamers were taken in hand for conversion at the Atlantic Navy Yards as rapidly as possible. Their withdrawal from commercial service had the unavoidable effect of making a present to neutral interests (mainly British and German) of the whole of the American trans-Atlantic passenger traffic.

In the Pacific the enemy's trade was also to be harassed. Two newly-completed 10,000-ton cruisers, the *Albany* and *Columbia*, under the command of Captain Appleton (of the former ship) as senior officer, were ordered to operate against Japanese trade with Australia, using Tutuila as their principal base. They were also to search for and destroy any Japanese cruisers they might encounter in this direction, an order that was to prove particularly fruitful, as will in due course be seen.

The activities of the Bureau of Construction and Repair were further increased, work being accelerated as much as possible on the ships already laid down, while additional units were ordered as follows :—

    6 cruisers of 12,000 tons with Diesel engines.
    50 destroyers of 1500 tons.
    4 aircraft carriers.
    20 ocean-going submarines.
    6 auxiliaries (supply ships and tenders).

To remedy the immediate deficiency in scouting vessels in the Pacific, a number of suitable merchant steamers on that side were armed for employment as auxiliary cruisers.

We must now turn to the main plan of campaign which had been devised by the Naval Operations Bureau, in consultation with their military *confrères*. This, in effect, was an adaptation of certain of the features of two earlier schemes, and the secret of its ultimate success lay in the care with which these features were selected and modified.

The two plans referred to, which had been prepared long before, but had not found favour hitherto, may be briefly summed up as follows :—

(*a*) An invasion of Hokkaido, the northernmost island of Japan Proper, by an army to be assembled in Alaska, the landing to be covered by a fleet based on Dutch Harbour, whence the expedition would take its final departure.

(*b*) The seizure of the island of Ponapi, in the eastern portion of the Caroline group (held by Japan under the Versailles mandate), and its conversion into an intermediate base from which either Guam or the Philippines, or both, could be threatened.

There were inherent difficulties about both schemes, but more particularly the first, owing to weather conditions in the waters to be traversed between Alaska and Hokkaido. As a matter of fact plan (*a*) was never seriously entertained by the American naval and military authorities, but to cloak their real intentions it was essential that the enemy should be deceived on this point. With the object of persuading the Japanese that plan (*a*) was being followed, the most elaborate arrangements were made. Several thousands of men, including those who for one reason or another could not be treated as first-class troops, were transported to Puget Sound, a few going direct to Dutch Harbour, the chief Unalaskan port, while every expedient that the united ingenuity of naval and military experts could suggest was put into operation for the benefit of possible enemy observers.   An appearance of secrecy was given to the proceedings by dispatching all transports from San Francisco, Portland, and Seattle under sealed orders, a practice which, once established, was found extremely useful when it was required to send troops and munitions to another quarter for the real expedition.   For convoy purposes on the Alaskan route it was found necessary to employ the older cruisers and destroyers, the latter being relieved of their coastal patrol work further south by armed yachts and other auxiliary craft. Dutch Harbour soon became a centre of naval activity, and it was allowed to leak out, for the benefit of enemy agents, that the battleships *Arkansas, Wyoming, Florida,* and *Utah* were to be dispatched there at a later stage in the proceedings, where, anchored behind booms and mine-fields, they would add to the appearance of preparation for something big.   Rumours were permitted to escape into suspected quarters of projected fleet movements in the direction of Dutch Harbour, and naturally the reported presence of four battleships was exaggerated until it was whispered that the greater part of the U.S. Navy had been concentrated there.   Stringent orders were at the same time issued that all naval movements were to be kept secret, a measure that went far to convince enemy agents of the imminence of serious attack from the direction of Alaska.   Japanese submarines which endeavoured to reconnoitre Dutch Harbour were driven off by patrol ships and airplanes— of which a large number had been directed to guard against such attempts—without being able to learn anything definite.   All this added to the uneasiness which began to be felt in Japanese official quarters, and although at first it was scarcely credited that the Americans would venture upon such a hazardous enterprise, the persistent reports of activity in Alaska, combined with remembrance of the previous daring attempt upon Port Lloyd, gradually encouraged a belief in the reality of an impending attack from the north-east. Well-planned strategy thus reaped its reward, and for as long a period as could possibly have been hoped the enemy was kept in a state of apprehension of a blow from a direction entirely opposite to the actual zone of activity.

In planning the real attack some use was made of plan (*b*), which was not, however, adopted in its entirety. Rear-Admiral Harper, whose knowledge of the various islands of the Pacific was extensive and peculiar, had carefully weighed the advantages and disadvantages of many of them as *points d'appui*, and strongly urged the rejection of Ponapi in favour of Truk (also known as Hogolu). This small sub-group, which is also part of the Carolines, lies some 450 miles to the westward of Ponapi, and although offering better facilities for harbouring a large squadron, is less well known than Ponapi, and therefore seldom visited by trading vessels. Its distance from Guam (600 miles) and from the east coast of Mindanao, the nearest of the Philippines (about 1700 miles), also rendered it preferable to Ponapi. If, as was believed, it could be seized and firmly held for a sufficient length of time, its possession would go far towards repairing the situation created when Guam was lost. It was decided that the expedition sent against the island must be launched from Tutuila, the nearest American possession, where it was found possible to concentrate the necessary forces without arousing enemy suspicions. The troops were provided mainly from the garrison of Hawaii, the pick of whom were gradually withdrawn and secretly transferred to Tutuila, while it was allowed to leak out that their destination was Alaska. The place of these troops was taken by newer formations, for which Hawaii became the training ground until they, too, were required for active service. Recruiting had meanwhile been proceeding on both a voluntary and compulsory basis, volunteers being called for at the same time that powers were reserved to draft any additional numbers needed. The first call was for 250,000 recruits, and the response was so excellent that a million men were examined at their own request at various enlistment bureaux throughout the States. Those selected reached a very high standard, both mentally and physically. Recruits considered fit only for garrison duty were drafted to special units, which were later sent to Alaska as part of the arrangements made for deceiving the enemy.

In the meantime, Japan was not without her troubles. China, having found that it was possible to create friction between Japan and neutral interests over questions of contraband of war and kindred matters, lost no opportunity of doing so. She found her chance in connection with certain neutral concessions for raising minerals which Japan needed for the prosecution of the war. American interests were active in endeavouring to prevent the export of such products to Japan, mainly by means of contracts with the neutral concessionnaires which bound them to deliver to other customers. Japan did not scruple to put pressure upon the Chinese Government to exercise their option of commandeering supplies irrespective of concessionnaires' engagements, a manœuvre made possible by a clause in the sale contracts reserving the right of cancellation by the concessionnaires in such event. But the Government at Peking, weak though it might be, was expert in procrastination and evasion, and Japan feared the effect on neutral opinion if she proceeded to use force to compel compliance with her wishes.

In these circumstances Japan endeavoured to gain her ends by a policy of mingled threats and bribery; but this had little effect, as American influence was at work behind the scenes, with a longer purse to back it. Recourse was then had to Li Ping-hui, the nominal Governor of Manchuria, who was for all practical purposes a vassal of Japan, and had an old score to settle with the Chinese Government. On the pretext that he was dissatisfied with the Central Government's methods in dealing with Manchurian external affairs, and ignoring the fact that Peking had no real voice in such matters since Japan had extended her influence over the country, Li Ping-hui demanded the resignation of the Premier, Hun Ying-fu, and his Cabinet, and the appointment of his own nominees to succeed them. On being met with a refusal, he set his armies in motion, and was soon in occupation of a number of villages in the province of Pechihli, beyond the Great Wall which divides Manchuria from China Proper. His troops were not only more numerous than those of which Peking could dispose at this juncture, but were superior in arms and equipment, and had the advantage of having been drilled by Japanese instructors. Li's old opponent, General Wang-Tsu, at this time was far away in the south of China with the best of his troops, engaged in crushing an incipient revolution. Probably, therefore, the issue would have turned in favour of Li; but before any decisive action had been fought, news was received that a serious revolt had broken out in Northern Manchuria, where influences from the Russian Far Eastern Republic had long been at work fomenting discontent. Stimulated by American gold, the spirit of resistance only needed the opportunity presented by the withdrawal of Li Ping-hui's soldiery to become active. Arms, ammunition and experienced leaders were imported from across the Amur, and in a very short time the whole of the northern province of Ho-lung-kiang was in a blaze, which extended rapidly southward into Kirin. The garrisons which had been left in a few of the more important places, such as Harbin, Kirin and Tsisihar, were able to hold out, but the districts away from the railway were speedily overrun by the insurgent peasantry. Leaving to some future date the settlement of his quarrel with the Government of Peking, Li Ping-hui hastily returned with the bulk of his troops to Mukden, there to concert measures with his Japanese advisers for dealing with the rebels who so seriously threatened his rule.

For the second time Japan's plans had miscarried, and she was now forced to content herself with the influence she was able to bring to bear upon the local governors of such provinces as Shantung, Hupeh, and Yunnan, where were situated the principal sources of supply for iron, petroleum, and copper. Though this method was expensive, and less satisfactory than dealing with the Central Government, it was found to answer sufficiently well for the moment, in so far as it ensured that the Japanese shipbuilding and munition programmes would not be held up by lack of raw materials.

In connection with the transport of petroleum from Hankow to Japan there were few difficulties, as the River Yangtse offered an excellent channel of communication, but one incident occurred which is worth recounting. Both the United States and Japan had for many years maintained gunboats on the Yangtse for police purposes and to protect their commercial interests, nor had the outbreak of war affected the position on this neutral waterway beyond causing each side to keep a watchful eye upon the other. But the apprehensions of a Japanese merchant captain now caused an explosion which was with difficulty localised. On December 29, 1931, the Japanese oil tanker *Yudachi Maru* had just left Hankow with a full cargo when she noticed that the U.S. gunboat *Palos* was some distance astern, apparently in pursuit, though as a matter of fact her movements were afterwards proved to have no reference to those of the oil tanker. No doubt the Japanese captain had been misled by imaginative stories circulating in Hankow as to the steps which the Americans were prepared to take to interfere with the traffic in which he was engaged. At any rate, he imagined himself to be chased, and having armed his crew with rifles which were carried as a protection against Chinese pirates, he actually ordered them to fire upon the *Palos*. The bullets were mostly wide or short of the mark, but one or two hit the hull of the *Palos*. Her captain, Lieut.-Commander O'Halloran, was naturally indignant at this unprovoked attack, and fired a warning shell over the *Yudachi Maru*, which in the meantime had increased speed to the utmost. Probably the affair would have ended more or less tamely had not the Japanese gunboat *Fushimi*, which was lying off the town of Wu-sueh, taken in the frantic radio appeals for help which the *Yudachi Maru* was broadcasting, and hastened up river under a full head of steam. Arriving just as the *Palos* had fired, the situation appeared clear, and the *Fushimi* answered the shot without hesitation. Thus protected, the *Yudachi Maru* speedily quitted the scene, leaving the two gunboats to fight it out. They were not unequally matched. Both carried identical armaments, namely, two 6-pounder guns, and neither could steam at much over 13 knots. The *Palos* displaced 190 tons, just ten tons more than the *Fushimi ;* and each carried a crew of about fifty. Neither ship had any armour protection, and as the range was short, casualties soon began to occur. The *Palos* was getting somewhat the better of it, having set the *Fushimi* on fire, when a newcomer intervened—again in response to the signals of the *Yudachi Maru*. This was the Japanese gunboat *Hodzu*, of 340 tons, built in 1923, and armed with two 12-pounders. Fearing he would soon be overmatched, and determined to settle with at least one of his opponents, Lieut.-Commander O'Halloran closed with the *Fushimi*, keeping her between him and the *Hodzu*. Owing to the smoke in which she was enveloped, and their preoccupation in fighting the flames, the *Fushimi's* people made no attempt to avoid the *Palos*, which rammed her amidships and opened a large rent in her hull. As the U.S. gunboat backed away, she came under a severe fire from the guns of the *Hodzu*, a shell from which killed the gallant O'Halloran. Finding the ship was leaking badly in the bows, which had been crumpled by the impact, the warrant officer who was now left in charge of the *Palos* beached her at a convenient spot just above Wu-sueh, leaving to the *Hodzu* the task of rescuing the crew of the sinking *Fushimi*. The *Palos* herself was a complete wreck, the whole of her upper works being shattered, while less than twenty men were left on their feet. The local Chinese authorities, making no secret of their hostility towards the Japanese, were prompt in rendering assistance to the survivors, who received every care and attention, while an armed guard of Chinese soldiers was placed over the wrecked American gunboat. But for this she would probably have been taken possession of by the Japanese, who were much incensed at the loss of the *Fushimi,* and were with difficulty deterred from attacking the Chinese sentries.

After some days of angry correspondence through the usual diplomatic channels, the Chinese persuaded both sides to submit the dispute to the British Consul-General at Hankow. His investigations showed clearly that the whole affair arose through the baseless misgivings of the master of the *Yudachi Maru,* who in consequence found himself rather unpopular in Japanese official circles, though the chauvinistic section of the public were disposed to regard him as a hero. To avoid a repetition of such incidents, it was arranged that the contending Powers should keep the British consular representatives advised of all intended movements of their gunboats on Chinese rivers, so that each might be informed through neutral channels of the whereabouts of the other, and so avoid unexpected encounters.

CHAPTER XIV

FEBRUARY–MARCH, 1932

American squadron under Captain Appleton sent to Samoa—Japanese squadron with transports enters neighbouring zone—U.S.S. *Columbia* taken at a disadvantage and sunk—Sound American tactics—Japanese squadron destroyed at Battle of Rotumah—Captain Appleton promoted and reinforced

EVENTS in the Southern Pacific must now be noticed. Captain Appleton's instructions included certain confidential references to the projected expedition to the South Sea Islands, for which his force was intended to pave the way He had under his command, in addition to the new cruisers *Albany* and *Columbia*, the aircraft-carrier *Wright* and eighteen destroyers. He was ordered to take every precaution to avoid rousing Japanese suspicions as to the ultimate object of his movements, and to make sure that no regular patrol of the area to the east of Truk was being carried out by the enemy. Compared with this the attack upon Japanese trade with Australia was to be regarded as a secondary consideration, to be dealt with when convenient. At the same time it would furnish a plausible explanation of movements which might otherwise set the enemy thinking.

Strangely enough, these orders coincided with a Japanese plan for seizing the American possessions in the Samoa group. In Tokyo it had been suggested that the most effective way of preventing the U.S. Navy from carrying out its rumoured intention of attacking the important Australian trade was to occupy Tutuila, the only position capable of being used as a base for such attack. A small expedition had been fitted out, comprising in all some 5000 troops, mainly *Kobi* (reservist) infantry. These, with artillery and munitions, were accommodated in ten transports, ships of moderate size, whose average speed fell below 11 knots. They were convoyed by a squadron made up of the four obsolete cruisers *Iwate* (flagship of Rear-Admiral Karuma), *Idzumo*, *Yakumo*, and *Azuma*, with ten second-class destroyers. The cruisers were all over thirty years old, and had long been relegated to subsidiary duties, but for an expedition of this kind they were quite useful ships. A couple of scouting seaplanes had been added to the equipment of each, and they had been otherwise modernised to a certain extent. Each was armed with four 8-inch and eight 6-inch guns. The destroyers were old 30-knotters of some 600 tons apiece.

The expedition assembled at Jaluit during the last week in February. It was timed to reach Tutuila at daybreak on March 5, when a landing, so the Japanese thought, could be effected without difficulty, having regard to the advantage of surprise and the absence of a strong garrison. Nor was there any reason why this programme should not have been carried through with complete success, but for the coincidence of Captain Appleton's mission in the same waters. On arriving at Tutuila that officer was employed for some days in arranging for the reception of the troops to be dispatched from Hawaii as part of the Truk Expedition. It had been decided to place most of the soldiers under canvas, and camp sites had to be selected within easy reach of water supplies. Although the area of Tutuila is only 40 square miles, this task kept Captain Appleton occupied for nearly a week in consultation with the Governor, who was also a naval officer. During this time the *Albany, Wright,* and two divisions of destroyers remained at Pago-Pago. The *Columbia* (Captain Parker) and the remaining six destroyers, having re-fuelled, were directed to cruise on a line to the north-westward.

On March 1 the *Columbia* ran upon an uncharted

shoal some 200 miles north of the island of Rotumah. She appeared to have scraped over a ridge of coral, upon which her after part still rested. Destroyers attempted to tow her clear, while her own engines worked at full speed, but no appreciable movement resulted. An inspection by divers showed the vessel to be firmly wedged between two masses of coral. It was then decided to lighten her by pumping 500 tons of oil fuel and water from her after tanks; this having been done, a second attempt was made to tow her off, but again without success. As night had now fallen, operations had to be suspended.

In the meantime Captain Appleton, advised by radio of the *Columbia's* plight, had ordered the *Wright* to proceed to her assistance, he himself intending to follow next day with the *Albany* and his remaining destroyers. At daybreak renewed efforts were made to drag the *Columbia* off the shoal, and at length, after hours of strenuous labour, she floated clear. But the damage she had sustained proved to be very extensive; portions of the keel had been torn away, and all four propellers were injured. It was at this juncture that two airplanes were observed coming from the north-west; and a machine from the *Columbia*, going up to investigate, sighted a squadron of enemy warships, convoying a number of merchant steamers. Closer scrutiny showed the hostile force to consist of a destroyer flotilla and the *Iwate*, *Idzumo*, *Yakumo*, and *Azuma*, old cruisers averaging 9600 tons. Their speed was low, but they had good armour protection, and their batteries of 8-inch and 6-inch guns, though of obsolete models, were likely to prove formidable in close action. The *Columbia*, being a ship of much later design, had a more powerful battery of 8-inch high velocity guns, but she was practically destitute of armour protection. True, her big guns were fitted with splinter-proof shields, but these afforded little or no real shelter to the crews, and more often than not they merely served to detonate shells which might otherwise have passed through without exploding. These drawbacks notwithstanding, Captain

o

Parker would have had small cause for anxiety if his ship had been good for her original speed of 33 knots or more, for he would then have been able to fight at his selected range, or alternatively to avoid action altogether. As things were, however, the crippled cruiser could barely travel at half her designed speed. It was therefore with a full knowledge of his dangerous situation that Captain Parker ordered his destroyers to leave him, and try to make contact with Captain Appleton's squadron, which was known to be on the way from Pago-Pago.

The Japanese squadron, leaving several destroyers to guard the convoy, now approached the *Columbia* at full speed. In order to make the most of his initial advantage in range, Captain Parker stood towards the eastward at his best speed, while the Japanese, changing their formation from line ahead to line abreast as the range shortened, were soon able to bring their forward 8-inch guns to bear. In the meantime the *Columbia* had endeavoured to knock out the leading Japanese ship before her low-powered guns could get into action. Despite a smoke screen thrown across the course of the advancing enemy cruisers by their attendant destroyers, which were steaming some distance to windward, the concentrated fire of the *Columbia's* heavy guns did a considerable amount of damage to the *Azuma*. One shell penetrated her deck and ignited a quantity of ammunition which had been brought up in readiness for closer action. The explosion and fire which followed put the *Azuma* practically out of action until she had repaired damages. She dropped astern, and did not appear again until the fight was nearly over.

But her consorts were now beginning to find the range, though for some time their practice was poor, probably because these ships were manned largely by elderly reservists and youths fresh from the training establishments. As they overhauled the *Columbia*, their 6-inch batteries were also brought into play. Still, for some time the *Columbia* contrived to hold her own, thanks to her superior fire control gear and more powerful guns. Unfortunately, this advantage was largely negatived by the Japanese airplanes, which by reporting the fall of each salvo enabled their ships to develop a most accurate fire, until the *Columbia* was being smothered with shell. She was soon in a deplorable state. Half her guns were out of action, and the crews of those still intact had been renewed more than once, so that she was no longer able to maintain a rapid or an accurate fire. In spite of all efforts to localise outbreaks, fires were raging at three points, and casualties had become so numerous that the medical staff could no longer cope with them. Some of the wounded, who had to be left where they fell, suffered a cruel death in the flames, for their comrades engaged in fighting the fires were either unaware of their plight or unable to reach them. Captain Parker and several of his officers had been killed early in the battle by a salvo from the *Iwate*, which wrecked the bridge and brought down the foremast and a funnel. Lieut.-Commander Isaacs, the senior officer surviving, continued to fight the ship from a less exposed position until he in turn fell, badly wounded by a splinter. In fear that some unauthorised person might offer to surrender before the ship sank—for it had been reported to him that she was leaking badly from hits on the water line, and that the pumps could scarcely hold the water—he had given directions for the seacocks to be opened. But the matter was taken out of his hands by the Japanese Admiral, who, observing the *Columbia's* fire to have slackened, and her manifest state of distress, promptly signalled his destroyers to attack. To supplement their efforts and at the same time to distract the attention of the American gunners, the eight airplanes which had hitherto been on spotting duty were also launched against the unhappy *Columbia*. A considerable number of bombs fell around her, but only four found the target, and these were too small to inflict serious damage, though they caused further casualties. But the doomed ship could still make her teeth felt, and she received the attacking destroyers with a slow but well-aimed fire. One shell exploded in the boiler room of the *Tachibana,* putting her out of action and causing the only deaths which occurred on the Japanese side during this phase of the action. This, however, was the *Columbia's* expiring effort. At least four torpedoes appear to have struck her, and before the second division of destroyers came within range it was apparent that she was about to founder. Rear-Admiral Karuma now signalled orders to cease fire, and sent his destroyers to close the sinking vessel. All her boats were smashed, and but for the timely help rendered by the enemy there would have been few survivors. As it was, the Japanese entered into the task of saving life with as much zeal as they had previously displayed in fighting, and the majority of those Americans left alive were rescued before the cruiser took her last plunge.

Rear-Admiral Karuma, in pursuance of his orders, continued his voyage to Samoa as soon as he had repaired damages. The *Tachibana,* which was the only ship in serious case, was taken in tow by a transport. When the squadron was sighted next day by the scouting seaplanes of the *Wright,* and it was apparent that another fight was impending, everything of value was removed from the crippled destroyer, her crew were distributed amongst the rest of the Japanese ships, and she was scuttled.

The battle that followed will long be remembered as a masterly example of sound tactics on the part of the American leader. Before closing with the enemy Captain Appleton had resolved to secure command of the air, for which purpose he concentrated his whole flying force—two seaplanes from the *Albany* and twelve from the *Wright*—upon the Japanese machines. These were all accounted for after a gallant fight, though not until they had shot down two of the American planes.

This much accomplished, Captain Appleton proceeded to hang on the flank of the Japanese squadron, pounding away methodically with his 8-inch guns. His speed advantage of about 15 knots enabled him to evade with ease all the enemy's efforts to close the range,

and Admiral Karuma found himself in the trying position of being hit continually without being able to
touch his opponent. Captain Appleton's tactics were
to train three of his guns upon each of the Japanese
cruisers, thus keeping the whole squadron under a
distant but accurate fire, for his spotting aircraft were
able to do their work without the least interference.

Stoically enduring his punishment in the hope that
some lucky chance would give him relief, the Japanese
Admiral refrained from useless endeavours to get to
grips with his elusive adversary, and held doggedly on
his course eastward, keeping his warships between the
Albany and the transports. Had nightfall been nearer
he might yet have won through; but as it was, his
position soon became desperate. Turn and twist as he
might, he could not for long avoid the regular salvos
of the American cruiser, nor did the smoke screen put
up by his destroyers have the desired result. In no
long time all four of the Japanese cruisers began to feel
the effect of this relentless hammering. Moreover, at
this stage of the action Admiral Karuma was confronted
by a new peril, for he noticed that the American
destroyers were working round his flank to get within
range of the transports. To counter this threat, he
ordered his own boats to attack the American flotilla,
which was considerably the stronger, and in the ensuing
mêlée the Japanese destroyers would have been wiped
out had not Karuma led his cruisers to the rescue.
While two of the Japanese boats were crippled in this
first brush, the Americans did not suffer to anything
like the same extent, since in conformity with orders
they broke off the conflict immediately the hostile
cruisers joined in. In the course of this fighting one of
the transports was hit by a torpedo, an incident that
added to Admiral Karuma's embarrassments. These
were crowding upon him thick and fast, for while his
attention had been engaged with the saving of his
destroyers, the *Albany* had so altered her position that
the transports now bore the brunt of her fire for several
minutes. Heavy casualties were suffered by these

ships, their decks being crowded with Japanese soldiers who were watching the fight; and two of the transports received structural injuries which caused them to leak, thus further reducing the speed of the squadron. Having sent destroyers alongside the damaged ships, Admiral Karuma circled round the convoy with his four cruisers, thereby laying himself open to further heavy punishment, as this close grouping of the Japanese ships afforded the *Albany* a better target than ever. The *Azuma* and *Idzumo* both began to show signs of distress, the former being on fire forward and the latter having lost her middle funnel; and the climax was reached when the *Yakumo* was suddenly enveloped in black smoke, while the report of a heavy explosion echoed over the sea. When the smoke cleared it could be seen that she had broken in two, evidently as the result of a magazine exploding. The flagship *Iwate* was now the only ship intact, but it was not long before her military main-mast, unsupported by any tripod, fell across the stern, jamming her helm and causing her to describe wild circles in the direction of the transports. At this moment the U.S. destroyers again rushed in to attack. Two were sunk by gun-fire, but they did not retreat until all the Japanese destroyers had been accounted for, while the *Iwate* herself received a torpedo which brought her to a standstill with a heavy list. Captain Appleton now began methodically to close the enemy, and as the range shortened the American fire increased in accuracy. To this murderous cannonade the *Idzumo* replied with little effect, for the smoke from the burning *Azuma* blinded her gunners and obscured their target. True to the fine traditions of the Imperial Japanese Navy, even the *Iwate*, though obviously sinking, kept several of her guns in action, and one of the shells from this ship inflicted the only serious damage that the *Albany* received—a hit that penetrated the hull forward, causing many casualties, and starting a leak which could not be mastered until the fight was over. But the succession of salvos which now struck the *Idzumo* speedily silenced her. In a few minutes she, too, was burning fiercely, whereupon the destroyers were again ordered to attack. Game to the last, the Japanese cruisers received these assailants with a fire that sent another of them to the bottom, but by the time the remaining boats had emptied their tubes the *Idzumo* and *Azuma* had both been torpedoed, and were no longer capable of offering serious resistance. Since the Japanese, on being summoned to surrender, still remained defiant, all that could be done was to pick up the survivors from the *Idzumo*, which soon foundered, and from the *Azuma*, which ship was now blazing from forecastle to mainmast, so that many of her crew were obliged to drop overboard to escape the flames. Eventually she blew up, leaving only the *Iwate* afloat. The Japanese flagship was now in such a position that no boats could have been launched from her port side, even if any had remained intact, and only one had been got out to starboard, where the water was nearly level with the rail. The Admiral's flag still flew from her foremast, but Captain Appleton dispatched his boats to her in the assurance that she could do no harm, even if she desired to repulse them. They arrived only just in time, for with a final lurch the *Iwate* went down, taking with her a large number of wounded. Quite 400 were rescued, however, including Rear-Admiral Karuma, who was injured in the arm. He was very much downcast at his defeat, and expressed a wish that he had not survived; but it is difficult to see how he could have done more in the circumstances in which he was placed.

There remained to be solved the problem of dealing with the transports. The torpedoed ship was sinking, and the *Wright*, which, owing to her low speed had only just arrived on the scene, was ordered to take her in tow. The troops from the sinking vessel having been transferred to her consorts, all but two of these were induced—with the assistance of Admiral Karuma, who went on board each ship to point out the futility of useless resistance—to haul down their flags and relinquish control to American naval officers. The remaining two were obdurate, and fearing that night would give them a chance to escape, Captain Appleton ordered them to be torpedoed, first warning them to have all available life-saving appliances in readiness. It was afterwards learned that this useless resistance was due to the fanaticism of certain military officers on board, who threatened to kill anyone hoisting a white flag or showing other signs of submission. In spite of all the humane efforts of the Americans, the sinking of these two transports entailed heavy loss of life.

The seven troopships that remained were taken to Pago-Pago, all soldiers being confined below under strict guard until arrangements could be made to transfer them in batches to the United States. In the meantime their presence caused not a little anxiety to the Governor of Tutuila, who realised that these thousands of prisoners would soon overrun the island if they succeeded in breaking loose and getting ashore. All arms except those actually in use by the Marine guard were placed temporarily on board the warships, so that if the worst occurred the prisoners would be able to offer no serious resistance.

The results of the battle of Rotumah, as it is officially called from the name of the nearest inhabited land, may be summed up thus :—

Japanese Losses.	*American Losses.*
Cruisers : *Iwate*	Cruiser : *Columbia.*
Idzumo	Destroyers : 5.
Azuma	
Yakumo	
Destroyers : 10.	
Transports : 10.	

On both sides the loss of life was heavy. In the case of the Japanese squadron, including the transports, it is believed to have been nearly 3,000. On the American side, upwards of 700 lives were lost, mainly in the *Columbia* and the destroyer flotilla. As a victory it was complete, and being the first unmistakable advantage gained by the United States in the struggle, there was no likelihood of its importance being minimised. Captain Appleton, who at the outset of the war had resigned his post as Assistant Chief of Naval Operations, rather than accept responsibility for a situation against which he had vainly protested, now found himself the hero of the hour. With characteristic modesty he contented himself with acknowledging the messages of commendation which reached him, and requesting that he might be permitted to continue his mission with the aid of another cruiser to replace the *Columbia*. He was gratified to learn that in response to this request three more cruisers were being placed under his orders. These were the *Troy*—a sister to the *Albany*—the *Memphis*, and the *Milwaukee*, the two latter being of the 7,500-ton *Omaha* type. Two fresh divisions of destroyers, to replace those sunk or injured in the battle of Rotumah, were also sent out. At the same time he was informed that he had been specially promoted to the rank of Rear-Admiral, irrespective of the ordinary rules regarding seniority. It is probable that his was the most popular promotion ever made in the history of the United States Navy; and the Government undoubtedly gained in public favour by their disregard of precedent in giving this gallant officer such well-merited advancement.

CHAPTER XV

MARCH–APRIL, 1932

Disquiet in Japan at news of Battle of Rotumah—Japanese raid on Dutch Harbour—Bad weather causes air operations to fail—Commander Nuzuki's daring dash into Dutch Harbour—U.S.S. *Charleston* sunk, but Commander Nuzuki taken prisoner—American cruisers interrupt Japanese trade with Australia—Similar operations in European waters by U.S. armed liners

A SENSATION bordering on panic was caused in Japan by the news of the annihilation of Admiral Karuma's squadron. Needless to say, the Government did its best to belittle the importance of the affair, stressing the obsolete character of the Japanese ships sunk, and hinting that the full extent of the American losses had not been disclosed. When these specious pleadings failed to satisfy the public, the authorities, as usual, cast about for some fresh enterprise which would serve to divert popular attention from the disastrous failure of the Samoa Expedition. After the position had been thoroughly reviewed by the Naval Staff, it was agreed that no better objective could be found than the base from which it was suspected the next American attack would be delivered. Although full and exact information was lacking, the reports of American activity in Alaskan waters had been so frequent and persistent that no doubt was felt as to the genuineness of the menace, and it was in any case desirable to obtain early intelligence of the strength of the forces likely to be met. The known presence at Dutch Harbour, in the island of Unalaska, of an uncertain number of naval units, including—it was believed—some ships of capital importance, focussed attention upon that base, which seemed to offer a promising point for attack. The composition of the force to be employed was only fixed after prolonged debate by the Naval Staff. Submarines were vetoed on account of the difficulties of navigation in the Bering Sea, more especially in the neighbourhood of the Aleutian Islands, which are surrounded by hidden dangers in the shape of submerged rocks, not all of which are accurately charted. Apart from this, fogs are so frequent in the locality that extreme caution has to be observed in approaching the islands. In the absence of precise intelligence as to the American strength, it was deemed advisable to employ vessels of high speed, but there was no intention of risking the most modern units. As a compromise, the aircraft carrier *Hosho*, of 9,500 tons displacement and 25 knots speed, built ten years previously, was assigned as the floating base from which to launch an air attack by twelve bombing seaplanes. These were to be accompanied by an equal number of combat machines to guard against possible interference from American aircraft. The *Hosho* was to be escorted by four light cruisers, *Tama*, *Kuma*, *Kiso*, and *Kitakami*—sister ships of 5,500 tons displacement and 33 knots speed, armed with 5·5-inch guns—and a flotilla of twelve 34-knot destroyers. The command of the expedition was confided to Vice-Admiral Soku-shima, whose flag was hoisted in the *Hosho*. Rear-Admiral Uyehara was in charge of the cruiser squadron, and Captain Okurami of the destroyer flotilla. The whole force was assembled at Ominato, a second-class naval station on Aomori Gulf, in the north of the island of Hondo. The departure was fixed for March 30, and it was calculated that the sheltered anchorage of Kashiwabara, at the north-eastern end of the Kurile chain, would be reached forty-eight hours later. But, as so often happens in these stormy latitudes, the squadron met with continuous bad weather and heavy head seas after rounding Cape Erimo, and it soon became plain that the schedule would have to be modified. Accord-ingly, after the ships had been battling against the mountainous seas for some hours, orders were issued to reduce speed and alter course to the westward, with the object of passing through Kunashiri Kaikyo * and gain the lee of the Kuriles. As expected, conditions in the Sea of Okhotsk proved easier than in the Pacific, and progress improved; but the haven at Paramushiru was not made until some hours later than had been designed, as Admiral Sokushima found it necessary on two occasions to anchor his squadron in order to regain touch. Even so, this portion of the voyage was an anxious one, as the islands required to be given a wide berth during the hours of darkness, and snow squalls frequently hid the ships from each other's view. Two days were spent at Paramushiru, waiting for better weather and repairing minor damages, after which a fresh start was made. As the squadron entered the Bering Sea it ran into a fog bank, which lasted, with occasional clear patches, for the next two days. Giving the Komandorski Islands a clear berth, a course was set to avoid the westernmost of the Kuriles and arrive off Akutan Island, to the N.E. of Unalaska, about noon on April 6, this being considered the direction from which the Americans would be least likely to apprehend danger. The misty weather, though it increased the chances of the expedition arriving without being observed, did not lighten the difficulties of navigation, and threatened to hamper the seaplanes when they came to deliver their attack. When about 50 miles S.W. of the Pribilof Islands, a vessel appeared unexpectedly out of the fog ahead of the squadron. She proved to be the United States Coast Guard cutter *Bear*, a wooden vessel built as long ago as 1874. Owing to her exceptionally stout construction and general fitness for work in ice-bound waters, due to her having originally been intended for the whaling trade, she had survived several proposals to scrap her, and was still in service on this remote station. She was at once summoned to surrender by the division of six destroyers which formed the vanguard of the squadron, and might well have done so without hesitation, since her armament consisted only of three

* *Kaikyo* is Japanese for strait.

6-pounders. But, true to the traditions of the Coast Guard service, her commander scorned to yield, and actually opened fire with his feeble weapons. Disdaining to waste shells on such a puny antagonist, the nearest destroyers used their machine guns to such effect that the guns' crews were almost immediately put out of action, and the *Bear* was then carried by boarding—the only recorded incident of the kind in the whole of the war.

Having captured the *Bear*, the Japanese Admiral determined to make use of her, calculating that her appearance was so well known throughout the Bering Sea that her movements were unlikely to arouse suspicion. She was manned by a prize crew under English-speaking officers, all on deck being directed to wear oilskins over their uniforms.

On approaching Akutan Island the fog, which had so far assisted the expedition by masking its progress, cleared under the influence of a S.E. wind, and haste was made to test the engines of the *Hosho's* seaplanes in readiness for the projected attack. One of the bombing machines in taking off from the *Hosho's* flight deck smashed her propeller and came down in the water. The other planes were satisfactorily tuned up and left for Unalaska with a rapidly rising wind, accompanied by falling barometer. After an absence of two hours they began to return singly and in twos and threes, till thirteen were back. By this time the wind was blowing with greatly increased force, and snow squalls were of such frequency that it remains a matter for wonder that any of the Japanese aircraft should have been able to find their way back to the rendezvous. That so many did so was due no doubt to the employment of directional radio signals, which enabled the planes to find their way through the blinding snow. Their reports varied but little. Owing to low visibility, the majority had failed to locate Dutch Harbour. Four had reached it, but could only say that a doubtful number of vessels, some of which could be identified as capital ships by their lattice masts, were to be seen. Bombs had been dropped over these, as well as along the shores of the harbour, but whether any damage had been inflicted could not be stated positively. At least one machine had found it impossible to release any bombs owing to spray and snow having frozen up the releasing gear. Altogether, therefore, the raid had to be regarded as a failure, nor was the loss of ten airplanes offset by the capture of the ancient *Bear*.

At Dutch Harbour the air raid had come as a complete surprise, though the actual damage done was infinitesimal. Most of the bombs fell either in the sea or on the beach, but one storehouse, containing nothing of military value, had been destroyed, and a patrol vessel of the trawler type had her bows badly shattered. In view of the tempestuous weather the American aircraft were not allowed to go in chase of the intruders, and there is no doubt that this inaction, though much criticised at the time by the uninformed, was sound policy. Scarcely had the last bomb fallen than there sprang up one of those violent white squalls known locally as williwaws, a phenomenon which was responsible for the disappearance of so many of the Japanese machines. One is known to have crashed in the interior of the island of Unalaska, where its fragments, with the remains of the pilot and observer, were found some months later. Another was seen by a fishing vessel to fall into the sea off Chernovski Harbour, on the opposite side of the island. Had American airplanes been dispatched in pursuit, they would in all probability have come to grief, as the weather in these regions renders flying an almost impossible feat under the conditions then obtaining.

Admiral Sokushima had been instructed to return to Japan as soon as he had done his utmost to deliver a telling blow at the U.S. naval base at Dutch Harbour. So far as the original project went, he had used every endeavour to carry out orders, and he therefore lost no time in making his way back with the main portion of his force. But in the secluded anchorage at Akutun (an abandoned whaling station) he had left the *Bear* and the destroyers *Isokaze* and *Yamakaze*, to carry out an operation which, if fortune had been kinder to the Japanese, might have brought the enterprise to a successful issue. Before dealing with this closing phase of the expedition, however, a word must be said as to the return voyage of Admiral Sokushima's squadron. The weather was exceedingly bad as far as the Komandorski Islands, when the wind died down and fog was again encountered. In groping a passage through this labyrinth, the ships became separated, and the destroyer *Amatsukaze* was run down and sunk by the cruiser *Kiso*, several lives being lost. Another misfortune was thus added to the record of the cruise. Extensive damage was sustained by several ships from the action of wind and sea, and the squadron eventually reached Ominato in a somewhat battered condition. The atrocious climate of the Bering Sea had proved a staunch ally to the American cause.

At Akutun the weather for some days precluded any movement. Advantage was taken of this delay to effect various small alterations in the deck arrangements of the *Bear*, the principal of which was the fitting of two pairs of torpedo tubes amidships. These had been transhipped from one of the cruisers previous to the departure of the squadron and were an important feature of the plan prepared by Admiral Sokushima and his staff. As soon as the weather moderated, the *Bear* proceeded towards Dutch Harbour, off which she arrived late in the afternoon of April 11. She was escorted to within a few miles of the port by the two destroyers, whose orders were to wait in the offing while the *Bear* entered the harbour, and then to take advantage of any movements of American warships that might ensue. They were also to succour any of the *Bear's* people who might succeed in getting out again, though this was regarded as a minor contingency, unlikely to occur.

In its early stages the programme proceeded without

a hitch. So familiar was the appearance of the *Bear*
that no suspicion was aroused at any look-out station
when she entered the channel leading between Spit
Head and the reef which runs out from Rocky Point
opposite. To forestall possible radio enquiries, her
maintopmast had been removed, and the mizzenmast
cut away by the board; this, with the rigging all in
disorder, was calculated to give the impression that her
aerials had been carried away in the recent severe
weather. A signal code book captured with the ship
provided means of answering any challenge by flag
or flashlight. Inside the harbour there was much mist,
which made it difficult for those on board the *Bear* to
distinguish ships clearly enough for identification.
But a crisis was precipitated by the U.S. cruiser *Charleston*, which was proceeding out of port after being weather-bound for some days. As she was passing the *Bear*
on an opposite course the officer in command of the
latter vessel, Commander Nuzuki, gave orders for the
two torpedo tubes which bore to be fired. Both torpedoes
sped home, and the *Charleston*, badly holed in engine-
and boiler-rooms, began to lose way. In spite of the
confusion caused by this utterly unexpected attack
from an apparent friend, guns were promptly cleared
and a hot fire opened on the *Bear*, which was hit two
or three times before the mist obscured the range.
The torpedoed cruiser appears to have been unable to
circulate news of her plight by radio, her dynamos
having failed when the engine-room was flooded. But
the sound of the torpedo explosions and the discharge
of the *Charleston's* guns had given the alarm, and as the
Bear continued her course up the harbour she was
challenged by a motor boat patrol. Commander
Nuzuki, whose mastery of the language, owing to some
years spent in the United States as a boy, was well-
nigh perfect, was quite prepared for this emergency.
He explained plausibly that the *Bear* had been dismasted
in a williwaw, and that he believed the *Charleston* must
have struck a mine and was firing her guns as distress

signals. He explained that he had been unable to offer any effective assistance himself, as the *Bear* had sprung a serious leak which was causing considerable anxiety. Quite deceived, the officer in charge of the motor boat sped the Japanese on their way with sympathy and good wishes. His disgust when he subsequently learned the real facts may be readily imagined.

Carefully keeping up the pretence that the *Bear* was in a semi-sinking condition, Commander Nuzuki proceeded to berth her between two large warships, whose tall lattice masts indicated them to be of importance. But here the luck which had hitherto stood by the Japanese deserted them. To deceive casual observers and possible spies, the U.S. Navy Department had taken over from the Shipping Board a number of laid-up steamers which were unfit for long voyages, and had carefully disguised them with dummy funnels, lattice masts, wooden turrets, guns, and superstructures, until they closely resembled battleships of the *Arkansas*, *Utah*, and *New York* types. In misty weather the illusion was complete, and Commander Nuzuki felt confident as he trained his tubes on his two neighbours that he was about to deal a smashing blow at American sea power. All four torpedoes struck the mark, as they could hardly fail to do, since less than half a cable's length separated the *Bear* from the make-believe battleships on either side of her. The force of the explosions was so great that it threw the *Bear*, whose displacement was only 1,700 tons, almost on her beam ends. Although two anchors had been dropped, both cables parted under the sudden strain, and the little Coast Guard cutter was flung heavily against the side of one of the dummy dreadnoughts. At the same time one of the lattice masts collapsed, covering the *Bear* with *débris*, and injuring most of those on her deck, including her commander. Patrol vessels speedily gathered round, some rescuing the small party of shipkeepers on board the sinking dummy ships, while others boarded the *Bear*. Commander Nuzuki had no alternative but to surrender,

P

and his chagrin was great when he found that he had practically wasted four torpedoes on ships of no fighting value. Nor was he to be consoled by the openly expressed admiration of his captors, who fully appreciated the coolness and ability shown in manœuvring the *Bear* into Dutch Harbour.

The *Isokaze* and *Yamakaze*, after waiting vainly for some hours in Unalaska Bay, eventually found their way back to Japan, where they reported that a number of torpedoes had exploded after the *Bear* had entered Dutch Harbour, with what results it was impossible to ascertain. The U.S. Navy Department kept all details of the affair secret, beyond a brief official announcement to the effect that the *Charleston* had been lost while navigating a narrow channel in misty weather, thus suggesting that the casualty was due to accident. At the same time it was purposely allowed to leak out in quarters suspected of communicating with the enemy that the *Charleston* had been torpedoed, and that two other vessels of greater importance had been sunk at the same time. This intelligence, which seemed to tally with the reports of the two destroyers, was eagerly accepted as fact by the Imperial Japanese Government, and embodied in a special *communiqué* to the Tokyo Press. In recognition of his supposed achievements Commander Nuzuki was awarded the third class of the Order of the Sacred Treasure, and promoted to the rank of Captain. These honours he had certainly merited by his endeavours, irrespective of the actual results.

From the American point of view the loss of the *Charleston* was more than counterbalanced by the misleading impression which was thus conveyed to the enemy. From this date until the end of the war many in Japan remained firmly convinced that two battleships were torpedoed at Dutch Harbour, and were readier than before to believe that an attack from the direction of Alaska was to be apprehended.

It is interesting to note that the *Bear*, which in spite

of the damage she received was not sunk, still survives as a storeship at Dutch Harbour.

In the meantime it must not be imagined that the squadron of fast cruisers under Rear-Admiral Appleton had been idle. With the larger force which he had now at his command, this zealous officer proceeded to give effect to the second part of his instructions by preparing an attack upon the important Japanese trade with Australia. For this purpose the *Memphis* was detached with orders to intercept all homeward-bound Japanese ships passing through Torres Straits. At the end of a fortnight she was relieved by her sister ship *Milwaukee*. It was rightly calculated that news of the loss of one or two ships on this route would be sufficient to cause a panic in Japanese commercial circles, and force insurance rates up to an absolutely prohibitive level. The effects would have been even more far-reaching but for a Government insurance scheme which had been prepared at Tokyo in anticipation of possible difficulties with the marine insurance market.

The joint operations of the *Memphis* and *Milwaukee* covered a period slightly exceeding a month during March and April, 1932. In this time they accounted for no fewer than thirteen Japanese vessels, including three or four bound for Australia in ballast. Most of the prizes carried valuable cargoes, such as wool, frozen meat, hides, butter and grain, besides some lead and copper. It is probable that many more cargoes intended for Japan would have been intercepted, had not Admiral Appleton given directions to his captains to refrain from interference with property covered by neutral flags. His views on this subject were approved by the Operations Bureau, since it was feared that such action might easily generate friction between the United States and countries whose benevolent neutrality was of value.

American cruiser activities in Australian waters would certainly have been continued for a longer period had it not been found that the Japanese were diverting the bulk of their trade to neutral bottoms, their own tonnage being still employed on the longer route around the Western Australian coast to Perth, Adelaide, and Melbourne. Owing to its comparative remoteness, this trade was less easy to molest than that passing through Torres Straits. Moreover, by this date it was desired to assemble all available cruisers for purposes of more direct military importance; for the expedition against Truk was now about to be launched.

The only incident worth recording in connection with this brief war on Japanese Australasian trade was the attempted capture of the *Soyo Maru*. This vessel, a steamer of some 7,000 tons dead weight belonging to the Nippon Yusen Kaisha, was keeping an inshore course when sighted by the *Memphis*. She refused to stop when fired on, and headed for the group of islands lying off Cape York. The captain of the *Memphis*, realising that unless he could stop the *Soyo Maru* she would escape into Australian territorial waters, directed his gunners to aim at her stern, in the hope of crippling the steering gear. The sternpost was hit more than once, but the master of the *Soyo Maru*, resolved to save his ship if he could, maintained his course at a speed approaching 15 knots, the best of which she was capable. The *Memphis* was doing more than double this, and as she gained upon the chase the latter was hit more frequently, several casualties being inflicted in addition to structural damage. Finding that her afterpeak was leaking seriously, and that this was affecting her speed, the Japanese captain headed for a patch of shoal water which lay nearly athwart his course, and in a few minutes his ship was stranded on a sandbank about three miles from Mulgrave Island. The American cruiser was preparing to approach and enforce surrender, when a timely diversion was created by the appearance of the Australian destroyer *Tattoo* from Thursday Island, attracted by the sound of gunfire. On ascertaining the position of affairs, the commander of the *Tattoo* informed the American captain that since the shoal lay within territorial waters, the *Soyo Maru* must be inviolate. Thus the intrepid master of the Japanese freighter succeeded in saving his ship, though it must have cost a considerable sum to pay for her salvage.

In European waters the trade war assumed a different character. It will be remembered that, owing to the dearth of regular cruisers, for the building of which the Navy Department had so often pleaded in vain before the war, a number of the fastest passenger steamers flying the Stars and Stripes had been armed for service as commerce destroyers. It was decided not to organise them in a single squadron, as first proposed, but that each ship on completion of her equipment should be dispatched to her cruising ground as an independent command, on the understanding that units must be ready to combine for joint action on receipt of instructions to that effect. As far as possible the original ship's company was retained on board each vessel, the officers being given commissions in the Naval Reserve, while the executive control of the ship was vested in a captain or commander, U.S. Navy. Another naval officer was carried in the larger vessels as second-in-command, while a few skilled gun-pointers were distributed among the crews with orders to train their own assistants. The armament usually consisted of 6-inch and 5-inch rapid-fire guns of old pattern, some being more or less worn pieces which had been removed from warships on replacement. Decks and bulkheads had to be stiffened to withstand the shock of discharge, while magazines and shell hoists were hastily improvised.

It was believed that only two of the large fleet of Japanese merchantmen engaged in trading between Europe and the Far East had a speed sufficient to stand much chance of escape from the majority of the American auxiliary cruisers. These two were the *Nagasaki Maru* and *Shanghai Maru*, both owned by the Nippon Yusen Kaisha, and built in 1923. Though comparatively small (5,272 tons gross), they were capable of steaming at 20 knots, a speed which the *Leviathan,* alone among the American ships, could exceed. Presumably the Japanese Government were alive to this circumstance, since it was about this time that the two liners in question received an armament of four high-powered 6-inch guns and two pairs of torpedo tubes. Unfortunately, this fact did not come to the knowledge of the U.S. Naval Intelligence Bureau until too late to be of any value.

The American auxiliary cruisers *Mount Vernon, George Washington, President Madison,* and *President Pierce* had orders to patrol the area between the Canary Islands and the coast of Norway, while the *Leviathan* was stationed in the neighbourhood of Brest as linking ship. This latter vessel served also as a transmitting station, through which the other cruisers were kept informed of all the known movements of enemy shipping. The cruising ground of each ship was modified from time to time in accordance with the requirements of the situation, but as a general rule the *Mount Vernon* and *George Washington* patrolled respectively to the north and south of the Straits of Gibraltar, the *President Madison* and *President Pierce* looking after the area north of the English Channel. The remaining three ships (*President Cleveland, President Jefferson,* and *President Taft*) were not ready for sea until some time after the others. When commissioned they were formed into a squadron and dispatched to the Mediterranean, where in consequence of their activities Japanese tonnage soon ceased to pass through the Suez Canal. As soon as the American cruisers had snapped up all the enemy vessels they could find in the Mediterranean, they proceeded to the Red Sea, but without accomplishing much beyond showing the flag there, as their orders forbade them to go beyond Perim.

These operations gravely embarrassed the Japanese, who were threatened with the complete stoppage of their supplies from Europe, except in so far as neutral tonnage could be employed for the purpose. Here again American influence made itself felt by competing for the chartering of all suitable vessels as they came into the market, much to the satisfaction of neutral shipowners, who saw rates steadily rising with no apparent limit. Underwriters also benefited, as increasing rates of premium could be demanded for the insurance of these vessels against war risks.

CHAPTER XVI

APRIL–JUNE, 1932

Armed Japanese merchant vessels make their appearance in the Atlantic—Severe action with U.S. armed liners—*Leviathan* and *George Washington* lost and *Mount Vernon* captured—Insurrection in Hawaii quelled with the help of tanks—Gallant act of Lieut. Logan—Inquiry into origin of revolt—American expedition from Samoa effects a landing at Truk

AMERICAN control of the situation in European waters had apparently been firmly established when the arrival at Madeira, on April 15, of the fast steamers *Nagasaki Maru* and *Shanghai Maru* suddenly put a new aspect on affairs. The two ships stayed only long enough to fuel and complete with fresh water and stores before proceeding on their voyage to London. The *George Washington*, duly apprised of their movements by the U.S. intelligence service, was on the look-out for them, and sighted their smoke some 80 miles to the S.W. of Cape St. Vincent. She rapidly closed with them at a speed of 18 knots, and was not surprised when they turned tail and made off to the westward. No suspicion appears to have been entertained that the enemy ships were armed, and rendered still more formidable by the installation of up-to-date fire control arrangements. Their guns were cleverly concealed behind dummy deckhouses when not in action.

The Japanese steamers allowed the *George Washington* to overhaul them slowly until she was within a little over 12,000 yards, whereupon they so increased speed that no further advantage could be gained by the pursuer. The American vessel opened fire with her forward 6-inch guns, but found the range too great for accurate shooting.

To her amazement the Japanese replied with telling effect, their well-judged salvos quickly dismounting one of the *George Washington's* guns and starting a fire forward.   Turning about to bring her other guns into action, the American ship presented her full broadside to the enemy, offering a big target for their rapid salvos, which demolished the forward funnel and the navigating bridge.   Under this storm of fire the remaining American guns were quickly knocked out, and the great ship was unable to send a single shot at her antagonists.   These now approached closer, steaming round their hapless victim and pounding her mercilessly until she was in flames fore and aft, while few of her complement above the water line had escaped injury.   Her radio cabin was demolished at an early stage, the last message dispatched being to the effect that she was in action with two enemy ships from whose fire she was suffering severely.

On receipt of this startling news the *Mount Vernon*, which was at Lisbon, proceeded at her utmost speed to the last reported position of the *George Washington*. That steamer when sighted was found to be completely disabled and burning furiously, so the new-comer found she must cope unaided with two opponents of equal speed and heavier armament.   In these circumstances the captain of the *Mount Vernon* deemed it wise to beat a retreat, since by so doing he drew the enemy away from his helpless consort, and towards the *Leviathan*, which his radio calls must soon bring to his assistance.

This stage of the action was protracted, as neither of the Japanese ships, with their bottoms fouled by the passage through the tropics, proved capable of catching the 20-knot *Mount Vernon ;* but they were able to keep her in sight until evening, when she ran into the port of Coruña, in the north-west of Spain.   Here she was blockaded for some hours, until next day she received news by radio of the *Leviathan's* approach.   Anchor was then weighed, and the *Mount Vernon* boldly attacked the blockading vessels, closing the range in order to use her guns with better effect. Though she succeeded in this, it was found that the Japanese shooting was more accurate, as in addition to their superior weapons and fire control installation, their guns' crews were picked men. Still the *Mount Vernon* was able to score several hits in spite of the punishment she was herself receiving, and her men were soon cheered by the appearance of the gigantic *Leviathan*, racing down from the northward. It is possible the battle might have ended differently, but for a fresh factor which was now brought into play by the Japanese. The action had developed into two single combats, the *Mount Vernon* fighting the *Nagasaki Maru* while the *Leviathan* engaged the *Shanghai Maru*, both Americans doing their utmost to close the range in order to neutralise their opponents' advantage in armament. To some extent they succeeded, as the speed of both enemy ships now began to fall off. Nevertheless, both the *Leviathan* and the *Mount Vernon* were suffering numerous casualties, and it proved impossible to subdue the flames that broke out after almost every hit with high explosive shell. With her speed of 23 knots the *Leviathan* was the first to get to really close quarters, when she had the satisfaction of seeing the *Shanghai Maru* suddenly veer off her course, describe an erratic segment of a circle, and approach the U.S. liner broadside to broadside, to all appearance out of control. Yet actually this proved to be a clever ruse on the part of the Japanese captain, who thus made an opportunity to discharge two torpedoes at the huge hull of his adversary. Their track was seen from the *Leviathan's* bridge too late to avoid them by use of the helm, and both exploded in quick succession amidships, tearing gigantic rents in the starboard side between the second and third funnels. With water pouring into the stokeholds, the ship at once began to lose speed, a circumstance of which the *Shanghai Maru* was quick to take advantage, drawing out of range before she could receive further punishment from the *Leviathan's* guns.

All this time the *Mount Vernon* and *Nagasaki Maru*

had been pounding away at each other on more or less level terms, for a lucky shot had crippled the Japanese ship's steering gear, throwing her out of her course and disconcerting the aim of her gunners until the emergency hand wheel could be manned. But by now the *Mount Vernon* herself had suffered severely, and when the *Shanghai Maru* joined her sister this reinforcement turned the scale. A further gallant attempt to close the range only resulted in an overwhelming fire being concentrated on the forecastle of the *Mount Vernon ;* her decks were ploughed up and half the bridge was blown away, together with much other superstructure, in the ruins of which the forward guns and their crews were buried. A dash was made for Spanish territorial waters, but the *Shanghai Maru* had already contrived to edge away in that direction, and steaming ahead of the *Mount Vernon*, so that the latter's stern guns would not bear, she kept up a fire so hot that the American liner was soon in a deplorable plight. Her foremast went by the board, and trailing alongside was drawn into the wake, fouling the propellers and thus destroying all chance of escape. Her two enemies now took up positions from which they poured in a methodical and devastating fire. In this extremity the survivors of the *Mount Vernon* had no choice but to surrender, and a white flag was hoisted at the mainmast as a signal to the Japanese ships to cease fire. A boat immediately sped across from the *Shanghai Maru* (her sister apparently had none left undamaged), the Japanese officer in charge demanding unconditional submission. As there was no possibility of help arriving, these terms were perforce accepted, whereupon an armed guard took possession of the crippled American liner, while the *Shanghai Maru* steamed off to ascertain what had become of the *Leviathan*. She found the great ship drifting helplessly, with a pronounced list to starboard. Passing neutral steamers offered their assistance, but it was considered dangerous to attempt towing, lest it should cause further bulkheads to give way. So a Norwegian steamer stood by in readiness to take off the *Leviathan's* crew in case of need, while the huge liner continued to drift in towards the coast. She eventually drove ashore close to Cape Finisterre, and, despite all efforts at salvage, became a total wreck—the largest ship lost throughout the war. The *George Washington*, after being towed for a long distance by a French tug from Casablanca, broke adrift in heavy weather and went to pieces on the Morocco coast.

The *Nagasaki Maru* and *Shanghai Maru* took the *Mount Vernon* into Vigo, where all three were busy for some days in repairing damages. No interference was to be feared from the *President Madison* and *President Pierce*, these ships having received radio instructions from Washington to do nothing until reinforcements were available. Since both vessels were inferior in force to those which had already been defeated, it would obviously have been folly to have allowed them to take the offensive. For the moment, therefore, the Japanese Naval Staff had scored a striking and unexpected success, due entirely to the prevision shown in making the utmost use of the best material that could be found. But, apart from its moral effect, very little permanent advantage was gained from this stroke, for American operations against Japanese trade had already inflicted severe losses which could not be recouped.

As an example of hard-fought duelling between armed merchant vessels, the events which have just been described were practically unique. In the war of 1914–18 the action in the South Atlantic between the *Carmania* and *Cap Trafalgar*, and that in the North Sea between the *Alcantara* and *Greif*, afford the nearest parallels. Perhaps the most striking feature of this battle in the Atlantic was the remarkable capacity which the Japanese ships showed for withstanding punishment. It is believed that the Japanese naval authorities had inspired the original design of the *Nagasaki Maru* and *Shanghai Maru*, so that their construction in some respects approached the cruiser model. No other

supposition adequately explains their astonishing powers
of resistance to gunfire.

A more remote field of operations now claims our
attention. Since the battle of Rotumah, described in
the preceding chapter, all had gone smoothly with the
preparations for the seizure of Truk. Troop movements
between California, Hawaii, and Samoa had proceeded
with regularity, and a sufficient number of trained soldiers
had been assembled at the last-named point. All was
in readiness for the next and most important step, when
early in May news was received of an alarming insurrection in the Hawaiian group. Whether it originated
locally or was inspired from Tokyo is a question which
has never been satisfactorily settled; but there is no
doubt that by some means a quantity of rifles had been
smuggled into the islands and conveyed to a central
point in Oahu, whence they were gradually distributed
among the large Japanese population of the group,
estimated at that date to number nearly 140,000 out of a
total of some 330,000. The contingency which now
developed had been a source of anxiety to the authorities
even before the war, and various plans for dealing with
it had been mooted. Some had suggested transferring
the entire Japanese population *en bloc* to the United
States in time of war, regardless of the difficulties of
transport and accommodation which this drastic
expedient involved. Another proposal was to form a
concentration camp in the island of Niihua, although it
is hard to see how such a vast multitude could have been
housed and fed in such a restricted area. In the end the
views of the local officials prevailed, and the Japanese
were allowed to remain undisturbed at their occupations,
which, being mainly agricultural and commercial, were
in large measure essential to the economic welfare of the
other inhabitants. If only the importation of arms had
been prevented, there is no reason to suppose that any
trouble would have occurred. But when thousands of
able-bodied aliens with rifles in their possession are at
large in a country which is at war with their own, it

is only a question of time and opportunity before an explosion takes place.

The opportunity occurred in connection with the arrangements for training recruits drafted to Hawaii. Two battalions of infantry had been stationed in temporary barracks erected at a spot five miles to the N.E. of Honolulu. Their arms, instead of being near at hand during the night, were piled in a building distant some hundred yards from their sleeping quarters. Sentries were posted, but being new to military life, these were not as alert as veterans would have been. It is impossible to acquit certain officers of culpable negligence in failing to make better arrangements for the safety of their station. The result of this supineness was that an armed body of Japanese, numbering several thousands, surprised the barracks on the night of May 17. They began by seizing the sentries at the armoury and taking possession of the weapons there. This done, the main portion of the barracks was surrounded and an entrance forced. Aroused from sleep and without arms, few offered much resistance, and those who did so were shot down without mercy, among the victims being the senior officer, Colonel Landauer, who thus paid for his carelessness with his life. So well had the Japanese plans been laid that not a man escaped to spread the alarm. The prisoners, confined under a strong guard, were marched away into the hills.

Following on this successful *coup*, the main body of insurgents took the road to Honolulu. They were organised on military lines, with Japanese Army reserve officers in charge of sections. On the way they were joined by contingents from other districts, and a series of positions in the central portion of the city, commanding the main approaches from the harbour, were occupied. Next morning the resident American population awoke to find their streets invaded by an enemy who seemed to have sprung out of the ground. The troops in the island, numbering over ten thousand, were not all assembled in a single place, but were scattered in various directions.

The largest body was at Schofield Barracks, twenty miles away, in the centre of the island, and found themselves surrounded by insurgents who had torn up the railway line and cut all telegraph and telephone wires.   Other detachments were at Forts Weaver and Kamehameha, at the entrance to Pearl Harbour; at Fort Shafter, to the N.W. of Honolulu; at Forts Armstrong, De Russy and Ruger, to the south-east, between the city and Diamond Head; and at a new magazine on the slopes of Mount Konahuanui, about ten miles north of Honolulu.   With the enemy holding the centre of communications, including the telephone exchange and railroad depot, the concentration of these troops was no easy task.   Several of the camps which had been formed around the forts had been attacked, but their sentries seem to have been vigilant, as nowhere had the rebels gained a foothold, though they still surrounded the forts in unknown strength.   In Forts Armstrong and De Russy, which are practically in Honolulu, there were barely 2,000 men, and not all of these were combatants.   The guns were mostly disposed with a view to repelling an enemy attack from seaward, and in any case it did not seem advisable to shell the city except as a last resort.   A fast launch was dispatched to Pearl Harbour to request assistance from the warships there.   Pending the arrival of help, all available men were employed in driving off the detachments of Japanese in the vicinity of the two forts.   This done, an advance was made along the streets leading towards the centre of the city.   Firing was incessant until both rebels and defenders learned by experience the folly of wasting ammunition.   As the day wore on, both sides were reinforced, the Japanese by further contingents from distant villages, the Americans by landing parties from the warships.   But it was only in the late afternoon that General McVey, the officer commanding in Oahu, judged himself strong enough to make a general attack.   Roofs were lined with riflemen and machine gunners, and the warships were ordered to throw shells into certain prominent buildings known to be occupied by the enemy. A large portion of the fleet had left on a cruise the day before, but about a dozen ships were brought round from Pearl Harbour. While their fire caused considerable structural damage, casualties among the Japanese were few, owing to the skill with which they took advantage of every bit of cover. An American bayonet charge was more successful, and after a short hand-to-hand fight the enemy positions were stormed. But on following the rebels across the open ground behind the buildings, the Americans found themselves enfiladed by a murderous fire from barricades and trenches at right angles to their line of advance, and were obliged to retreat. On regaining the shelter of the buildings they had just quitted the plan of attack was reorganised, and while some kept the rebels busy with a steady fire, other parties spread out on either flank to take them in the rear. These movements were not executed without heavy casualties, and at the close of the day it was felt that other methods must be devised if the enemy was to be turned out of his positions without long and arduous trench warfare.

The situation was saved by the arrival in port that night of a transport carrying a complete "tank" section. The tanks were of a light and handy type, eminently suitable for such an emergency. They were brought ashore without delay, gangs working all through the night to complete their discharge and assembly. Fortunately their crews had been embarked in the same ship, so the necessary trained personnel was not lacking. On the following day they led the advance with complete success, for the Japanese, taken altogether by surprise, were evidently disheartened by this unexpected diversion. Bursts of machine-gun fire from the tanks broke up every attempt to rally, and the victory was rendered complete by the arrival of strong reinforcements from Fort Shafter, whose garrison had been relieved by a body of troops and seamen marched overland from Pearl Harbour. These made a flank attack on the retreating Japanese, who now broke and fled in various directions. Their retirement was covered by a series of fires which broke out simultaneously, having evidently been kindled to delay pursuit. Several streets were involved in this conflagration, which added considerably to the heavy bill for damages caused by the revolt. Many of the Japanese wounded perished miserably in the burning houses. This marked the turning point of the insurrection, and though the last spark of rebellion was not quenched until some weeks later, it never again assumed dangerous proportions.

At the time this truth was not fully realised, and as soon as the fire had been mastered and order restored, strong detachments patrolled the city to guard against the possibility of renewed attack in the night. Next day steps were taken to reconquer the rest of the island, which appeared to be largely in the hands of the enemy. The garrison of Schofield Barracks, having driven off their assailants and repaired the railroad, were now in communication with Pearl Harbour, and with this aid systematic arrangements were made to round up the rebels. On the previous day a series of heavy explosions from the direction of Mount Konahuanui had caused grave misgivings as to the safety of the magazine there. It was now ascertained that Lieut. Logan, the Coast Artillery officer in charge of this depot, had for many hours maintained a stubborn resistance to the assaults of a strong force of insurgents, who finally burst their way in by sheer weight of numbers. Although severely wounded, Lieut. Logan contrived to ignite a train which had been laid in readiness, and blew up the whole magazine, killing some hundreds of Japanese and injuring many more. This desperate act completely wrecked the plans of the rebels, who had counted on seizing the large quantity of rifles and ammunition stored in the magazine. There is no doubt that by his heroic action Logan appreciably hastened the end of the revolt.

In the other islands, where fewer weapons were available, the outbreak was not so serious. At Hilo, the largest town in the group after Honolulu, the disturbances

Q

only amounted to rioting. In fact, the movement was manifestly aimed at the American naval and military establishments in Oahu. In the hills the Japanese insurgents contrived to maintain themselves for some two or three months by a form of guerilla warfare scarcely distinguishable from brigandage; and the American War Department has placed it on record that the new military formations derived invaluable experience from the operations involved in the suppression of these dying embers of revolt.

All Japanese captured with arms in their hands were deported to Panama and employed as labourers in the Canal Zone. Those who surrendered voluntarily within a certain period were dealt with more leniently. The many thousands of Japanese still left in Hawaii were segregated as far as possible, and kept under surveillance by the military police.

A court of inquiry which sat at Pearl Harbour to probe into the origin of the revolt found no positive evidence of outside instigation, though many prisoners quoted the ringleaders as having declared that they were acting under the orders of the Japanese Government. A Japanese farmer named Morimoto, who had been captured while leading an attack upon Fort Ruger, assured the examining officers that the rising was planned to coincide with the arrival of a Japanese army of invasion, of whose coming the insurgents had been secretly apprised. This witness, it is true, bore a dubious character, and although he stuck to his evidence under severe cross-examination, the court appears to have remained sceptical. Another witness, named Sodo, who had also been captured with arms in his hands, flatly contradicted Morimoto, and insisted with considerable vehemence that the revolt had been planned from beginning to end by certain Japanese residents of Hawaii. In the opinion of several officers present in the court, Sodo's vigorous denial of Japanese official complicity in the plot was overdone, though there was no means of testing his statements.

The only other fact bearing upon the question is a

reference in a book published at Tokyo a few months after the war. Its author, Captain Amakasu, a former naval officer, speaks vaguely of a projected expedition against Hawaii, the date given coinciding with that of the actual revolt. This expedition, Captain Amakasu states, was not proceeded with, " as our scouts were unable to obtain the intelligence which was essential to the success of the undertaking; but," he adds, " matters had already gone so far that warships and transports were assembling at Yokosuka for the voyage to Hawaii, and the plan was cancelled only ten days before the convoy was due to sail."

In view of this testimony it is impossible to dismiss the suspicion that the Tokyo Government had some share in kindling the flames of rebellion. It would, in any case, have been a perfectly legitimate action from their point of view, for the creation of domestic embarrassments for an enemy State is one of the most time-honoured methods of waging war.

The rising might, of course, have proved a far graver affair than it actually turned out to be. Even as it was, many American lives and much valuable property had been sacrificed. Nor was the trouble without effect on the general military situation, for it delayed by at least three weeks the sailing of the expedition to Truk, and to that extent may be said to have prolonged the war.

The expedition, which finally sailed from Pago-Pago on June 18, consisted of 4000 picked troops, with machine guns and field artillery. The troop transports, escorted by two divisions of destroyers and the aircraft-carrier *Wright*, pursued a route which as far as possible avoided all islands of importance, leaving the Ellice and Gilbert groups out of sight to the north, and Fiji and the Solomons to the south. Two strong squadrons of fast cruisers, each accompanied by an aircraft-carrier, kept station some 20 miles ahead and to the northward of the transports, while 40 miles astern came the main battle fleet with its attendant destroyers, submarines and auxiliaries. So large an assemblage of vessels could not be expected to cross even such a vast ocean as the Pacific without being sighted, but by the formation adopted the presence of the transports was effectually screened. Indeed, the only ships which caught a glimpse of the expedition were a British cruiser bound from the Solomon Islands to Fiji, and a merchant steamer carrying phosphates from Nauru. The former only reported what she had seen to the British Admiralty, while the merchant vessel, being without radio gear, had no opportunity of disclosing the news until she reached Sydney a fortnight later, by which time it was too late for any harm to be done.

The expedition covered the distance of 3000 miles from Tutuila to Truk in ten days, the average speed being rather below 13 knots. A certain amount of bad weather was encountered, which lengthened the voyage by a day or two. Eventually, however, the islands were reached without misadventure, and the landing, which took place on June 28, was quite peaceful, no resistance being offered by the two or three Japanese officials who represented their Government. It is doubtful whether the native inhabitants of these remote islands appreciated that a war was in progress; nor would it have interested them if they had known. During the voyage radio signals were reduced to a minimum; but once the island was occupied full details were transmitted to Honolulu and thence to Washington in order that further preparations might proceed without delay. Since it was desirable that the enemy should be kept in the dark until the last possible moment, no intimation of the seizure of Truk was given out in the United States. So far as could be ascertained, Japanese cruisers were not in the habit of visiting Truk, but to guard against a surprise visit by enemy ships, the strictest possible watch was kept by airplanes, flights of which relieved each other in patrolling the group of islands. Four of the fastest cruisers were held ready with steam in their boilers, in case it should prove necessary to run down and destroy an intruder, and shortly after the landing had been effected all ships were refuelled from the attendant oilers and colliers. Long afterwards it was discovered that the expedition had narrowly missed running into the Japanese South Sea squadron, under Rear-Admiral Kokuyama, which had called at Ponapi on a cruise from the Philippines to Jaluit, in the Marshall Archipelago, the day before the descent on Truk, so that the bad weather which delayed the U.S. fleet was a blessing in disguise.

The Truk or Hogolu Islands, which had thus become an advanced war base of the United States Navy, constitute the largest group in the Carolines, and were among the ex-German insular territories which fell to Japan under the Versailles mandate. The dozen or more basaltic islands of the group form, as it were, the jagged rim of a great lagoon, some 40 miles in length and about the same in breadth, studded with rocky islets. This lagoon is accessible by six or more navigable passages, each deep enough for the heaviest battleships, though patches of shoal water and the strong tide rip render it necessary to proceed with caution. Eten Harbour, the principal settlement and seat of the Japanese administration, is located between Eten and Dublon Islands. The passage into the harbour is clearly marked by pole beacons, which the Japanese had omitted to remove on the outbreak of war. The lagoon itself, as Rear-Admiral Harper had reported, was found to provide anchorage facilities for the entire fleet, and though there were not a few submerged rocks and areas of foul ground, the clear water enabled these dangers to be avoided by keeping a sharp look-out from each masthead when conning the ships to their berths. So far as natural advantages were concerned, it would have been difficult to find a place more admirably suited to the purposes of the expedition. Why the Japanese had neglected to take even the most elementary precautions against the seizure of Truk will always remain a mystery. True, there were so many islands in the South Seas which lay exposed to a sudden *coup* that the

protection of all would have been physically impossible;
but the geographical situation of Truk was such as to
endow it with obvious strategic importance, and the
failure to provide the simplest defences—there was not
even a long-range radio station—was an error for which
Japan was to pay dearly. The easy and bloodless
seizure of this valuable position stood in marked contrast
to the abortive expedition against the Bonins.   But the
whole history of successful warfare is largely a record of
initial mistakes having been retrieved by the wisdom
born of painful experience, and this war was to be no
exception to the rule.

CHAPTER XVII

JUNE–AUGUST, 1932

Japanese dismay at loss of Truk—Divided counsels in Tokyo—Sinking
of a monster Japanese submarine—American forces occupy islands
of Jaluit and Ponapi—Operations of dummy battleships deceive
Japanese airmen—Grave discontent in Japan—More trouble with
China

THE seizure of Truk aroused much more excitement in
Japan than in the United States, where the public did
not immediately grasp the full significance of this move.
But the Japanese were quick to see what it portended.
The very contingency they had striven to avert at all
costs, and the prevention of which had been one of their
main objects in going to war, had now come upon them
like a bolt from the blue. Subordinate only to the prime
motive of stamping out incipient revolution had been
the desire to expel American influence from the western
half of the Pacific. This aim, they imagined, had been
achieved once and for all by the conquest of the Philippines and Guam. Yet, with the fall of Truk, the
American flag had re-invaded the forbidden zone, where
its naval power was once more in a position to make
itself felt. Disconcerting as this was, it might prove to
be only the prelude to graver events. The islands, it
was true, lay at a great distance from Japan, but to
Guam they were sufficiently near to constitute a serious
menace, and if Guam were lost, the way would lie open
to an attack upon the Philippines—or even, perhaps,
upon Japan itself. While the authorities at Tokyo were
still considering means of coping with the new situation,
rumours of a further peril came to their ears. It should
here be interpolated that the Japanese naval and

231

military leaders were handicapped all through the contest by the absence of reliable intelligence as to the plans and movements of their enemy. Espionage in the United States could not be practised by natives of Japan on account of their racial characteristics, which no disguise served effectually to conceal. Moreover, the few Japanese permitted to remain in the country were kept under close observation, and none were allowed to reside in or near the limits of any naval or military district. A certain number of white persons are known to have been in the pay of Japan, but even when these contrived to obtain information of value, they had no means of transmitting it promptly. Their reports could only reach Tokyo by slow and devious routes, generally *via* South America or Europe, the delay in most cases rendering the news quite worthless. The expedition to Truk furnished a notable example of this. According to the Japanese historian Nakabashi, a full report on the projected expedition, giving its destination and accurate particulars of the force to be employed, was compiled by a Japanese agent in San Francisco at least three weeks before the date of sailing. This report was telegraphed in code to a confederate in Callao, by whom it was to be relayed by cable to Japan; but for some reason unexplained, it did not reach Tokyo until a fortnight after the expedition had landed at Truk. From time to time, other items of important news from their agents in the United States did arrive at Tokyo headquarters with surprising promptitude, but almost invariably they proved to be deceptive. Some Japanese writers, displaying a lamentable lack of humour, have indignantly charged the American Government with being " treacherous " in this matter, though it is surely permissible to hoist an enemy with his own petard whenever the opportunity occurs. The American intelligence system, on the other hand, became increasingly efficient as the war progressed, thanks in large measure to the willing assistance of Chinese nationals; though, for obvious reasons, it would not be wise to dwell too closely on the methods which, in the later stages of the war, enabled Washington to

receive timely warning of important Japanese movements. It is, however, no longer a secret that the
decisive naval engagement of the war was indirectly
brought about by the skilful dissemination of reports
which entirely misled the Japanese high command. On
July 8, that is, ten days after the American landing at
Truk, messages were received at Tokyo from two different
agents in the United States—neither of whom was known
to the other—asserting most positively that the Truk
expedition was merely a blind to divert attention from
an impending attack on Guam, which was to be launched
by 40,000 troops, covered by practically the entire
American battle fleet. Both agents insisted, moreover,
that the rumours of an impending raid on Hokkaido had
been put about with the same object, and that no such
raid had ever been seriously contemplated. While it
was, of course, impossible to verify these reports, colour
was lent them by the stories told by neutrals who had
recently arrived in the Far East from the United States
and Canada. One of the English journals published at
Hong Kong printed a circumstantial account of the
American preparations to recover Guam by a sudden
attack in overwhelming strength, this being but the first
move in a great offensive campaign, which was to be
carried on with the utmost vigour until the Philippines
were again in American hands. Further, it was hinted
that the war would then be carried to the coasts of Japan
proper, and allusions were made to the gigantic fleet of
aircraft which was building for the express purpose of
laying waste Tokyo and other great Japanese cities
when the Americans had secured a base within striking
distance. While these reports were disbelieved in
Japanese naval circles, the military leaders took them
more seriously. Differences of opinion thus developed,
not for the first time, between the two services, but as
the influence of the army always prevailed when vital
questions of national defence had to be settled, the
Supreme War Council eventually decided that no further
operations of importance, whether by land or sea,
should be undertaken until the situation had become

clearer—in other words, until the enemy had shown his
hand. This meant that Japan was to remain strictly on
the defensive at the very moment when it best suited
American plans. Pursuant to the decision of the
Supreme Council, no attempt was made to recapture
Truk, though it had previously been resolved to send a
powerful force to eject the intruders from these islands,
and a squadron had already assembled at Guam for the
purpose. Had it arrived promptly, matters might have
fared ill with the Americans, whose improvised defences
were not yet in a condition to sustain a determined
attack. As it was, they remained unmolested save by a
solitary Japanese submarine, the adventures of which
must be briefly recounted. On the outbreak of war
Japan had completed six very large submersible cruisers,
as noted in a preceding chapter. Each of these vessels
displaced more than 7,000 tons, carried two 8-inch guns
in a turret, besides lighter artillery and torpedo tubes,
and could travel on the surface at a speed of 23 knots.
They were credited with a radius of 24,000 miles, and
their decks, turrets, and conning towers were stoutly
armoured. One of these boats, adapted for mine-laying,
had planted mine-fields in Hawaiian waters. A second
was believed to have cruised as far as Panama, though
the identity of this craft was never clearly established.
On the whole, however, little had been seen or heard of
these gigantic submersibles, and it was assumed in
America that they had failed to make good on active
service. Such was indeed the fact. Either the design
was fundamentally at fault, the construction defective,
or the *personnel* insufficiently trained, for the vessels in
no case fulfilled expectations. The first to be completed
was the *Nagasaki*—all submarines of the cruiser type being
named after Japanese cities. After narrowly escaping
disaster on her trials, owing to the difficulty of manœuvring the unwieldy hull below water, she was taken in hand
for extensive repairs, which were barely completed when
the war began. In due course she departed on a cruise to
the American coast, where her powerful armament might
have made her an extremely unpleasant visitor. She

did not arrive there, however; nor was she ever heard of again.   Somewhere in the abysmal depths of the Pacific her hull lies rusting, but how and where she came to grief will never be known.   The *Hakodate*, second of the series, made one cruise to the South Seas without accomplishing anything of note, and was then attached to the battle fleet.   Suffering constantly from machinery troubles, which materially reduced her nominal speed of 17 knots, she became more of a hindrance than a help, finally ending her brief career one day when the fleet was at sea by coming to the surface a few yards ahead of the battleship *Yamashiro*, whose stem crushed her like an egg-shell.   In view of the circumstances, there is no manner of doubt that the submersible had got out of control, and broached surface at the wrong moment. Others of the same class, such as the *Kobe* and *Osaka*, were so frequently laid up with defective engines that they cannot be said to have played any part in the war. Japanese opinion of the type is evidenced by the fact that the last two vessels were never completed, both being broken up for their metal after being launched to clear the slipways.   It was the *Nagoya* of this class that appeared at Truk a fortnight after the American occupation, but whether she came by special order or was merely on a roving commission remains a matter of surmise.   Her movements indicated, however, that she knew the islands to be in enemy possession.   On the morning of July 12 there were lying in Eten harbour the cruisers *Columbus* (Captain Bateman) and *Hartford*, eight destroyers, the airplane-carrier *Alaska*, and a number of transports and auxiliaries.   Six miles off shore the destroyers *Melvin, Clemson, Reid,* and *Thornton* were patrolling, the first pair to eastward, the other two rather more to the north.   Two seaplanes were also up, and the dirigible *Jackson* was on the point of ascending from the mooring mast by which she was attached to one of the auxiliary ships.   Nevertheless the enemy was able, in spite of this vigilant watch, to spring a surprise.   A look-out man in the *Clemson* was the first to sight the huge submarine as she came to the surface midway

between the destroyer and the shore, the sun flashing on
the glistening turrets and conning tower as they rose
out of the sea. Signalling to her consorts, the *Clemson*
wheeled round and dashed at full speed for the enemy,
firing from every gun that would bear, while the other
destroyers also converged swiftly on the scene. Though
several shells burst against her long grey hull, the submarine did not attempt to dive. Instead, she moved at a
good pace in the direction of, but parallel with, the
islands. Her turret swung round, a tongue of flame
spurted from one of the great guns, and a 250-pound
shell hurtled over the destroyer's bridge, missing it by
inches. Swerving to throw off the enemy's aim, the
destroyer fired shot after shot at the big hull, but still
without apparent effect. This time the submarine,
having turned a few degrees to starboard, let go a salvo
from both guns with deadly effect, one shell raking the
Clemson fore and aft and exploding with tremendous
force just above the steering gear. Brought suddenly
to a standstill, the destroyer drifted helplessly, exposing
her full broadside, which was promptly holed on the
water-line by a second shell. Having disposed of one
antagonist, the monster next opened fire on the *Melvin*,
whose commander, realising the futility of attacking
thick armour with 4-inch guns, was manœuvring to
use his torpedoes. One of his triple tubes had been
discharged, and the other was about to be fired, when a
heavy shell burst on deck. This must have touched off
one or all of the remaining torpedoes, for the *Melvin*
instantly disappeared in a smother of flame and smoke.
Avoiding by use of the helm (but only in the nick of
time) the torpedoes which the *Melvin* had launched, the
submarine now directed her fire against the *Reid* and
Thornton, making such excellent practice that the two
boats were compelled to turn away and throw up a
smoke screen. Under cover of this they dashed in again
and let go their torpedoes, only to find that the enemy
had forestalled them by putting on speed and reaching
a position far ahead of that in which they had supposed
him to be. As the screen lifted he sent a shell into the

Reid, while at the same moment his anti-aircraft guns spat at one of the American seaplanes which had approached the area of combat. Unfortunately, this machine carried no bombs, and could therefore do nothing except pepper the *Nagoya's* deck with Lewis-gun bullets, which laid low a few of the Japanese sailors. But the return fire was too hot for comfort, and the seaplane had to beat a retreat. Up to now the submarine had had things very much her own way. She had sunk one destroyer, totally disabled a second, and damaged a third, at the cost of half-a-dozen men killed or wounded and a few dents in her armour. But by now the alarm was given, and the cruiser *Columbus,* advised by radio-phone of the situation, was steaming out of the harbour to take a hand in the game. As she rounded Salat island and made for the open sea the submarine was reported from her masthead look-out to be seven miles distant, bearing S.S.W. As this was well within the range of the cruiser's 8-inch battery, fire was opened at once, and with such precision that the target was straddled at the second salvo, though no direct hit was observed. Apparently the *Nagoya* had no stomach for the duel, for she proceeded to dive, but it was several minutes before the top of her conning-tower vanished, and the last shot from the *Columbus* pitched only a few yards away. Captain Bateman now steamed out to sea at high speed, zigzagging to avoid torpedoes, but remaining near enough to cover the four destroyers that had followed him out of the harbour and were now trying to pick up the enemy with their hydrophones. The *Nagoya* was quickly located by the throb of her electro-motors, for the enormous depth of water in this locality rendered it impossible for her to lie on the bottom, where, with engines stopped, she might have escaped detection. She was thus compelled to keep her motors running, and so to reveal her position to the hunters. Four depth charges of the 750 lb. model were heaved over, set to explode at 150 feet, and before the tortured sea had subsided after the mountainous upheaval the enemy's bows were seen emerging, a short distance away from the destroyer *Pillsbury*. With admirable presence of mind, the captain of this boat launched three torpedoes at the mark, besides opening fire with his guns. The cruiser, now some three miles distant, could not use her guns for fear of hitting the destroyers, but her intervention was not required. Whether the submarine had already sustained fatal damage from the depth charges is uncertain. If so, the *Pillsbury's* torpedoes only gave her the quietus, for two of them hit her squarely, opening gaping holes in her side. With a convulsive shudder the giant submarine rose higher out of the water, until half her length was exposed, while the destroyers pumped a stream of shell into the unarmoured bottom. There she hung poised for a full minute, then gave a sudden lurch and vanished from sight, leaving a veritable sea of oil to mark her grave. To make assurance doubly sure the hydrophones were put in action again, but no sound came up from the cavernous depths into which the *Nagoya* had plunged. Long before she reached the bottom her sides must have been crushed flat by the irresistible pressure of the water. The defenders of Truk had, of course, no means of knowing whether or not they were in further danger of attack. To them it seemed likely enough that the big submarine was the precursor of strong enemy forces on their way to make a desperate bid for the recovery of the islands. Everything possible was done to improve the defences. Guns were emplaced in positions from which they commanded the sea approaches; mines were laid across the three main entrances to the lagoon, namely, the North-East, the Uligar, and the Neurui passages; hydrophone stations were erected at three different points on the island to give timely warning of submarines, and a patrol was maintained from dawn to dark by seaplanes and a small dirigible. As the base was developed and its fortifications strengthened the peril of serious attack, and even of raids, steadily diminished, but the first few weeks were a period of intense anxiety for the garrison. Nothing happened, however, for the reasons indicated above. The Japanese high command had no intention of embarking upon any considerable enterprise at a distance from home waters until they knew more about the enemy's plans; and it was long ere enlightenment was vouchsafed to them. Meanwhile the Americans were taking further steps to safeguard their line of communication with the advanced position at Truk. Ponapi, in the Carolines, and Jaluit, in the Marshall group—both of which lay within submarine range of the Samoa-Truk route—were suspected of serving as Japanese naval bases, and it was accordingly decided to reduce them. Simultaneous descents upon both places were planned, the Ponapi force sailing from Truk, while that destined for Jaluit proceeded thither direct from Tutuila. In each case the operation was completely successful. At Ponapi, where no resistance was encountered, the troops got ashore and took possession with the utmost ease. No Japanese combatants were found in the islands, but a couple of dismantled seaplanes and a magazine of naval stores showed the post to have been used as a minor base. The Jaluit expedition was not quite so fortunate. A few Japanese Marines who were stationed there to man the battery of four 6-inch guns, showed fight, but a bombardment by the warships and a gas attack by aircraft soon overcame this opposition, and after a brief delay the invaders made good their footing with only a score of casualties. Apart from the elimination of the submarine danger to the Samoa-Truk route, the capture of these islands was of some strategic importance. Jaluit, in particular, was conveniently situated as a port of call between Hawaii and Truk, and from this time forward it was feasible to dispatch men and supplies to the advanced base direct from Hawaii, via Jaluit, instead of by the longer route over Samoa. Now that the broad scheme of strategy mapped out by Rear-Admiral Harper had begun to develop, the moment was fast approaching for another bold but well-considered move. Needless to say, nothing so foolhardy as a direct attack upon Guam was meditated. But the Japanese, bearing in mind the earlier attempt against the Bonins—which, as they well knew, was thwarted more by ill-chance than their own efforts—might conceivably be persuaded that Guam had now become the true American objective. It was to foster this belief that Japanese emissaries in the United States had been allowed to glean full information of the coming attack, nor did they suspect how the transmission of their reports to Tokyo had been kindly facilitated by the authorities. There were, moreover, officials in Washington who could have explained the apparent leakage of intelligence which enabled travellers on returning to the Far East to spread the most circumstantial rumours of an impending expedition to Guam. That the Japanese War Council, or at least the military members, finally accepted these inspired rumours as authentic is made clear by their subsequent policy. A few days after the seizure of Truk a division of four American battleships quietly departed from Dutch Harbour, where it had been stationed for several months. Had the presence of this force in a remote haven of Unalaska been suspected by armchair critics in the United States, they would assuredly have condemned in unmeasured terms what seemed to be a futile and dangerous dispersion of strength. But things are not always what they seem, least of all in modern warfare; and though to all appearance it was the *Arkansas*, *Wyoming*, *Florida*, and *Utah* which sailed out of Dutch Harbour one misty morning in early July, they were, in fact, only counterfeit presentments of the battleships whose names they had usurped, being large freighters skilfully camouflaged as fighting ships. Their guns and turrets looked most formidable, though fashioned out of lumber. One big shell would have blown any of these " dreadnoughts " into matchwood, but their mission was to deceive, not to fight. The use of " dummy " ships was no new stratagem. It had been employed by the British Navy during the world war, and, if certain historians are to be trusted, by the Japanese themselves in their contest with Russia. But on this occasion the ancient ruse was destined to have consequences of the last importance. In addition to the four ships named, six others had been prepared at Puget Sound Navy Yard, so that a fleet of ten of these make-believe battleships was now available. They included replicas of the *Maryland, Colorado, California,* and *Tennessee,* the most powerful units of the real battle fleet. Rendezvousing at Portland on July 15, this bogus armada proceeded by easy stages to Truk, where it arrived on August 7. Three days later, accompanied by the airplane-carrier *Alaska* and two flotillas of destroyers, it made a sweep to the north-west, approaching to within 150 miles of Guam, where an enemy submarine was sighted. Here the fleet turned back, and a few hours later found itself assailed by several large Japanese planes which had come speeding out from Guam, eager to bomb the first American battleships seen in these latitudes since the outbreak of war. Some trying moments were endured by those on board when the hostile planes began dropping bombs, for a single hit might have betrayed the disguise, and in that case the whole strategic conception, of which this cruise was but a preliminary, would have fallen to the ground. Not even in the excitement of action could the Japanese airmen have failed to draw conclusions from the spectacle of massive guns and turrets flying aloft under the impact of their bombs. Fortunately, however, the anti-aircraft guns of the destroyers kept the intruders at an altitude too great for accurate practice, and before they could summon up resolution to attack at closer quarters they found themselves hunted in turn by the chaser planes from the *Alaska,* which soon drove them off. This momentary excitement over, the fleet pursued its leisurely voyage back to Truk. The fates had indeed been kind on this occasion, for everything had gone according to plan. Confronted with detailed reports both from their submarines and aircraft, Japanese headquarters could no longer doubt that the United States battle fleet, or a major portion of it, had carried out a reconnaissance in force in the direction of Guam, and what should this signify but that the long-foretold attack was imminent? To

R

appreciate what followed it is necessary to emphasise the fact that Guam, in Japanese eyes, was something more than a lonely islet in the broad Pacific. It had stood to them as a symbol of alien power in the Far East, a fortress which sooner or later might become an impregnable stronghold, from which an American fleet could dominate their own waters and menace the very threshold of Dai Nippon itself. True, the Washington Treaty had bound the United States not to fortify Guam or otherwise exploit it as a naval base, but to the Oriental mind paper guarantees have always counted for little. For these reasons the conquest of the island in the first month of war had evoked enthusiasm out of all proportion to the actual achievement. Judge, then, of the corresponding reaction that ensued when news leaked out—as evil news invariably does, no matter how rigid the censorship—that Guam might soon be attacked in overwhelming force. Hitherto the Japanese war authorities had remained austerely indifferent to public opinion. Several newspapers which had ventured mildly to criticise the measures adopted by the War Council to conserve foodstuffs and other prime commodities—of which, thanks to the activity of American cruisers, a severe shortage was already making itself felt—had been punished by suspension, fines, and the imprisonment of their editors. Freed from the restraints imposed by the constitutional safeguards that operated in peace time, the Government and their reactionary supporters carried things with a high hand. The whole country was administered by what, in everything but name, was martial law. This arbitrary policy was slowly but surely cooling the patriotic fervour which the people had displayed on the outbreak of war. Though the Diet still met, the party truce proclaimed in February, 1931, had long since been broken. Liberal politicians were denied a hearing, many suffered violence at the hands of hired bullies, in the pay of the reactionaries; and half-a-dozen, who had dared to protest against the Government's cavalier methods, now languished in gaol. In short, the nation was no longer united. Among the poorer folk who had to subsist on a meagre allowance of food—ostensibly the same for everyone, but which the wealthier classes were able to supplement with delicacies that could be purchased openly, despite Government edicts to the contrary—symptoms of war-weariness were becoming very pronounced. Several hundred thousand of them were conscripted for various branches of war work at a pittance based on Army rates of pay. They were subjected to a severe discipline, every infraction of the rules being visited with harsh penalties. As early as the autumn of 1931, surreptitious peace meetings had been held at Yokohama, Osaka, Kobe, and other industrial centres. Whenever the police got wind of these assemblies they were ruthlessly broken up and wholesale arrests made. But official repression was powerless to check what was rapidly becoming a nation-wide movement. Far-seeing observers had warned the ruling caste that war as a remedy for revolution might eventually inflame the very disease it was meant to cure. But although alive to the critical posture of affairs, the Government had by no means abandoned hope of a successful issue. To still the angry mutterings of the people and convert their sullen discontent into patriotic enthusiasm, it was only necessary to win some really brilliant victory. This, indeed, was urgently to be desired from every point of view, for fresh complications were now embarrassing the Japanese Government. Some weeks previous to the fall of Truk, the Chinese Government had assumed a tone of which there was no mistaking the significance. Peking had reaffirmed its determination to enforce the embargo on the export of war munitions from Chinese territory, and Japan's attention was drawn to the fact that the coal, iron, and other minerals she was raising from Chinese mines under her control and sending to Japan came within this category. She was accordingly invited to put an immediate stop to the traffic. Compliance with this request would have paralysed the Japanese munitions industry, which could not carry on for a week if bereft of raw materials from the mainland. The Government was therefore compelled to temporise, for an open breach with China was the last thing they desired to court at the present juncture. But Peking was not to be gainsaid. In a stern Note, which was practically an ultimatum, Japan was again requested to suspend at once the export of products from her Chinese mines, failing which the Central Government proposed to take all necessary measures to uphold the sovereign rights of China. A week later, no reply having been received, Peking declared war. This action was admittedly due in part to American diplomatic pressure, but not entirely so. The exploits of General Wang-Tsu, which had paved the way for the unification of the Empire, had stirred the sluggish national spirit of the Chinese people, making them less tolerant of alien encroachment upon their soil. And it was against Japan, as the worst offender in this respect, that their anger was chiefly vented. But hitherto they had not felt themselves strong enough to resist her pretensions by actual force. Now, however, General Wang-Tsu was in command of an army 400,000 strong, trained and thoroughly seasoned in the hard-fought civil warfare which has been previously described. This host, although deficient in modern equipment, especially in artillery, was yet sufficiently powerful to give a good account of itself. It was most ably led by General Wang-Tsu and the officers who had served under him in the civil struggle. Above all, it took the field with the hearty good-will of the Chinese nation at large, a moral asset not to be despised. The major operations of this army will be dealt with in their proper place; but at this point we must return to events in the naval sphere.

CHAPTER XVIII

AUGUST–OCTOBER, 1932

American plans to induce Japanese fleet to fight—Further manœuvres with dummy battleships—Japanese expecting a fleet action—Feint against Guam distracts Japanese attention while Angaur is occupied—Improvement in U.S. position—Strength of Japanese battle fleet at this time

IT has been shown that the Japanese war leaders could not afford to wait indefinitely for the next move of their adversary; still less dare they risk anything in the nature of a severe reverse, such as the loss of Guam, or even of the minor but strategically important Pelew Islands, which their naval advisers believed to be the immediate objective of this American thrust into the Western Pacific. As it happens, the naval view was the correct one. The plan adopted by the U.S. Bureau of Operations was to advance step by step to a position from which an invasion of the Philippines could be launched, and Angaur, in the Pelew group, was the position selected. It was believed in Washington that nothing short of intervention by the Japanese battle fleet was likely to frustrate the methodical fulfilment of this plan. Thanks to the base established at Truk, and to the naval forces now working therefrom, it was possible to make the route to the Pelews fairly safe from attack by Japanese cruisers or submarines; and although Angaur might prove to be lightly fortified, this contingency had not been disregarded. Thus the only uncertain factor was the Japanese battle fleet. The general opinion was that Japan would not risk this force save in the last extremity.

Whether she would consider a threat to **Angaur**

sufficient justification for throwing in her fleet was doubtful. It seemed more probable that she would reserve her battleships to strike a hammer blow in defence of some position of greater importance, such as Guam, and it was upon this assumption that the whole scheme of American strategy now rested. Information received at Washington from Far Eastern sources tended to verify Admiral Harper's premises. There was no doubt that the Japanese regarded Guam as one of the vital points which must be defended to the last, for moral no less than for strategical reasons. So much having been postulated, it remained to devise a method of compelling the Japanese fleet to fight under conditions favourable to the American cause— that is, in an area distant from its home bases, and at the moment selected by the American Commander-in-Chief. Difficult as the problem appeared to be, it was not deemed insoluble. How the solution was achieved will now be made clear. The voyage of the pseudo-battleships to Truk, and their subsequent cruise towards Guam, have already been chronicled. This latter movement took place during the week of August 10–17. Ten days later it was repeated, on much the same plan as before, but with certain modifications. On this occasion the fleet steamed 50 miles further, thus arriving at a position only 100 miles to the southeast of the island. Again it was sighted and attacked by aircraft, this time with more disastrous results. While the action was at its hottest, and the Japanese machines were advancing bravely through a barrage of fire, a heavy explosion was seen to occur just alongside the *California,* quickly followed by a second upheaval. Other detonations were observed, but whether from bombs or torpedoes did not transpire. The great ship was soon in distress and plainly sinking, though on an even keel, and in a surprisingly short space of time she had gone to the bottom, apparently taking most of her crew with her, for only fifty or more survivors were picked up by the destroyers. Intoxicated with their wonderful success, the Japanese aviators pressed on to attack the other battleships, throwing them into such confusion that one dreadnought was seen to ram her next ahead, which had turned suddenly to port, and was thus struck a glancing but powerful blow almost amidships. The damaged ship was identified by several Japanese pilots as the *Oklahoma* or her sister, the *Nevada*, and reported as such on their return. It became clear that she, too, was doomed, for when last sighted she was heeling over at a dangerous angle, and several crowded boats were pulling away from her. Further observation was impossible, for by now the chaser planes from the *Alaska* were up, and in the ensuing combat they shot down all but four of the Japanese machines. These four had been deliberately spared, in order that news of their tremendous success should be promptly borne to Guam, and thence to Japanese headquarters. It was just as well that the *Oklahoma's* end did not come until these witnesses had left, else they might have been diverted by the sight of ponderous turrets and 65-ton guns floating gently away from the deck of the " battleship " as she foundered ! To explain that the crushing disaster that seemed to have befallen the squadron was a cleverly contrived piece of stage management is, perhaps, superfluous. No Japanese bomb had fallen within effective radius of any ship, but at a certain moment explosive charges had been detonated alongside the spurious *California*, giving a realistic impression of bomb hits close to the waterline, where they would prove most destructive. Then the sea cocks had been opened in such a way as to ensure the ship's sinking on an even keel, since too clear a view of the underwater bow or stern section of the mock battleship would have betrayed the trick immediately. The ramming of the *Oklahoma* had also been arranged beforehand. All those who had taken part in this elaborate comedy could congratulate themselves on the faultless manner in which it had been performed. Whether the desired results had been produced remained to be seen, but it was confidently believed that they had. That "faked" battleships should deceive the eye of trained naval officers, as the Japanese naval air pilots were, may seem incredible, until the contributory circumstances are weighed. In the first place, the attack had been delivered at a considerable height, from which position a warship is most difficult to identify. Secondly, the view below was obscured by the smoke-screen which the fleet's destroyers had put up, and still further by gun smoke and bomb splashes. Thirdly, it is a psychological fact that even the clearest-headed men, when engaged in some hazardous feat of arms, are liable to see things as they wish to see them rather than as they are—a phenomenon which explains the contradictory versions of sea battles fought in earlier wars and the long list of apocryphal losses suffered by the enemy which each side compiles from the reports of men present, who honestly believe they are speaking the truth. It is, therefore, in no way surprising that the Japanese airmen who got back to Guam should have reported, in all good faith, that two of the finest American battleships had been sunk, one by their bombs, the other in collision. At Tokyo, where the tidings caused frantic jubilation, their accuracy was never questioned. More than this, the apparent ease with which two great dreadnoughts had been destroyed, one of them by bombs of less than maximum power, engendered a belief that the American type of battleship was more vulnerable to attack than had ever been suspected. Truly Oriental in their contempt for everything pertaining to Western civilisation, even Japanese naval experts found no difficulty in persuading themselves that all American dreadnoughts were structurally defective. This theory had a momentous effect on their plans. Up to now, reckoning one American ship of given tonnage the equal in fighting power of a Japanese ship of the same type, they had felt no confidence in the outcome of an action in which their small fleet would be pitted against a much larger number of American battleships. But if the latter were weakened by some fundamental fault in design or construction, as Japanese experts now believed, numerical superiority would avail them little, and there was, in consequence, no reason to dread the result of an encounter with the American main body. Considerations of this nature, added to the pressing need for some dramatic success, led the Supreme Council to revoke their ban on active operations at sea. The naval command was instructed to make all preparations for a decisive engagement. Squadrons and individual vessels detached on special service were to be instantly recalled, with the view of effecting a concentration of all available ships. This accomplished, the fleet was to be held in readiness to put to sea in full strength at the shortest notice. Every unit, from battleship to submarine, was to sail with its maximum load of fuel. Other orders directed the assembly at Guam, where a large air base had been established, of all efficient naval aircraft except those required for coast defence. Furthermore such fleet auxiliaries— *i.e.* tankers, colliers, repair ships, ammunition ships, and tugs—as were momentarily stationed at other bases, such as Ominato, Kure, and Sasebo, were ordered to proceed at once to Yokosuka. Finally, all navy yards were instructed to lay aside everything but the most urgent work and hold themselves ready to deal with the long list of ship casualties that might be expected in the event of a great engagement taking place. These preparations naturally occupied time, but in less than three weeks they were completed. On September 17 the entire fleet sailed for the Bonin Islands. Meanwhile submarines had been dispatched from Guam to keep an eye on enemy activities at Truk. It was a duty attended with some peril, for the Americans were now very much on the *qui vive*. Their listening posts gave immediate warning of any submarine that came within ten miles of the islands, and both the air and destroyer patrols had been reinforced. One of the Japanese submarines, *I 59*, venturing too far in, was discovered and sunk by depth-charges on September 14, and other boats narrowly escaped the like fate. Beyond reporting the arrival at Truk of numerous warships and merchantmen, which appeared to be transports, the submarine scouts were unable to gather any information of value. It was accordingly resolved to try other methods. On September 20 the airplane carrier *Hosho*, escorted by destroyers, steamed out of Port Lloyd and stood towards the south-east until within 150 miles of Truk, where a squadron of four scouts and eight combat planes took off from her deck. Their orders were to avoid action if possible, but in any case to fly over Truk and make a careful survey of the shipping in port, and to use their cameras freely. Reaching the islands an hour after sunrise they ran into a haze which made observation difficult, though it probably saved them from premature detection. They planed down to a low level and had made a complete circuit of the position and adjacent waters before being molested. But now a heavy fire was opened from the ships and batteries, and air patrols were speeding to attack them. Five machines were lost before the pursuit could be shaken off. On returning to the *Hosho* the survivors were able to report the presence in Truk of at least eight large men-of-war, presumably battleships; four big cruisers, many destroyers, and a dozen vessels of mercantile build, intelligence that received visual confirmation when the photographs they had taken were developed. This news satisfied the Tokyo Naval Staff that a great expedition was about to be launched from Truk; but whereas they held the Pelew Islands to be its goal, the War Council persisted in regarding Guam as the American objective. While the debate was yet proceeding, messages came from the sea that appeared to vindicate the accuracy of the Council's judgment. A Japanese submarine patrolling to the north of Truk signalled that it had sighted a great fleet of vessels steering on a north-westerly course and had got sufficiently close to recognise ten battleships and at least a dozen transports. When sighted, this armada was 70 miles to the north of Truk. Consequently, if making for Guam, as the course denoted, it had still nearly 550 miles to cover, a voyage that would take some 40 hours to complete, assuming the collective speed of the transports to be 14 knots. Though marvelling at the rashness of the enemy in venturing upon such a desperate enterprise, the naval staff could no longer doubt that Guam was about to be attacked. Not a moment was lost in issuing the necessary orders. Less than three hours after the submarine's radio signal had been received, the Japanese battle fleet had left the Bonins with instructions to proceed at utmost speed to Guam. "Everyone in the fleet was confident that we were steaming to fight the greatest sea battle in our history," writes Mr. Nakabashi, the naval historian, who was present in one of the ships. "There was no question of our failing to come upon the enemy and bring him to action soon after he had reached Guam. From the Bonins, our point of departure, to that island was some 860 miles, and we were steaming at 20 knots. We reckoned, therefore, upon reaching Guam three to four hours later than the enemy fleet, which, although it had a shorter distance to travel, was restricted to a speed 6 knots below our own by the presence of its slow transports. Enthusiasm ran high in the fleet. We had heard from the flagship that the enemy had only 10 battleships. Where were the rest? Perhaps they were coming up from some other quarter, for the Americans had already committed so many strategical blunders that no one would have been astonished to see them split up their battle fleet on the eve of action. All the better for us. We had 11 battleships, all faster than the enemy's; we had more cruisers and destroyers, and probably more aircraft as well. It would be strange if we could not fall upon the audacious invaders and utterly destroy them. From Admiral Hiraga (the commander-in-chief) to the youngest bluejacket, all were animated by a single resolve : to win a resounding victory for Emperor and fatherland." We cannot do better than follow the eloquent historian in his lucid account of ensuing events. All that day and throughout the night, he tells us, the Japanese fleet steamed on at high speed, keeping only two or three knots in reserve for the moment of action. On board the flagship *Nagato* messages from submarine and air scouts—the latter operating from Guam—were coming in continually, in each case reporting the steady advance of the enemy towards Guam, though one of the later signals mentioned that the ships appeared to have slackened speed. "At 4 p.m. on October 3, thirty-five hours after leaving Port Lloyd, we had covered approximately 700 knots, and had thus approached to within 150 sea miles of Guam. The following day might deliver the foe into our hands ! Then, like a cold douche, came a signal from the flagship : ' Scouts report enemy fleet altered course at 3.30 p.m. and now steering due east. Raise speed to 22 knots.' Whatever this might presage, our battleships were now ordered to work up to within a knot of their maximum speed. Could the quarry be slipping through our fingers ? The tension was extreme. Some mercurial officers who had been loudest in forecasting an early victory now went about with gloomy faces. Still, we continued to hope until, at 5 p.m. the Admiral signalled : ' Enemy has turned and is retreating south at full speed.' At once we knew that our hopes of battle were dashed to the ground. True, we might, by a long stern chase with full pressure in our boilers, have overtaken the flying foe before he could regain his lair at Truk, but the risks of a dash into enemy waters, with our ships running short of fuel, would certainly not be countenanced by the higher command. At 5.30 the flagship made the expected signal, ' Reduce speed to 12 knots.' The chase was over, and we were now cruising slowly towards Guam, which was no longer in danger of attack. If we had failed to destroy the enemy, we had at least thwarted his design, and saved a vital position from possible capture." It is to be feared, however, that even this crumb of comfort must be denied to the gallant narrator. Guam had never been in the least danger. The expedition whose approach had been so closely shadowed by Japanese scouts, and which had brought the Japanese battle fleet racing down from Port Lloyd, was nothing more than a collection of dummy battleships and empty transports, the latter being old merchant vessels more or less useless for any other service. The ruse had served a double purpose: it had tested and proved the Japanese readiness to fight a fleet action at this stage of the war; secondly, it had diverted attention from any possible interference with the real expedition against the Pelew Islands, which had sailed from Truk a few hours in advance of the decoy armada. Transports conveying the troops for the Pelews had come direct from Hawaii, reaching Truk a week after the Japanese air reconnaissance of that port. Two days later the battle fleet also arrived, having called on the way at Jaluit, where the destroyers and cruisers had refuelled. When the Pelew expeditionary force sailed on October 2, taking a southerly route to avoid submarines from Yap, the battle fleet covered it for two-thirds of the distance (1400 miles), though standing further towards the west. At the same time a squadron of fast cruisers made a cast far to the north, from which direction the Japanese fleet must come, if it came at all. But all doubts on that head were set at rest on October 4, when American submarines which had previously been sent to scout to the north of Guam reported having seen many Japanese battleships steaming south at full speed, obviously bent on intercepting the " live bait " squadron of dummy ships, which at that time were approaching Guam. It was thus perfectly clear that the Japanese main fleet was at least 800 miles distant from Pelew, and therefore in no position to molest the expedition, which was now only two days' steaming from the objective. Nothing was to be feared save cruisers or submarines. As we saw, however, practically all such craft had been recalled from the South Seas nearly a month before, to join the great concentration at Yokosuka. Angaur, the principal settlement in the Pelews, was duly reached on October 6.

A reconnaissance by destroyers having drawn fire from a battery of 6-in. guns which commanded the approach, planes from the airplane-carrier *Harvard* flew in and plentifully distributed phosphorus gas and explosive bombs over the position, whose defenders were quickly put out of action. The actual landing took place without the loss of a single life, and at 9 p.m. on October 6 8000 troops were ashore. Without an hour's delay the Control Force, which experience in previous landings at Truk, Jaluit, and Ponapi had made highly efficient, began its work of unshipping guns, stores, and equipment. In less than a week Angaur had been rendered safe against a surprise attack by the mounting of 7-inch and lighter guns, and the establishment of an aerodrome. The defences proved their efficacy on the 12th, when two Japanese planes from Yap, coming to spy out the land, were pursued and shot down in flames. When news of this successful descent upon the Pelew Islands reached Japan, it created universal dismay, and in many quarters absolute despair. The War Council had to confess itself outwitted at all points, nor did the polite reminder of the naval men, that they had foreseen this precise development and vainly urged the taking of measures to defeat it, allay the mortification of the military chiefs. That the position had now become extremely serious, not to say desperate, was clear to all. By a succession of bold yet well-considered moves the Americans had contrived to modify the whole strategical outlook to their advantage. At the beginning of the war they had been confined exclusively to the eastern sector of the Pacific, apparently with no prospect of breaking the fetters imposed upon them by geographical circumstance. In a fruitless effort to burst through the invisible but rigid cordon they had, in defiance of the elementary laws of strategy, launched their foolhardy enterprise against the Bonins, only to meet with the disaster their folly had invited. But the lesson learned at such bitter cost had not been in vain. From the defeat of the Bonins expedition dated the inception of that new and sounder strategy the fruits of which were now being garnered. With the seizure of the Pelew group the end of the war had been brought within sight, for it could not be long ere Japan was compelled to play her last card as the alternative to owning defeat. At first sight the American position was still far from satisfactory, and might even have been termed precarious. For while the new post at Angaur was now too strongly defended to be capable of reduction by anything less than a powerful force, it was dangerously remote from any large American base, Hawaii being 3,800 and Tutuila 3,600 miles distant. Moreover, the line of approach to Angaur both from Hawaii and Tutuila was outflanked by the Japanese fortress of Guam, and still more so by the island of Yap, which lay only 300 miles to the north-east. Five hundred miles to the west was the coast of the Philippines, in the harbours of which the Japanese might secretly assemble an overwhelming force for the reconquest of the Pelews. To many onlookers it must have seemed as if the United States, in venturing so far towards the west, had thrust its head into the lion's jaws. But a closer survey tended to modify this view. Before establishing themselves at the Pelews the Americans had methodically secured control of all potential enemy bases lying athwart the main route to the islands, and by promptly making use of these bases for their own ships had been able to institute a fairly efficient patrol along the whole line of communication. Though errant Japanese cruisers or submarines might cause trouble, or even serious loss, by striking at the convoys which were now continually passing to and fro along the route in question, such raids could exert no decisive influence on the fortunes of the campaign. Somewhere behind the line of patrols lay the United States battle fleet, no longer tethered to its eastern bases, but henceforth able to strike with full weight at any point between Hawaii and the Philippines, thanks to the floating fuel reserves now available at Jaluit, Ponapi, Truk, and Angaur. Japan could not hope to recover her lost

islands and so arrest this insidious advance into her
own waters until she had defeated the hostile fleet.
Nothing less would suffice to retrieve the situation.
To ignore the challenge and keep her battleships inactive would leave the Americans free to extend their
hold on the western sector of the Pacific by seizing the
Mariana Islands, an operation which had now become
feasible. Notwithstanding their lack of definite intelligence, the Japanese well knew the military power
of the United States to have grown enormously in the
past 18 months. It was not improbable that within
this period the Navy had doubled its strength in every
type of vessel except battleships, nor was it impossible
that the battle fleet had been reinforced. By virtue of
her infinitely superior wealth and industrial resources,
the United States could by this time have equipped
herself with all the materials essential for waging aggressive warfare overseas, while her army might now run
into millions. New tonnage, it was known, was pouring
out of her shipyards, and this shipping furnished her
with all the transports and auxiliaries needed for an
amphibious expedition of the first magnitude. While
the cost of the war to date had been immense, it had
not seriously depleted her coffers. She had an in-
exhaustible supply of foodstuffs and raw materials of
every description. Her people, despite an ingrained
aversion to war, were displaying by a hundred signs
their inflexible determination to continue the struggle
until a lasting and honourable peace had been won.
Now that the tide of war was running so strongly in
their favour they were less inclined than ever to accept
a patched-up truce. All this was known to the rulers
of Japan, who were at the same time painfully conscious of their own less enviable position. The war
had been in progress a year and a half. How much
longer could Japan afford to continue a struggle which
had already taxed her strength to the utmost? She
might, at a liberal estimate, carry on for a further six
months, always provided her home front stood firm.
But the popular temper was not such as to inspire the

Government with confidence on this point. Were it possible to achieve some undeniable success, decisive enough to impress American public opinion with the futility of going on with the war, all might yet be well. Japan had previously caused it to be known through neutral intermediaries that she was willing to entertain reasonable terms of peace. She was prepared to waive an indemnity on condition that the insular territories she had wrested from the United States were confirmed to her. These feelers, however, had produced no encouraging reaction in America, and in the meantime the loss of the Pelews had divested such proposals of whatever claim to attention they might otherwise have possessed. But if the gravity of the outlook was realised in Tokyo, there was as yet no disposition to sue for peace on the enemy's terms. The War Council still pinned its faith to the fleet, which was intact both as to material and morale. With this weapon a blow might be struck at the enemy's heart. How to employ it under the most promising conditions now became the Council's prime concern. Since the American line of approach lay far to the southward, the Bonins were no longer suitable as a main war base for the fleet. Guam would have been ideal for the purpose so far as position went, but it had neither the anchorage room nor shore facilities requisite for a great naval force. Cavite, in Manila Bay, was accordingly selected as the main base, in spite of the considerable distance which separated it from Angaur. The resources of the arsenal at Cavite had been greatly extended under the Japanese occupation, and reliance was placed upon patrols operating from the eastern shores of Mindanao to send warning of any important American movements in time for the main fleet to intervene if Guam—or, as seemed not unlikely, Mindanao itself—were threatened. On October 15, therefore, the whole fleet arrived at Manila, having come by way of the Balingtang Channel to evade observation. But its passage did not go unremarked, for two U.S. submarines, $V\ 7$ and $V\ 11$, which were cruising to eastward of the channel, had

s

sighted the vast procession of ships and duly flashed word to the proper quarter. Since the climax of the naval war was fast approaching, and a clash between the two fleets had become only a question of weeks, it is desirable at this juncture to examine the composition of the rival forces. The effect of the Washington Treaty, signed in February, 1922, had been virtually to stabilise the American and Japanese battle fleets from that date to the outbreak of war, nine years later. At the beginning of hostilities each country had decided to augment its fleet by new construction, but the gigantic battle-cruisers which Japan was rumoured to have laid down had, in fact, never got beyond the stage of paper design. Foreseeing that these vessels could not, in the most favourable event, be ready for service in less than two years, the Japanese had wisely resolved not to dissipate their energies in building ships which were unlikely to play any part in the war, and which might even be rendered obsolete before completion. Other means of reinforcing the exiguous battle fleet lay readier to hand. In the *Kaga* and the *Akagi* they had two vessels which, originally designed as capital ships, had afterwards been converted into airplane carriers to save them from destruction under the ruling of the Washington Treaty. Of these, the 23-knot *Kaga* had never been a complete success, the special functions of an airplane carrier requiring her to be swifter by at least seven knots than the battleships with which she co-operates. The *Akagi* had given more satisfaction, thanks to her speed of 28 knots; but the completion in recent years of the *Hosho* and other fast carriers had provided the Japanese Navy with an ample contingent of such vessels. Consequently, as soon as war appeared imminent, the naval authorities decided to restore the *Kaga* and the *Akagi* to their original designs, since in this way the battle fleet would gain two units of matchless power. The work was put in hand immediately, and to ensure prompt completion most of the guns and armour plates needed to equip the two ships were ordered in Europe.

By June, 1932, both the reconditioned ships were ready for sea. The *Kaga* was now a battleship of 40,000 tons and 23 knots speed, mounting ten 16-inch guns, her vital parts encased in stout mail. The *Akagi* emerged as a battle-cruiser of 44,000 tons, with a main battery of eight 16-inch guns, and capable of steaming at 30 knots. Each in its way was a more powerful ship than any unit of the United States Navy. Their completion brought the Japanese strength up to 12 capital ships. Five were battle-cruisers, with a squadron speed of 28 knots; the other seven were battleships, averaging 22 knots. Of heavy guns this fleet mounted 114 in all, thirty-four being of 16-inch and the remainder of 14-inch calibre. There were also in service four airplane carriers; twenty-three cruisers, including a number of large vessels armed with 8-inch guns; approximately 100 destroyers, and ninety-four submarines of varying tonnage and power. Against this fleet the United States could marshal in the Western Pacific sixteen battleships,* twenty-three cruisers, 115 destroyers, and eighty submarines, with five airplane carriers. The battleships mounted in the aggregate 170 big guns, viz. twenty-two of 12-inch, 124 of 14-inch, and twenty-four of 16-inch calibre. In speed they were inferior to the Japanese, none having a legend velocity above 21 knots, while the older ships, in spite of new boilers, were not good for more than 20 knots. On the other hand, five of the Japanese battleships could steam at 23 knots and two at 22 knots. To the five Japanese battle-cruisers the Americans could oppose no ships of equivalent speed and armament. If, therefore, the Japanese battle fleet was outnumbered numerically and in gun-power, its higher mobility conferred upon it a tactical advantage of the greatest importance. In all other types the two navies were fairly well matched. Since the Japanese destroyers, as a class, were larger, swifter, and more heavily armed than the American boats, these attributes went far to balance the disparity

* At this period the *Utah* and *Arkansas* were absent from the fleet undergoing repairs in home yards.

in numbers. The United States battle fleet, it will be noticed, had not been increased by new construction. Four battle-cruisers, of 52,000 tons each, had been designed early in the war, but, for the same reasons which had restrained the Japanese from proceeding with their new capital ships, these American vessels were built at a very slow rate, and at this time were not even launched. The main constructional effort had been devoted to smaller craft, the demand for which was insatiable. Of these a considerable number was now in service. At one stage of the war the re-armament of several battleships with guns of a larger calibre than those already on board had been seriously contemplated, on the strength of reports which declared the Japanese to have equipped several of their battleships —*Fuso*, *Yamashiro*, *Ise*, and *Hiuga*—with eight 16-inch guns apiece, in place of the twelve 14-inch weapons originally carried. While these reports were accepted as authentic by many naval officers, who seem to have overlooked the technical objections involved, they were scouted by Admirals Muller and Harper, to whose firm opposition it was due that the dangerous experiment of re-arming six American battleships with heavier guns than they were designed to carry was never attempted.* In regard to *personnel*, that imponderable factor which nevertheless counts for much more than material, there seemed little to choose between the rival fleets. During the preceding eighteen months the American crews had been trained to a high standard of proficiency. The percentage of " green " men was now negligible. If the American system of discipline was less draconic than the Japanese, it appeared to give excellent results. As for the officers, the most striking difference was that the average age of American

* It is pertinent to recall that Admiral Jellicoe, when commanding the British Grand Fleet in the world war, was at one period misled by similar rumours into a belief that the Germans had re-armed their 12-inch gun battleships with 14-inch artillery, though the technical difficulties of making such a change would have been well-nigh insuperable. Needless to say, the rumours eventually proved to be unfounded.

senior line executives was considerably above that of corresponding Japanese ranks. Some of the American captains were elderly men. Not a few of the Japanese captains were still in their thirties; several of the Japanese flag officers were barely over forty. Although the impending battle was to be fought at a period when Japan had sustained a series of reverses, there was nothing indicative of a decline in the morale of her sailors. All the evidence points the other way. Practically every Japanese commentator insists that the navy as a whole was thirsting for battle and supremely confident of victory. But the conduct of the Japanese fleet during the action itself renders this assurance superfluous. As most American critics generously admit, had the enemy possessed an additional squadron of battleships the outcome of the duel might have been other than what it was. The Japanese did all that brave and skilful seamen could have done, proving themselves worthy successors of the men who had built up Nippon's sea-power at the Yalu and Tsushima. From every angle of view, the great naval action off Yap was an historic event to which both combatants may look back with sentiments of patriotic pride.

CHAPTER XIX

Both fleets prepare for an early conflict—Americans make a false attack on Yap—Japanese main fleet leaves Manila for Yap—Its composition—Japanese discover they have been outwitted and must fight

For the American naval command it now remained only to make the last and decisive move in their well-conceived plan of campaign. If this succeeded they could count with some confidence on sweeping the Japanese main fleet from the board, either by destroying it or reducing it to a state of military impotence. Its disappearance might not bring the war to an immediate end, but it would inevitably pave the way for measures certain to achieve that purpose at no distant date. Now that the Japanese fleet was known to be at Manila, no time was lost in pressing matters to a conclusion. Admiral Hiraga's presence there was taken as evidence of Japan's determination to fight a general action rather than submit to the loss of further territories in the South Seas. And so the obvious method of tempting him out was adopted : namely, the dispatch of an expedition to Yap, which lay some 300 miles to the north-east of Angaur. Though the operations in view entailed certain risks, there was no hesitation in accepting them. The month following the arrival of the Japanese fleet at Manila was a period of strenuous preparation at every American base. Since Angaur was within airplane radius of the Philippines, the ships detailed for the expedition were ordered to assemble at Truk, where they would be less liable to observation. Once more the squadron of imitation battleships was allotted a highly important *rôle.* This time, however, they were to be joined by a real battleship, the *Florida*, for an object that will duly transpire. Twelve of the freight steamers which had taken part in the feigned attack on Guam were also to be employed again in the guise of "transports." According to the plan, this composite force, attended by a division of cruisers and screening destroyers, was to reach Angaur from Truk on November 16. If it were there observed by Japanese air or submarine scouts no harm would result; in fact, it was very desirable that this should happen. Twenty-four hours later the expedition was to sail for Yap, and not merely approach to within range of the island, but so manœuvre as to suggest that a landing was about to be attempted. The port was to be shelled by the *Florida's* 12-inch battery, aided by the light guns with which her make-believe consorts had been equipped for the sake of appearance. If the fire was returned—and the Japanese were known to have fortified the island—at least one of the false battleships was to simulate damage, but the *Florida* was forbidden to expose herself to serious punishment. The sham attack was to be continued for several hours, and at a suitable opportunity three of the "transports" would move in as though about to disembark troops. As it was more than likely that these ships would be heavily attacked, and perhaps even sunk, they were manned by crews who had specially volunteered for the duty. In the meantime news of the attack would promptly reach Japanese headquarters at Manila, for Yap possessed a high-powered radio plant with which the Americans had studiously refrained from interfering, though their airplanes from Angaur might easily have destroyed it had this appeared desirable. Further, it was probable that the expedition would have been sighted and reported by Japanese scouts while on its way to the island. There was scarcely any doubt that the Japanese battle fleet would hasten at full speed to the relief of Yap. They might suspect a strategem, it was true, but having no means of verifying that suspicion they would almost certainly elect to take the risk. If, as was surmised, the Japanese Commander-in-Chief had explicit orders to prevent at all costs the enemy's seizure of fresh territory, he would have no option but to take his fleet in the direction of Yap the moment he heard of the peril which seemingly threatened the island, without pausing to determine whether the attack was genuine or merely a ruse, such as had been practised in the case of Guam. From Manila to Yap is a voyage of 1,160 miles. It was accordingly calculated that the Japanese fleet, steaming at 18 knots, would appear on the scene in sixty-five hours. Of course it might happen that Admiral Hiraga would travel at his utmost speed, in which case he would be liable to arrive ten hours earlier, that is, at 5 p.m. on the 20th. There was the further possibility that he might be cruising away from his base when the news reached him, a contingency not to be disregarded in view of the fact that American patrol submarines had already sighted his fleet at sea a week after its first arrival at Manila. In these circumstances a rigid schedule of movements was not feasible. The most that could be done was to arrange for the timely appearance of the United States battle fleet at the critical moment. Fortunately, this was not difficult. Admiral Templeton was instructed to sail from Truk on November 15, steering a course towards Angaur. While his battleships were not to go nearer than 100 miles, most of the destroyers and other vessels that had need to replenish their bunkers would enter the harbour at Angaur and quickly refuel there, what time the battleships, screened by the remaining destroyers, held their position at sea until the smaller craft rejoined. This done, the entire force would make for a specified position 70 miles to the east of Yap, its arrival being timed to coincide with the approach of Admiral Hiraga towards the same island. Ample margin was provided for an earlier or later coming of the enemy. To ensure early warning of his approach, no less than twenty American submarines were strung out on a longitudinal line of patrol 150 miles to the west of Yap. Through some section of this line the Japanese fleet was bound to pass, and whether it came in daylight or in darkness, the chance of its getting through unobserved was very slight, for every submarine was equipped with hydrophones. The boats, it should be added, had strict orders not to attack any hostile ships steaming eastward, that is towards Yap. They were to reserve their torpedoes for the enemy on his return from the impending battle. When word of the Japanese approach came to Admiral Templeton he was to head north at full speed, and, passing between the islands of Yap and Uluthi, stand towards the north-west until precise intelligence of the enemy's position and course came to hand. In this way, it was hoped, he would be able to interpose his entire force between the Japanese and their Philippine bases before action was joined. Meanwhile the decoy squadron off Yap was to remain there until ordered to retreat by radio signal from the Commander-in-Chief; but the signal would not be given until the Japanese fleet was within a few hours of the island, since a premature withdrawal of the squadron might decide Admiral Hiraga not to continue his run to the eastward, the immediate peril to Yap having passed. While the false battleships and transports, their mission fulfilled, were to return to Angaur under light destroyer escort, the subsequent movements of the *Florida* were to be determined by events. If possible she was to rejoin the main fleet on its passage north about Yap. Such, then, were the dispositions which, it was hoped, would compel the enemy to accept action in waters remote from his bases and thus enable a decisive result to be obtained. At this time, it should be remembered, the Japanese firmly believed two of the best United States battleships to be at the bottom of the Pacific. Moreover, if they did not know positively of the absence of other vessels in American dockyards, they could be virtually certain that one or two capital ships were undergoing repair and therefore not immediately available. They thus assumed that Admiral Templeton had at most fourteen battleships under his command, and probably not more than thirteen. As we know, however, he had sixteen. Since the Japanese themselves could muster twelve capital ships, all of which were swifter than the American vessels, it is not surprising that they should welcome the opportunity of giving battle under what seemed to them highly propitious conditions. On the American side there was no tendency to minimise the formidable nature of the operations that lay ahead. It was one thing to force an encounter with the hostile fleet; it would be quite another to defeat that fleet when it was encountered. The American superiority in number of heavy ships and weight of broadside was none too great, while the higher speed of the Japanese would give them a tactical advantage which, if skilfully exploited, might well prove decisive. The Japanese Admiral could take advantage of this extra speed either to choose his own range or to make good his retreat if the American fire became too hot. So far as the United States fleet was concerned, its sole chance of getting in a mortal blow lay in developing from the very outset an accurate and overwhelming fire. These considerations having long been evident to the American naval command, every effort was made to improve the shooting of the fleet. Gunnery practice had taken place frequently during the previous year, special attention being paid to firing at extreme range. The turret-gun elevation in eight ships had been raised from 16 degrees to 25 degrees, thus increasing their effective range by 4,000 to 5,000 yards. This change had been proposed as far back as 1923, but reasons of international policy had caused it to be deferred until the outbreak of war. To avoid unduly weakening the Fleet by detaching several vessels simultaneously, each ship was dealt with in turn. The process had therefore occupied nearly eighteen months, and there still remained five vessels which had not yet had their guns raised. Spare guns were held ready to replace those worn out by frequent target practice, with the result that the artillery of the fleet was at all times maintained in a thoroughly efficient condition. As the war progressed various improvements prompted by experience were made in the fire-control installations. In short, nothing that human foresight could suggest for the improvement of gunnery had been neglected. That the Japanese had also devoted attention to this branch of naval preparedness was deemed highly probable. But even if the quality of the shooting on both sides were fairly equal, it was felt that the American preponderance of fifty-six big guns ought to turn the scale. Finally, the fleet possessed in the *Lexington* and *Saratoga* two airplane carriers of unrivalled speed and capacity. All initial dispositions having been made, the Yap expeditionary force, commanded by Rear-Admiral Hubbard with his flag in the *Florida*, sailed from Angaur at 7 a.m. on November 17. At the same moment Admiral Templeton, a hundred miles to the east, was preparing to take his fleet to the appointed position near Yap, there to await intelligence that might herald the clash of battle. The force from Truk had not proceeded far when it received proof of the enemy's vigilance. Torpedoes were fired at the leading ship by a submarine, fortunately without result, the intruder being driven off by destroyers. But twenty minutes later the American radio operators were intercepting messages in a strange code : it was the submarine scout flashing word of what he had seen to Admiral Hiraga at Manila. Two hours afterwards a couple of large Japanese airplanes, probably from Mindanao, came in sight, but did not attempt to attack. Since there was no longer any question as to the discovery of the expedition it was rightly conjectured that the Japanese fleet would very soon be speeding towards Yap. Steaming at 14 knots, and zigzagging to confuse the aim of lurking submarines, Admiral Hubbard held on towards the northeast until early on the morning of November 18, when the island came within sight. His squadron was promptly assailed by Japanese airplanes, which were met and repelled by combat planes from the *Alaska* before they could get within attacking distance. Leaving his " transports " astern, in charge of half the destroyers, Admiral Hubbard, with his ships in battle formation, steamed slowly past the harbour and, at a range of 18,000 yards, opened with his 12-inch guns. Drawing no response, he closed in to 14,000 yards, at which distance the 6-inch guns of his dummy " battleships " were able to join in the cannonade. Thereupon a battery ashore began a slow but well-directed fire, the height of the splashes denoting shells of 7-inch or 8-inch calibre. When one of these pitched uncomfortably near the *Florida*, Admiral Hubbard turned away, for his orders forbade him to imperil this ship. As he turned, his next astern, the pseudo *Arizona*, was hit in the funnels. The position of the battery having been signalled by one of the spotting planes aloft, the *Florida* endeavoured to silence it, but the need for husbanding ammunition prevented a really effective bombardment from being maintained. Though it received at least two direct hits, the shore battery continued to fire at intervals all day and succeeded in hitting three of the dummy battleships—one of which, as prearranged, left the line and steamed slowly out to sea, listing heavily as she went. The fact that yet another enemy battleship had been disabled was doubtless communicated immediately to Admiral Hiraga, whose confidence in a coming victory for his fleet must have soared at the news. At 6 p.m. three of the " transports " approached the shore and manœuvred as if on the point of lowering boats, while to cover the operation the *Florida* and her consorts increased their fire. But at this stage of the proceedings several light guns on the island, hitherto silent, began throwing salvos with great accuracy. Before the three " transports " could withdraw all were hit more or less severely, the *Roanoke* being holed repeatedly and having a number of casualties. Had the hidden guns ashore been of heavier calibre—they were 12-pounder field pieces—nothing could have saved the ships from destruction. As it was, the *Roanoke* foundered during the night, though not before the survivors of her volunteer crew had been taken off. As darkness fell upon the scene the defenders of Yap must have congratulated themselves on their successful resistance. They had, it seemed, held out all day against half the American fleet, inflicting serious damage on more than one ship and visibly frustrating an attempt to land troops. Perhaps, however, the more thoughtful among them were surprised at the comparative feebleness of the attack, and still more so at the temerity of the foe in allowing his transports to come within range of unsilenced guns. Admiral Hubbard, on his part, had no reason to feel dissatisfied with the day's work, since events had fallen out precisely as desired. Remaining during the night at a distance of 30 miles to the south-east of the island, he closed in again shortly before dawn on the 19th, when the performance of the previous day was repeated, except that the *Florida* this time discharged her big guns but rarely. All that day the desultory cannonade continued, punctuated by attacks from Japanese planes. These, however, were too few in number to break through the American cordon of air patrols, and in no case did their bombs take effect. At 4 p.m. a submarine twice torpedoed the dummy battleship *Utah*, which was only kept afloat by the special buoyancy devices with which she had been fitted. Towards nightfall the principal shore battery ceased firing, either from lack of ammunition or because the guns were disabled. To keep up the pretence of a landing operation, four " transports " again approached the shore, whence they were met by a dropping fire from isolated field-guns in well-concealed positions. Loath to expose the gallant volunteer crews of these ships to further loss, Admiral Hubbard finally ordered them out of range. They had played their part well. Sixty hours had now passed since the expedition had left Angaur, and presuming the Japanese Commander-in-Chief to have heard from his scouts very soon after its departure, he might now be only five or six hours away. There was consequently not much time to spare. On the other hand, it was of vital importance that the garrison of Yap should feel themselves endangered up to the last moment, lest reassuring messages from them should cause the oncoming Japanese fleet to halt. Nor was

Admiral Hubbard unmindful of his orders to await direct instructions from the Commander-in-Chief before breaking off the sham attack. But shortly after 9 p.m., when he had ceased fire and was making his dispositions for the night, he received the long-expected signal from his superior officer. This bade him proceed at full speed, with six of his destroyers, to join the main body, which was then about to pass between Yap and the Uluthi islands on its way to cut off the Japanese fleet. The dummy battleships and transports were ordered to return to Angaur, steering a course well to the eastward, which it was hoped would take them clear of any lurking submarines; while as an additional protection the remaining destroyers were to accompany them. Thus at 9.15 p.m. the *Florida* parted from her consorts and proceeded at 19 knots to the rendezvous, leaving the " scarecrow squadron " to make the best of its way back to Angaur. It need only be added that the *Florida* joined the fleet shortly after midnight, her arrival bringing Admiral Templeton up to his full strength of 16 battleships.

To learn what the Japanese were doing while these events were in progress, we must revert to the pages of Mr. Nakabashi,* who gives a clearer and more coherent narrative than is to be found in the official history :—
" During the morning of November 17, a report from Submarine *Ro. 60*, patrolling north of the Pelews, came to hand, announcing it had sighted a large fleet of enemy warships and transports steering N.N.E. The submarine had attacked with torpedoes, though without scoring a hit, and after being hunted by destroyers had emerged six miles astern of the enemy squadron, which was observed to be maintaining its original course. From this intelligence we assumed that the threatened invasion of Yap was about to take place. But how could the enemy be so misguided as to launch such an expedition under the very nose of our fleet? Did not his apparent recklessness indicate some deep-laid scheme to

* *The Japanese Fleet in the American War,* by Nakabashi Rokuro. Seikyo-sha Publishing Office, Tokyo, 1933.

ensnare us to our undoing? Such thoughts, we know, passed through the mind of our Admiral and his staff. But they were no longer free agents. The War Council had issued its decree : ' At the first hint of peril to Yap or Guam, throw in your whole force.' Here was something more than a hint, yet still Admiral Hiraga would have hesitated had he been left free to obey his own intuitions. The enemy was doing precisely what he might be expected to do if he wished to bring about a decisive naval action. Already the transfer of our fleet from the north to the south must have convinced him of our resolve to fight if new insular territories were menaced. Possessing this knowledge, his course was obvious. He need only arrange a spurious attack upon one of our outlying islands, having previously disposed his main force in some advantageous position, to be sure of bringing our fleet to action under such conditions as suited him best. All this seemed clear as daylight to Admiral Hiraga and his staff.* But their orders left them no latitude. When news of the suppositious attack on Yap was received there was no time and still less inclination to solicit fresh instructions from Tokyo. For sailors to attempt to reason with soldiers on a point of naval strategy had always proved futile. Soldiers had directed the conduct of this war so far, and would direct it to the end, despite the fact that it was, and had always been, essentially a struggle in which sea-power was the key factor. But though some of our officers thought they penetrated the American design, they nevertheless welcomed the challenge to decisive combat. Believing the enemy to have been weakened by the loss of several battleships—a belief, alas ! that was to prove illusory—we were willing, nay, eager, to engage him. And so the fleet made ready to sail. All ships had steam raised in their boilers, for the summons which had now come had long been anticipated; but the ships of the

---

* It is of great interest to observe how closely these revelations coincide with the conclusions reached by the American naval strategists who had mapped out the plan of campaign, piecing scattered fragments of evidence into a theory that events confirmed in the minutest particular.

1st Cruiser Squadron, besides several destroyers, were taking in fuel at the oil wharves, and there was no time to wait for these vessels, which were ordered to follow after as quickly as possible. Mine-sweepers having reported the channel clear, the fleet moved out by divisions, the first ships passing Corregidor at 10.30 a.m. The spectacle was a magnificent one as this, the greatest navy ever seen under the flag of Nippon, steamed out to meet the enemy. First went two destroyer flotillas and Rear-Admiral Uyehara's 4th Cruiser Squadron (*Myoko, Ashigara, Yonezawa,* and *Itsukushima*), the blue water of Manila Bay creaming beneath their sharp prows. They were followed by the aircraft carriers, upon whose spacious decks were seen many airplanes, among which moved blue-clad aviators and mechanics. Next in stately array came the battle-cruisers under Vice-Admiral Wada, headed by the colossal *Akagi,* and the smaller but still formidable *Kongo, Hiyei, Haruna,* and *Kirishima.* In the wake of these mastodons steamed the flagship *Nagato,* embodied for tactical purposes in Rear-Admiral Shimizu's 1st Division, which comprised also the *Kaga* and *Mutsu*; and, finally, the 2nd Division—*Ise, Hiuga, Fuso,* and *Yamashiro.* Astern of the battle columns came the 2nd, 3rd, and 5th Cruiser Squadrons, thirteen ships in all. When the 1st Cruiser Squadron caught up with the fleet, Admiral Hiraga would have twenty-one cruisers at his disposal. Of the thirty-three submarines at Manila, the fastest were ordered to follow the fleet at their best speed, eventually to take up such positions as the Commander-in-Chief might direct. The slower boats were also to make for Yap. While it was doubtful whether any submarines except those already patrolling in the vicinity could reach the theatre of operations in time to take part in the actual battle, Admiral Hiraga hoped that they would eventually be on hand to deal with disabled ships of the enemy and perhaps to harass his retreat. As our battle divisions came abreast of Corregidor island the garrison paraded, and their hearty ' Banzais ' came rolling to us across the intervening

water. Cheering them in return, we passed on. No
sooner were we clear of Manila Bay than the fleet took
up its cruising formation—the heavy ships in three short
columns, the airplane carriers ahead, and the cruisers
and destroyers forming a complete screen around us.
Our speed was 18 knots, but since all boilers were now
under steam we could increase our velocity at very
brief notice. Overhead blazed the sun in a vault of
intense blue, unflecked by a single cloud. Visibility
was high, but range-taking at this juncture would have
been rendered difficult by heat refraction. Almost as
far as the eye could reach were the forms of ships, large,
medium, and small. From the funnels of many smoke
was pouring forth, and each ship left a foaming wake of
vivid white as she cleft her way through the glassy sea.
None but visual signals were permitted, for even the
short-range radio might have betrayed us to enemy
scouts. Half-a-dozen times during the day we took in
messages from our patrols, all reporting the enemy's
advance towards Yap. By midnight we had covered
more than 200 knots, but still had some 950 knots to
traverse. It was clear that our destroyers would reach
the scene with their bunkers half emptied. That,
however, would not matter if we met and defeated the
enemy out of hand, in which case the boats could subsequently draw from the heavy ships enough oil to take
them back to port. The night was quite uneventful.
No enemy submarines or airplanes were observed, though
twice we had cause to suspect that radio messages were
being sent from craft invisible to us yet near at hand.
At 10 a.m. on the 18th we had a message from Yap,
reporting hostile battleships within sight of the island,
bearing S.W. At 10.45 came a second report : ' Ten
battleships bombarding us; fleet of transports lying
out of range. Our batteries are in action.' This time it
looked as if the enemy must be earnest. On the previous
occasion, when Guam had been his ostensible objective,
he had never actually approached the island nearer than
several hundred miles, but now, at Yap, he was actually
shelling the defences. What could this mean but that a

T

landing was to be attempted? Further news was now awaited most anxiously, for if the defences were quickly subdued and a landing effected, the covering battleships might withdraw long before we could come up with them. For this reason our Commander-in-Chief turned the fleet on a course slightly more to the south-east, which would bring us across the track of the enemy if he eventually returned towards the Pelews. But as additional messages came in it was obvious not only that Yap was offering a stubborn resistance, but that the attack was being conducted with a singular want of vigour. At 5 p.m. we heard that the defences were still intact, and that the Americans were firing mainly from their secondary armaments, few heavy projectiles coming ashore. Four hours later the island reported the sharp repulse of an attempt to land, three enemy transports having been badly hit before they could steam out of range. At 10 p.m. came a message: 'Enemy no longer in sight.' All night long we remained in communication with our gallant comrades at Yap, in breathless anticipation of news that the attack had been resumed; for if the enemy had really given up his enterprise our hopes of bringing him to action would be dashed. Conceive, then, the relief we felt on learning at 8 a.m. that hostile battleships were again off the island and had reopened their bombardment. But again, we asked ourselves, why does he persist in this crazy operation, knowing as he must that our fleet is racing eastward at full speed? Why expend his ammunition and risk damage to his ships in this senseless undertaking when he might soon have to bear the brunt of attack by our whole fleet? By this time Admiral Hiraga was full of suspicion as to the genuineness of the enemy's manoeuvres, but still he was constrained to go on. If he turned back and Yap did, after all, become the prize of the Americans, how should he justify himself? In truth, we had now no choice but to conform to the enemy's movements, a course that became inevitable when we yielded him the initiative, as, thanks to the blunders of the Supreme War Council, we had done.

It lay with him to make a thrust in this direction or in that, while we, ignorant whether such movement was genuine or feigned, had nevertheless to change our guard to meet it. It must be confessed, however, that few in the fleet outside staff circles suspected a deception in this particular instance. Too many of our officers, imbued with a contempt for American intelligence, were ready to believe the enemy capable of any mistake, however flagrant. To this overweening confidence in our intellectual superiority may be traced not a few of our misfortunes in the war. But at present we had little time for moralising. Frequent messages from Yap recorded the continuation of this second day's bombardment, and although the ships' fire was not heavy, it had by now subdued the main defences. That evening we fully expected to hear of a landing. Instead, there came at 7 p.m. a report that four transports had been driven off by the fire of field guns. Two whole days, therefore, had the enemy squandered in a half-hearted attack on an island whose defences were of the feeblest ! At 9 p.m. came the usual report : ' Enemy withdrawing to sea. We are endeavouring to repair our batteries, but have only two guns left in action.' By now we had come within 360 miles of the island, and at the present rate of travel would reach it at 5 p.m. the next day. If the enemy resumed his assault in the morning he could not escape us, since by turning more to the south we should cut athwart his line of retreat. We must, in any event, continue our voyage throughout the night. At dawn we received from Yap a message reporting that the enemy was no longer in sight. This, though indicating that the attack had been abandoned, was not sufficiently definite for us to act upon, since at any moment the American fleet might return and continue its futile bombardment. But as the morning hours passed without bringing such news the Admiral at length concluded that the enemy, having got wind of our coming, had finally given up his designs upon Yap and was returning to his base at Angaur, or, more probably, to Truk. This supposition was confirmed at 2 p.m., when two of our

swiftest airplanes, which had been sent ahead to reconnoitre, sighted nine American battleships and many
transports some 200 miles E.S.E. of Yap, steaming
slowly towards the south-east.* Once more, it seemed,
the foe had escaped us. But two problems remained
unsolved : what could have reduced the American
squadron which had bombarded Yap from ten units to
nine, and where was the rest of the American fleet?
As to the first, we could only hope that one battleship
had fallen a victim to gunfire from the island, or perhaps
to our submarine patrols. As to the second puzzle,
we judged the remainder of the fleet to be at Truk or
somewhere in that neighbourhood. In any case it was
not within reach. The urgent need of the moment was
to determine our next step. As we were now scarcely
60 miles from Yap, the Commander-in-Chief decided
to push on to the island, where the small craft could
refuel. By that time we might have received fresh
intelligence to guide our future movements. So at
2·30 p.m., reducing speed to 16 knots, we pursued our
way to Yap, having meanwhile detached planes to
reconnoitre the Pelews and surrounding waters. Once
more we had drawn blank. There seemed no end to this
aimless game of hide-and-seek with an opponent who,
whatever his other defects, had proved himself master
of the art of mystification. Then, of a sudden, philo-
sophic apathy was transformed into breathless excitement. Again there came news that the enemy fleet had
been sighted—not, however, where we supposed it to be,
some hundreds of miles to the east, but almost due west
of us, and only 100 miles away ! At first we flatly
refused to believe the apparently impossible tidings,
which came from patrol submarine *Ro. 57.* But our incredulity was soon resolved by messages from another
submarine scout, who reported ' Great enemy fleet in
sight,' giving a position and course which coincided
closely with the previous message from *Ro. 57.*
Instantly the Admiral ordered the fastest airplanes to

* This, of course, was the " scarecrow squadron " on its way back
to Angaur, making a wide *détour* to the east, as instructed.

make for the position indicated, and a few minutes later we saw machines rising from the decks of their carriers. At the same moment the fleet was ordered to turn eight points to port in succession, which had the effect of changing our course from due east to due north.   Even as this order was obeyed a thrill ran through the whole fleet.   By instinct rather than knowledge we knew the hour of action to be approaching.   In my ship (the *Nagato*) we prepared quietly for battle.   Nothing remained to be done when, half an hour later, we heard that course had again been altered, this time six points to port—which meant we were heading straight for the enemy—and the signal ' Action Stations ' flashed from the flagship.   But in spite of this suppressed excitement, one asked one's self repeatedly :   What does it all mean ?   How is it possible for one great enemy fleet to be in the west and another in the east?   Can it be that the Americans have created entirely new battle squadrons?   But in that case, why have they divided their forces, instead of keeping them united in one overwhelming armada? "   As our eloquent Japanese historian proceeds to devote several pages to speculative answers to the questions he himself propounds, we will now take leave of him and transfer our attention to the United States Fleet.

CHAPTER XX

NOVEMBER, 1932

Composition of U.S. fleet—Conflict in the air precedes main action—
The Battle of Yap—Superior strength of American forces results
in victory after desperate fighting—Japanese lose five capital
ships, Americans only two

WHEN Admiral Templeton sailed from Truk the force
under his immediate command was organised as
follows : Fleet flagship, *West Virginia.* Battleship
Divisions : No. 1, *Colorado, Maryland,* with *West
Virginia* incorporated for tactical purposes. No. 2,
California (flagship of Vice-Admiral McArthur, Second-
in-command), *Tennessee, Idaho, Mississippi.* No. 3,
New Mexico, New York, Oklahoma, Nevada. No. 4,
Pennsylvania, Arizona, Texas, Florida, Wyoming.
Cruiser Divisions : No. 1, *Hartford, Olympia, Columbus,
Atlanta.* No. 3, *Albany, Kansas City, Los Angeles,
Portland.* No. 4, *Troy, Cleveland, Denver, Wilmington.**
No. 5, *Cincinnati, Richmond, Raleigh, Detroit.* No. 7,
Omaha, Memphis, Milwaukee. No. 8, *Pittsburgh, Huron,
St. Louis.†* Six destroyer squadrons, numbering 115
destroyers. Air squadrons Nos. 1, 2 and 3, comprising
the carriers *Lexington, Saratoga, Alaska, Montauk* and
Curtiss,‡ carrying between them 190 airplanes. Two
submarine divisions, each of five V-class boats, with a
speed of 21 knots. On this cruise the fleet sailed without

---

* The twelve foregoing ships were all of the new 10,000-ton class,
built from 1925–26 onward.

† These three were old armoured cruisers, but still good for about 19
knots.

‡ A new vessel, named after the *Curtiss* sunk at the battle of Lubang
in March 1931 (*vide* Chapter II).

its auxiliaries, none of which were fast enough to accompany the main squadrons when steaming at full speed. But no less than thirty of these auxiliary vessels, mostly fuel and repair ships, were at this moment on their way from Truk to Angaur, the movement being part of the comprehensive dispositions ordered by the Bureau of Operations. As the waters around Yap had always been regarded as the predestined zone of battle, the dispatch of these auxiliaries to Angaur would ensure the timely provision of fuel and repair facilities for the fleet when the action was over.

It was at 3 p.m. on November 20 that the Japanese Admiral heard for the first time that the whole American fleet was in a position 160 miles W.N.W. of Yap, which placed it only 100 miles from his own force. He thus found himself cut off from his base by an enemy whose presence in that quarter he had never suspected. Even had he wished to avoid action, he could not have done so now, for his superiority in speed was not sufficient to enable him to slip away round either flank of the American fleet. Part of his force must inevitably be brought to action. Moreover, his destroyers had not enough fuel left to take them back to port if they travelled under full power. We know, however, that he had made up his mind to fight.

The rival fleets were now drawing together at a collective speed of 40 knots. The American battle divisions were in line ahead disposed abeam, with two cruiser squadrons thrown out in advance, one on either beam, and one astern. The air scouts on each side were speedily in touch, and in spite of much mutual interference they contrived to keep their respective admirals informed of each enemy manœuvre. The action began as it had often been predicted the next great naval battle would begin—by a violent and reciprocal air offensive.

In view of his adversary's superior speed, Admiral Templeton was particularly anxious to disable one or more of the Japanese major ships at an early stage of the combat, hoping and believing that rather than desert

his crippled vessels Admiral Hiraga would stay and fight
it out to the bitter end.   Accordingly at 3.20 p.m. fifty
planes, the majority being bombers and torpedo-carriers,
took off from the *Lexington* and *Saratoga* with orders
to concentrate their attack on the leading battleship
of the first column they sighted.   In forty minutes they
were within view of the Japanese fleet and were rushing
to attack when suddenly a powerful flight of enemy
machines, which had been patrolling at a higher level,
came dropping down to intercept them. To give any
detailed account of this scrimmage in the air would be
impossible.   In the first minute of the fierce *mêlée*
nearly a dozen planes went down out of control.   Thrice
amidst the crackle of machine-gun fire did head-on
collisions take place, the Japanese aviators never hesi-
tating to ram when otherwise baulked of their prey,
preferring to immolate themselves rather than allow
the American bombs to reach their ships.   Less than
half the American machines broke through and made for
the Japanese fleet, which received them with a hurricane
of fire.   How different now were the circumstances
from those which aviation enthusiasts, deceived by
artificial peace tests against helpless targets, had
pictured !   From the ships below, turning and twisting
at high speed, came a veritable stream of shell, the
incessant detonations of which caused the planes to rock
as in a gale of wind.   The air was alive with steel
splinters and poisoned with acrid fumes.   Still the indo-
mitable pilots held on, and were almost within range
when six Japanese machines crossed in front of them at
lightning speed, leaving a thick curtain of yellowish
vapour in their wake as they passed.   As the American
fliers drove through this curtain they were instantly
conscious of a choking sensation, accompanied by rack-
ing head pains.   Through some culpable oversight they
had not been equipped with gas masks.   The omission
was fatal.   All but two of the planes dived headlong
into the sea, their pilots having been disabled by the
noxious fumes.   The occupants of the remaining two
machines—one a bomber, the other a torpedo-plane—

which had passed through the gas screen before it had properly developed, got but a whiff of the poison, and though deathly sick were able to carry on. But being half-blinded and choked, it is not surprising that they should have mistaken a cruiser squadron for a battleship division. Both accordingly attacked the *Myoko*. The torpedo-plane was just about to release its weapon when apparently it was hit by a shell and blown to pieces. The bomber got one hit on the cruiser and was then shot down, the pilot and observer, Lieuts. Cuthbertson and Martyn, being saved by a Japanese destroyer. Although the *Myoko* was badly smashed up about the forecastle, she was not put out of action. Such was the result of an attack that had cost nearly forty machines, barely a dozen of the planes having survived. While this raid was in progress the Japanese, on their part, had launched a similar offensive against the American fleet, though with scarcely better fortune. True, they blew a hole in the *Pennsylvania's* upper deck and gassed eighty men in the *Texas*, but all but seven of their machines were brought down. Even at this early phase it was made clear that a decision must be achieved by weapons other than the air arm. Since the supply of aircraft on each side was strictly limited, neither felt disposed to risk any further machines in this way until conditions became more favourable. At 4.30 p.m. the advanced cruiser screens were in contact and hard fighting at once developed. Rear-Admiral Blaine, leading the 1st Cruiser Division, found himself attacked by eight large Japanese vessels, and but for the prompt arrival of the 3rd Cruiser Division, under Rear-Admiral Appleton, matters would have gone ill with him. In this first bout the *Hartford*, *Olympia*, and *Portland* all sustained damage and heavy casualties, but they had the satisfaction of seeing an enemy cruiser, the *Ashigara* blow up and sink. A Japanese detroyer dash at the 1st Division was repulsed with shattering loss to the assailants. As the outposts thus tested each other's mettle the heavy squadrons were drawing rapidly within gun-range. The direction of both fleets was roughly W.N.W., but the lines were converging when, at 5.15 p.m., the range then being 28,000 yards, Admiral Hiraga altered course three points to port and increased his speed. At the same moment his cruisers again advanced, striving to roll up the American cruiser divisions by sheer weight of numbers. Simultaneously three Japanese destroyer flotillas broke through their line of cruisers and steamed straight for the American van, putting up a thick pall of smoke as they went. But sharp eyes aloft perceived what was happening and flashed word of it to Admiral Templeton. Taking advantage of their greater speed, the Japanese were trying to cut across the head of his line at right angles— in other words, to " cross his T "—a manœuvre that would have brought his leading divisions under an annihilating fire. To counter the attempt he turned away four points, signalling his leading division to open fire on the enemy's van. The target was invisible to the gunners, but the spotting aircraft constantly transmitted information as to the enemy's position, range, speed, and course. At 5.25 p.m. the *Colorado* opened with a two-gun salvo, the shots pitching slightly ahead of and over the leading Japanese ship, which was taken to be the *Mutsu.* Sights having been adjusted, the *Colorado, Maryland,* and *West Virginia* began firing full salvos, and at each discharge twenty-four tons of steel went roaring towards the enemy. Sharp and fast from the aircraft spotting officers came radio-phone reports : " Salvo one, 600 yards over," with data as to change of rate and deflection. At the third salvo came the welcome signal " Straddle," and at the fourth and fifth " Several hits on leading ship." Fire was now switched on to the second vessel, either the *Nagato* or the *Kaga,* two hits being recorded in the eighth salvo. Considering the enormous range the practice was good, but it involved a heavy expenditure of ammunition for a minute percentage of hits. Still, the few shells that did get home proved very destructive, falling at a steep angle and penetrating through the decks to explode with stunning force inside the ship. Though the *Nagato* was struck but twice, she seemed to be severely damaged forward, and temporarily dropped out of the line.   One 16-in. shell hit the *Mutsu*, wrecking her second turret and putting the guns out of action. Unwilling to risk graver injury, Admiral Hiraga turned away and opened the range, whereupon the American fire promptly ceased. The Japanese manœuvre had been foiled. Determined now to bring his superior weight of broadside to bear, the American Admiral signalled for full speed and swung his line four points inward, accomplishing this move under a screen of smoke put up by his destroyers, while overhead his airmen attacked the hostile planes with such fury that the latter had no time to observe what was passing below. Before the smoke had thinned sufficiently to reveal his approach, Admiral Templeton's leading divisions were within 17,000 yards of the enemy's centre, upon which they opened a terrific cannonade. No less than eight ships were concentrating on the *Ise* and *Hiuga*, which thus became the target for about ninety of the heaviest guns. All the American vessels were firing with the utmost rapidity, averaging only forty seconds between each full salvo. To observers ahead, watching this line of grey leviathans, their sides seemed to explode at regular intervals in gouts of flame and brown smoke. Every minute more of the American battleships were coming up to join in the terrible drum fire that was now smiting both the centre and rear of the Japanese fleet. Admiral Hiraga strove desperately to draw out of range, but the damage that several of his ships had received had reduced his squadron speed to 20 knots, and he no longer had the advantage in mobility. At this, the fiercest stage of the action, many noteworthy episodes occurred, one or two of which must be recorded. The five Japanese battle-cruisers had not hitherto been closely engaged, as except for the *Akagi* their armour protection was too light to withstand severe pounding, and Admiral Hiraga had therefore held them in reserve, to await an opportunity favourable for their intervention. But his position was becoming so desperate that he resolved to take a bold step. At 5.40 p.m., therefore, he made certain signals to Vice-Admiral Wada, whose five magnificent battle-cruisers at once turned 16 points and raced eastward at full speed, just beyond range of the American guns. On the way they fell in with Admiral Winthrop's 4th Cruiser Division, which was covering the left flank of the battle fleet against destroyer attack. By now Admiral Wada's ships were beginning to turn northward again, and as they broke through the smoke pall they sighted Winthrop's division only 10,000 yards away. The Japanese were swift to seize the chance thus presented. A burst of fire came from the *Akagi's* huge 16-in. guns, promptly echoed by the 14-inch batteries of her consorts, and in less than a minute the cruiser *Troy* was a shattered wreck, lying on her beam-ends, with half the crew dead or wounded. The *Cleveland* also got her death wound, and both the *Denver* and *Wilmington* were hit before they could steam beyond reach of those murderous broadsides. Even as the sound of this heavy cannonade far astern warned Admiral Templeton that something was amiss, his air scouts notified him of a new development. Having disposed of the 4th Cruiser Division Admiral Wada held on his northerly course for another five minutes and then swung sharp to the westward, his five battle-cruisers, thanks to their much greater speed, now drawing parallel with the rear of the American line, consisting of the 4th Battleship Division. Originally the *Florida* and *Wyoming*, as the two weakest ships, were ahead of the three more powerful units of their Division, but as the action progressed and the line was advancing at full speed to fall upon the Japanese centre, the *Florida* and *Wyoming* had dropped behind and were now several cable-lengths astern of the rest. Upon these two ships fell the concentrated salvos of Admiral Wada's battle-cruisers. In the few minutes that elapsed ere the rest of the Division—*Pennsylvania, Arizona,* and *Texas*—realised the position and came to the aid of their hard-pressed comrades, the Japanese guns had taken a heavy toll. Hit a dozen times by 16-inch and 14-inch shell, the *Wyoming* was leaking badly and had lost way. Her foremast and both funnels were gone, the stern group of turrets was disabled, and water was entering the starboard engine-room through a hit below the water-line. Still worse was the plight of the *Florida*. One of the first shells from the *Akagi* had struck the conning-tower, killing Admiral Hubbard and most of his staff. The ship was thus temporarily out of control, and before she could be steadied on her course she was hit by three full salvos. Then an amazing thing happened. One, or perhaps two, of her after magazines must have exploded, for the whole stern section of the ship blew up, and those who were watching expected every instant to see her go to the bottom. But although practically one-third of her hull had been blown away, the battle-ship still kept afloat, and afloat she remained when the enemy passed on to seek other prey. Not until half an hour later did the *Florida* take her final plunge. The delay enabled all her surviving officers and men to be saved, but 350 had perished. Having delivered this brilliant stroke and inflicted such heavy loss on the American rear, Admiral Wada would have done well to retrace his course and join the main fleet, since by now he had drawn upon himself the attention of all the American battleships. Moreover, he had saved the situation, his surprise attack having relieved the strain on the Japanese centre; for the American Commander-in-Chief, on finding part of his line between two fires, had hauled off to the north-east and was now coming down to deal with this daring antagonist. But whether Admiral Wada stretched his orders or became momen-tarily seized with the lust of battle is a question upon which even the Japanese historians are at variance. It is certain, however, that he held straight on to the west and fought a running action with more than half the American battle fleet before finally turning away to rejoin Admiral Hiraga. But by then it was too late. Before the *Florida* and *Wyoming* were battered into silence their guns had done good work, inflicting heavy punishment upon the *Akagi* and the *Haruna*.

The former's thick armour saved her from serious injury, but the *Haruna* had a big hole just forward of the bow turret, and steaming as she was at 29 knots a great deal of water from the bow wave poured through this rent. Very soon she was perceptibly down by the head and it became necessary to slacken speed. In the meantime the *Akagi, Hiyei,* and *Kongo* had all suffered in exchanging salvos with the other American battle-ships, the *Hiyei* having a turret blown up. It was at this juncture that Admiral Wada, belatedly thinking of discretion, tried to disengage his squadron, relying on his great speed to do this without difficulty. But the *Haruna* had now dropped to 22 knots, nor could she maintain this pace for long without putting a perilous strain on her bulkheads. As more water entered her bows she slowed to 18 knots and then to 16, at which moment the other battle-cruisers were racing past her on their way to rejoin the fleet. The Americans, observing the *Haruna's* crippled condition, were plying her with shell, and so intense was the fire focused upon her that she was frequently obscured by a forest of great waterspouts. Admiral Wada may well have hesitated as to his course of action. To stand by his stricken consort meant the destruction of his whole squadron, yet to leave her to her fate was an act which, however necessary, must have been repugnant both to him and his gallant comrades. His next movements were marked by an indecision which was not, perhaps, unnatural in the circumstances. For a few minutes he circled round the *Haruna*, drawing upon his other ships part of the fire which had scourged her; but this manœuvre did not suffice to avert disaster. Riddled with shell, waterlogged, and unmanageable, the *Haruna* was clearly doomed, and now American airplanes were winging down to finish her off. Seeing that no more could be done, Admiral Wada steamed away at his best speed, leaving the great ship in her death-throes. She did not sink until 6.40 p.m., her exceptionally well subdivided hull having withstood five torpedoes from the airplanes before its buoyancy was finally destroyed.

Out of her complement of 1,200, over 300 officers and men were picked up. This, however, was not the only loss that Admiral Wada had to lament. During his headlong flight his ships were hit frequently by shell, and the *Kongo*, with her steering gear damaged, sheered out of line just as the squadron was leaving the zone of fire. A minute later she was attacked by six American airplanes, which charged home regardless of a heavy fire and planted two torpedoes in her side. Though still afloat she could now barely move, and as other planes were swooping down to lance her vitals anew, Admiral Wada saw the futility of lingering on the scene. With his squadron reduced to three units, all of which bore the scars of battle, he held on his course, tormented by the persistent airplanes which followed in the hope of claiming yet another victim but eventually winning through to the battle fleet without further loss.

Incidentally, the torpedo-plane had once more demonstrated its complete superiority over the bombing machine as an instrument of naval combat. The heaviest bombs carried by planes which it was possible to operate from the carrier ships were 600-pounders, and in no case did these prove effective against capital ships, though several smaller vessels were destroyed by them. Nothing less than a 1,000-pounder bomb appeared to be capable of inflicting vital injury on a capital ship, and missiles of this calibre could not be transported by ship planes, though well within the capacity of machines flying from a shore base. While the action so far had surpassed in fury every other sea fight of modern times, the issue still hung in the balance. During the heaviest phase of the cannonade against the Japanese centre the *Hiuga* had been hit repeatedly, and but for Admiral Wada's timely intervention both this ship and the *Ise* would probably have been destroyed. As it was, the *Hiuga* had half her guns out of action and 3000 tons of water in her hull. The *Ise* could still use most of her armament, but was terribly battered, and with her rudders disabled was compelled to manœuvre by means of her screws. But even in these critical

moments the Japanese gunners had fired with cool precision, and their handiwork was painfully apparent in the American line.   The *New Mexico* presented a most extraordinary spectacle.   While turning suddenly to avoid her next ahead (the *Mississippi*), whose steering gear had been damaged, she was raked by successive salvos which swept her deck like a giant's broom.   Her funnel, both cage masts, and most of the superstructure were wrecked.   The main mast in its collapse fell diagonally athwart the two after turrets, effectually masking their fire for the rest of the day.*
In the unarmoured 5-inch battery a heavy shell burst among the crews who were standing by to repel destroyer attack, and caused dreadful carnage.   The salvos which wrought such havoc in the *New Mexico* were believed to come from the *Nagato*, whose firing was observed to be particularly accurate all through the battle.   The *Mississippi* was also handled very roughly by this ship and the *Mutsu*, and only kept her station in the line with difficulty.   It was now 7 p.m.   Taking advantage of the diversion created by his battle cruisers, Admiral Hiraga steamed at his utmost speed towards the north-west, his rear ships being now some 30,000 yards ahead of the American van.   But for the loss in speed suffered by certain of his vessels he could easily have shaken off pursuit; but he was forced to suit his pace to that of the crippled *Hiuga*, whose speed was reduced to 17 knots.   Still, night was coming on, and if the enemy could be kept at bay for another hour or two the fleet would be safe, for the Americans were unlikely to press the chase so far to the westward, if only because their fuel would be running low.   Moreover, they had several damaged ships to embarrass their movements.   The 2nd Division, which had suffered most, was now the Japanese van, while the 1st Division, comprising the three most powerful ships—*Kaga*,

---

* Being merely secured to a ring on the upper deck, the cage masts in the American ships were liable to fall if the deck in their vicinity was damaged by shell fire, and several did so fall, in some cases with disastrous results.

Nagato, and *Mutsu*—followed in its wake. Further astern the destroyer flotillas kept a smoke-screen permanently in the air, and planes from the carriers fought gallantly to keep the American aviators from coming within sight of the fleet. These precautions notwithstanding, two or three American machines were able to report its movements, and Admiral Templeton, realising that the last chance of getting in a decisive blow was slipping away, resolved to strike while yet there was time. Leaving the more badly-injured ships in charge of cruisers and destroyers, he pressed forward with twelve battleships at a speed of 20 knots, and at 7.20 p.m. had the satisfaction of finding the quarry again within reach of his guns. In view of the failing light and the Japanese smoke clouds, long-range practice controlled by aircraft would have been ineffective, so Admiral Templeton did not begin firing until the range was down to 16,000 yards. Then his 1st and 2nd Divisions opened with all guns, to be reinforced soon afterwards by such ships of the 3rd and 4th Divisions as had been able to maintain the pursuit. The principal target was the *Kaga*, but other ships were directed to concentrate on the *Mutsu*, and, as the range still further decreased, the *Nagato* also. Most American versions of this phase of the action lay stress upon the grim grandeur of the scene. In the gathering dusk every flash of gun or exploding shell was intensely brilliant, and the tall columns of water thrown up by falling shot stood out against the gloom like giant wraiths emerging from some spirit world of the undersea. Though the distance was short for the big guns that were in action, visibility was so poor that hits were infrequent, and at 7.30 p.m. Admiral Templeton ordered salvo firing to cease while the line forged steadily onward, from time to time checking the rangetakers' figures by a sighting shot. At 7.45, after " browning " with salvos of shrapnel and high-explosive the Japanese destroyers which had been putting up the smoke screen, he sent two of his own destroyer squadrons to drive them off. This was accomplished, though not without serious loss to the

U

American boats.   At 8 p.m., the range then being down to 13,000 yards, and visibility, thanks to the partial dispersion of the smoke screen, somewhat improved, the Admiral reopened with all guns on the Japanese battleships, which immediately replied.   At this comparatively short range hitting began almost at once, and there were moments when the *Kaga* seemed to be spouting flame at every seam, so continuous were the shell bursts on her sides and decks.   Nor did the ships ahead of her escape their due meed of punishment. Every man in the American fleet, knowing this to be the final chance of settling accounts with the enemy, did his utmost to ensure a crushing victory.   But although engaged in so unequal a combat, the Japanese fought with iron determination.   At 8.05 the *Colorado* had her forward turret wrecked, and almost simultaneously received two hits which drove in her armour and started a dangerous leak.   With her guns still roaring she dropped out of the line, but not before she was able to claim a share in disabling the *Kaga*, which was now heavily on fire and losing way.   In truth, the great Japanese battleship had taken her death blow. The merciful darkness hid her gaping wounds, but flames were leaping from rents in her hull and only one turret remained in action.   As she came abreast of the American line practically every ship turned its guns on her.   Under this torrent of levin-bolts she seemed to crumple up.   Louder than the din of gunfire and bursting shell were the explosions that now racked her as the fire reached the forward magazines.   The end came in one mighty volcanic eruption that shook the heavens, lighting up the whole sea with the glare of noonday.   Then all was darkness again, and though American destroyers dashed to the spot on an errand of mercy, they found no trace of ship or crew.   A vessel of 40,000 tons, manned by 1500 souls, had been utterly blotted out.   Scarcely had the reverberations of that terrific blast died away ere the American guns were seeking a new victim.   It was now the turn of the *Mutsu* to feel their concentrated fire.   An amorphous shadow in the deepening night, she steamed doggedly ahead, jets of flame from her guns alternating with the golden-red splash of shell as they detonated against her armour or flimsier topworks. And then there happened a thing so strange, so inexplicable, that even the Japanese historians differ as to its meaning. Let us quote Commander Elmer, of the *Tennessee*, whose narrative of the battle,* distinguished as it is by a cool, objective appraisal of every incident, is of greater value for documentary purposes than the more dramatic versions penned by some of his colleagues. "At 8.25 p.m.," he writes, "the *Kaga* having previously blown up, our division was hotly engaged with the *Mutsu* and *Nagato*, while some of the van ships were already reaching out at Japanese battleships still further ahead, believed to be of the 'Fuso' class. Suddenly our spotters reported the *Mutsu* to have turned eight points to the right, which of course meant that she was coming straight at us. Ships sometimes yaw in this way when their steering-gear is hit, but they are always brought back to their proper course by manœuvring the propellers. As the enemy battleship now presented her bows to us we naturally raked her, our gunners firing more rapidly than I had believed possible. Through my periscope I saw her simply smothered with big-calibre shell, and expected every instant to see her turn again to resume her original line of direction. But to my astonishment she came steadily on, and though her head had pointed first to our van, the progressive advance of our line was such that if she held on her present course she would intersect our division just astern of the *Tennessee*. Could it be that her officers, believing themselves doomed, had decided to commit hara-kiri on the grand scale? As the range closed to 12,000, then to 11,000, and even to 10,000 yards, we fired and fired till the guns grew hot and the paint on their chases rose up in blisters. But though the target was now so conspicuous, and coming

* "Extracts from a Naval Officer's Diary," by Quincy A. Elmer. *Atlantic Monthly*, May, 1934.

nearer every moment, I am afraid the unusual sight of a big battleship charging headlong at us upset the nerves of the gunners, not only in our ship but in the whole fleet, for I observed that many of the salvos were going wide. The *Mutsu* herself shot with wonderful accuracy from her six remaining guns. Since the *Colorado* had fallen out our fleet had been led by the flagship, *West Virginia*, and I saw this vessel hit by salvo after salvo from the onrushing enemy, who seemed resolved to dash right through our line. Had anyone told me beforehand that even the largest battleship could endure the converging fire of more than a hundred big guns at a range of only five miles without being sunk outright, I should have laughed at him. Yet this was the very ordeal that the *Mutsu* was now enduring, and she was still above water. But as she came nearer and yet nearer I could see her, as it were, disintegrating under the rain of sledge-hammer blows. Her massive heptapod foremast was a tangle of twisted steel. The first funnel had vanished, while the second stack, riddled like a colander, was tilting sideways at an acute angle. Almost every second some piece of *débris* flew into the air : now it was a great fragment of deck plating or casemate armour, then a boat derrick, and next a whirling mass of objects that may have been men. At this point-blank range our shells seemed to be tearing through the ship from end to end. And still the *Mutsu* came on. But now her bows were so deep in the water that shells began to smash through the forecastle deck and plunge into the machinery. At 8.40 p.m., the range being then down to 7,000 yards, the Japanese battleship had stopped and was drifting broadside on to us. Her people had no intention of surrendering, for two guns still kept up a slow fire, so there was nothing for it but to finish her off. We gave her two more salvos, and when last I saw her she was heeling over at 35 degrees, clearly on the point of sinking. Our airmen, who now came up, claim to have sunk her with their torpedoes, but it was really our guns that had done the work." It was now close on

9 p.m. If in this running fight the Japanese had lost two of their finest battleships, they had succeeded in inflicting heavy damage on their pursuers. The flagship *West Virginia*, hit a dozen times by 16-inch shell at close range, was making water rapidly. Two turrets were disabled, and there were more than 400 casualties, including the Commander-in-Chief, who had been knocked senseless by a splinter of steel. Only by getting all the pumps to work could the flow of water into the forward compartments be checked. The *Colorado*, also, had ceased to be effective and had fallen miles astern. The *Maryland* was intact so far as fighting equipment went, but many of her executives had been killed. Few of the remaining ships had escaped hits of a more or less serious character, and barely half-a-dozen were in a condition to maintain their full speed. But Vice-Admiral McArthur, upon whom the command had devolved when Admiral Templeton was struck down, could not bring himself to abandon the chase without making one more effort. Straightening out his depleted line, he steamed on in his flagship, the *California*, at 18 knots, firing at such enemy ships as were still visible in the growing darkness. At the same time he ordered half the available airplanes from the carriers to attack the head of the enemy columns with torpedo and bomb. But at this juncture the Japanese played their last card. Just as the leading American ships had reopened on the *Nagato*, a swarm of destroyers bore down upon them in two columns, to port and starboard respectively. They were immediately fired on by the battleships and cruisers, but the rush was not stopped until they had got within range. Admiral McArthur turned his line towards the approaching torpedoes, most of which passed harmlessly through; but the cruisers *Albany* and *Portland* were hit, and another torpedo got home on the battleship *Oklahoma*. Then the Japanese destroyers found themselves assailed by a squadron of American boats, and those that broke away from the deadly grapple had to steam back through waters that were lashed into foam by the tempest of shell. Forty

boats began the attack, and eighteen returned. But their devoted valour saved the remnants of the Japanese fleet, for the American air attack, delivered a few minutes before, had been only partially successful. The Japanese ships, when located, were so shrouded in smoke as to be all but invisible, and although magnesium flares were dropped to illumine the scene, torpedoes and bombs had to be launched more or less at random. The only vessel badly hit was the battle-cruiser *Kirishima*, which besides being twice torpedoed was deluged with phosphorus gas. This ship struggled gamely on for a time, but eventually had to be beached off the coast of Mindanao, where she became a total wreck. It was now 9.30 p.m. The night was dark, and a falling glass presaged a storm. Touch with the enemy had been lost, and with so many ships disabled Admiral McArthur judged it useless to continue the pursuit. While the full extent of the Japanese losses could not be determined, they were known to be severe. If the battle had been rather less decisive than had been hoped for, it had certainly eliminated the Japanese fleet as a commanding factor in the situation—at least for some months to come. When the chase was abandoned the American force found itself, roughly, 450 miles to the north-west of the Pelews, the nearest friendly base. For Angaur, therefore, a course was set, the disabled ships being taken in tow by their more fortunate consorts. Heavy weather was encountered towards midnight. Before long the cruiser *Albany* became waterlogged and had to be scuttled, Rear-Admiral Appleton transferring his flag to the *Los Angeles*. Five destroyers injured in the battle were also sunk when it became impossible to take them any further. Other vessels, including the *West Virginia* and the *New Mexico*, were only kept afloat by the indefatigable exertions of their *personnel*, and at more than one period during that trying voyage it seemed as if one or both of these great ships were doomed. But if the bad weather was a misfortune in one way, it was an undoubted boon in another, for it saved the fleet from attack by enemy submarines.

Twice in the night and once on the following day the submarine alarm was given, but if torpedoes were fired none took effect.   At 5 a.m. on the 21st a tragic incident occurred.   In the grey light of dawn a big submarine was observed by the American destroyers, which at once opened fire, and when the craft had disappeared dropped many depth-charges, two of which took effect. The submarine then emerged again for a few moments, and was identified as an American boat, the *V 6 ;* but before anything could be done her shattered hull plunged to the bottom.   She had got out of her station during the night and was trying to regain it when mistaken for an enemy.   Only one officer and three men were saved, out of a company of eighty.   The bulk of the fleet reached Angaur about noon on the 22nd, having taken nearly forty hours to cover a distance of 450 miles, and some of the more badly damaged units did not arrive till much later.   Thanks to the facilities now available at Angaur, it was possible to begin emergency repairs without delay.   Within a fortnight all the battleships except the *West Virginia* were able to sail for Hawaii.   While the fleet had lain at Angaur Japanese airplanes from Mindanao had attempted to raid it, but the American air patrol proved too strong, and no enemy machine reached the ships.   The result of a great naval battle is not to be measured solely by a comparison of respective losses.   In the Jutland action, fought during the world war, the British were strategically the victors, though their casualties in ships and men far outweighed those of the German fleet.   On the present occasion, however, there was no question as to which side had triumphed, both tactically and strategically.   With a much smaller force at their disposal, the Japanese had sustained by far the heavier loss.   Out of a total of twelve capital ships, no fewer than five had been accounted for—*Kaga, Mutsu, Kongo, Haruna,* and *Kirishima.*   Moreover, all the seven remaining vessels had been damaged to an extent that would keep them in dock for a considerable period.   Losses among the cruisers and destroyers had also been severe.

As an effective unit the Japanese battle fleet had ceased to exist. On the American side, only two big ships had gone—*Florida* and *Wyoming*, neither of the most powerful type. Fourteen battleships survived, with two in reserve in the United States. Consequently, when its wounds had been healed the American fleet could take the sea with a strength of sixteen battleships. Three cruisers had been sunk, together with twenty-three destroyers, but these gaps would speedily be filled by new craft approaching completion. Thus from every point of view the victory had been overwhelming and decisive. It came as a fitting climax to the well-planned scheme of strategy mapped out by the Bureau of Operations, of which, as is now universally known, Rear-Admiral Harper was the guiding genius. The United States had at length gained command of the sea in the main theatre of war. It only remained to exploit this advantage by putting such pressure on Japan as would compel her to yield to the inevitable.

CHAPTER XXI

NOVEMBER, 1932–MARCH, 1933

Hopeless position confronting Japanese Government—Chinese armies overrun Manchuria—Sakhalin surrendered to Russia—Guam becomes American again—American armies effect landings in Luzon—Defeat of Japanese Army of Occupation and fall of Manila—Bloodless air raid on Tokyo followed by an armistice—Terms of peace—A war which benefited neither combatant

UPON the Japanese Government and nation the tidings of this great naval disaster fell as a veritable thunderclap. The leaders of the Opposition now demanded the resignation of the Cabinet on the score of incompetence; the naval members of the War Council bitterly reproached their military *confrères* with having deliberately thrown away all chance of victory in defiance of the advice of those who had pointed out the danger; while the public, on the full implication of the defeat being explained to them in the newspapers, clamoured for the heads of those who had brought the country's affairs to such an evil pass.

Other misfortunes came thick and fast. On the outbreak of war with China, Japan had endeavoured to maintain her ascendency by the occupation of certain points of strategical importance; but these garrisons were gradually isolated by General Wang Tsu's forces and compelled to surrender or withdraw. Nor was this the end. Having freed China Proper from the domination of the hated foreigner, the Celestial Government directed its energies to Inner Mongolia, from which territory Japanese interests also found themselves excluded. Following upon this, General Wang Tsu in person led his armies across the Manchurian frontier at Chinwangtao during the last days of October. On finding his sway challenged, Li Ping-hui, already uneasy, flew to arms, but again he proved himself no match for the redoubtable Wang. Though he brought his best troops into the field, regardless of a renewed insurrection which promptly burst into flame in Northern Manchuria, they only served to make his fall more striking. In a pitched battle north of Newchwang, Li's soldiers were crushingly defeated, and those who did not seek safety in flight eagerly proffered their allegiance to the new power. Li himself, who had imprudently endeavoured to rally his flying forces, found himself made prisoner by his own men and led before Wang as a hostage. The Chinese Government, on the advice of their general (who could afford to be magnanimous), contented themselves with exiling Li to a distant province, where he might meditate on the futility of human ambition.

To make matters worse, a division of Japanese troops which had been hurrying to the support of their ally arrived too late to save the situation, and found itself in a hostile country, enveloped on all sides by superior Chinese forces, estimated at nearly 200,000 bayonets. After a gallant attempt to cut its way through to the coast, this force was swamped by sheer weight of numbers, and the remnant surrendered after exhausting its ammunition. Wang Tsu, quick as ever to follow up an advantage, moved with the bulk of his forces along the railroad into the Kwangtung Peninsula, bent on investing the Japanese base at Riojun (Port Arthur) before reinforcements could be thrown in. Dairen, the commercial port which the Chinese call Talien-wan and the Russians Dalnii, could offer no effective resistance, and became the headquarters of the Chinese army and siege train. For the Japanese Government to assemble sufficient strength to relieve Riojun was impossible without stripping Korea of its army of occupation, a step which in the unsettled state of that country was clearly out of the question. In view of the increasing unrest in Japan itself, which had already led to some ugly rioting in the industrial centres, the Government hesitated to dispatch a relief expedition from home—more especially since, with the command of the sea wrested from them, the Naval Staff refused to take any responsibility for the safety of transports on the short voyage from Sasebo to the Yellow Sea.

Feeling itself tottering, the Cabinet over which Prince Kawamura still presided seems to have determined on a policy of inaction. The depleted Japanese battle fleet under Admiral Hiraga, after executing temporary repairs at Cavite, had been withdrawn to Yokosuka, where it remained completely idle for the rest of the war. To guard the Philippines a few small cruisers and other light forces remained in the vicinity of Manila, but Rear-Admiral Uyehara, the flag officer in command, was given strict orders to remain on the defensive—an attitude which does not encourage enterprise, and which on this occasion did nothing to hinder further loss of territory. Although for some weeks the Japanese army of the Philippines—amounting to about 100,000 men, 75 per cent. of whom were in the island of Luzon—was left unmolested except by blockade, this was only because the first concern of the Americans was to reduce Guam. The defenders of that base, with their battle fleet swept from the board, can have entertained no hope of relief; but like true Japanese, they put up a strenuous fight. Their resistance was gradually worn down by the American tactics, which combined a steady long-range bombardment with frequent gas bomb attacks from the air; and on December 8 the Stars and Stripes again floated over the island. No American naval units sustained any important damage during this operation.

Manila Bay being closely blockaded by a squadron comprising a dozen cruisers and six divisions of destroyers, the problem of landing troops for the reconquest of the Philippines had to be faced. Taking a leaf from their opponents' book in the operations of March, 1931, the American High Command sought to mislead the enemy. This was rendered easier by the superiority of the American air force, which subsequent to the attempted raid on Truk from Mindanao had gained a complete ascendency over the Japanese airplanes. Repeated feints were made at disembarkation, all on the east coast of Luzon, with the result that large Japanese forces were concentrated in the neighbourhood of Albay and around Dilasac Bay. This had an important influence on the result of the real landing, which was made near Lauag, in the north-west of the island, on December 28. The casualties were heavy, as a Japanese battalion which was rushed to the spot fought almost to the last man in its endeavours to prevent the Americans gaining a footing. But its sacrifice proved vain, for by the time Japanese reinforcements reached Lauag the invaders had established too strong a hold to be driven out. More and more transports discharged their soldiers and munitions under cover of gunfire from the warships, until the offensive could be taken and an advance made to the southward, the right flank of the American army being protected by cruisers and destroyers.

The Japanese continued to fight a stubborn rearguard action during the next forty-eight hours, until they reached a strong line of carefully prepared entrenchments south of Lingayen, behind which the main Japanese army, nearly 50,000 strong, seems to have been massed. But in the meantime a second landing had been effected near Dilasac Bay, which the Japanese had neglected to observe so closely since the real menace had materialised at Lauag. The second army of invasion made a forced march across the island, brushing aside every obstacle which its surprised opponents sought to interpose, and arrived in the vicinity of Lingayen in time to take part in the battle which now developed. The Japanese Commander-in-Chief, General Kimura, finding this new enemy threatening to outflank him, swung round his right in an attempt to preserve his position, his plan apparently being to hold up one U.S. army with a comparatively weak detachment while he concentrated in superior numbers on the other invader.

But the efficient American air scouts were quick to detect this manœuvre, and General Kimura soon found himself committed to a fierce battle on both fronts, with no prospect of reinforcement should the tide turn against him. In numbers the combatants differed but slightly, but the American forces derived great assistance from their bombing airplanes, whereas every machine the Japanese sent up was instantly overwhelmed by a superior concentration. Such a conflict could have but one end. Kimura himself managed to secure his retreat to Manila with some 15,000 men, but the bulk of his army was surrounded and forced to capitulate, though not until nearly half its fighting strength was *hors de combat*. The American casualties were also severe, exceeding 11,000, and would have been much heavier but for the assistance rendered by the air squadrons, the gas bombs from which proved particularly effective. It was, in fact, the most desperately fought land engagement of the whole war, and both nations have reason to feel proud of their share in it. Officially known as the battle of Lingayen, a monument is now being erected at a spot some distance to the south of that town to mark where the carnage was heaviest. The funds for this cenotaph have been jointly contributed by American and Japanese members of a society which has been formed for the promotion of a better understanding between the two countries.

On the night following the battle the Japanese cruisers and destroyers in Manila Bay made an attempt to break through the American cordon of blockade. The *Abukuma, Yubari*, and at least three destroyers made good their escape. The others were driven back, two destroyers being sunk in a sharp action, during which the U.S.S. *Kansas City* was torpedoed and had to be abandoned.

A few days later the remaining vessels were destroyed, by order of Rear-Admiral Uyehara, with methodical thoroughness, it being apparent that Manila could not long hold out against the superior forces that were being concentrated against it. The very complete way in which these warships were rendered unfit for further service affords an interesting comparison with the ineffective scuttling of the Russian Fleet at Port Arthur before the surrender in 1905.

Manila capitulated on January 8, 1933. General Kimura and his garrison were allowed to return to Japan on their parole not to take any further part in the war. This arrangement has been harshly criticised in some quarters, but it should be widely known by now that General Clay, who was in chief command of the American military forces in Luzon, had private orders to avoid useless bloodshed in view of the anticipated early cessation of hostilities. Moreover, the news of the Manila garrison's surrender on these lenient terms undoubtedly hastened the reduction of isolated Japanese detachments in other parts of the group, since the majority of the soldiers were heartily sick of the struggle and only too anxious to get back to their homes.

By this time it was evident to all that the war was approaching its end. China, the country for whose control Japan had risked so much, was now a completely independent power, and Korea showed every promise of following this example if outside aid were forthcoming. Sakhalin had been surrendered in its entirety to Russia in order to avoid bringing a fresh adversary into the field; and a new Cabinet of pronounced democratic tendencies had replaced that of Prince Kawamura in Tokyo. Since the defeat of the Japanese fleet at Yap had given American cruisers a free hand to prey upon enemy commerce, the shortage of commodities had now become more marked, and this circumstance, coinciding with an acute financial crisis, was reducing the island Empire to desperate straits.

Credit must be given to the Officer Commanding the U.S. Flying Squadron (Rear-Admiral Symonds) for an adroit move which, made as it was just at the psychological moment, is known to have had a decisive moral effect. The Flying Squadron, consisting of the airplane-carriers *Alaska, Curtiss, Lexington, Saratoga,* and *Montauk,* formed part of the U.S. fleet which was cruising off the Pacific coast of Japan during the last week of January, 1933, with the object of enticing the enemy out of Yokosuka. On the night of January 30, fifty airplanes were sent to make a demonstration flight above Tokyo, upon which city a number of bombs were dropped. These missiles were coated with luminous paint, and although attached to parachutes which arrested the violence of their descent, they created a panic in the thronged streets of the capital. But when it was seen that none of the bombs exploded, curiosity soon overcame alarm, and the strange projectiles were carefully examined. It was then discovered that each contained a bundle of leaflets printed in Japanese, explaining that rather than waste more lives in a futile quarrel, the American nation preferred to appeal to the good sense of the Japanese people, with whom they had no real grounds for dissension. Attention was drawn to the fact that China, the nominal cause of the war, was now managing her own affairs without external assistance. Stress was also laid on the argument that two nations living on opposite sides of the greatest ocean in the world would be far better employed in peaceful trading than in reciprocal homicide. Though many of these " bombs " were confiscated by the police, thousands of the leaflets fell into the hands of the people.

Broadcast in this novel way, such propaganda could not fail to make a strong appeal to the war-weary Japanese masses, whose demand for peace became so insistent that the Government was forthwith constrained to sue for an armistice. This request was acceded to by the United States on February 4, a complete truce being observed by both belligerents until the Treaty of Peace was signed at Shanghai on May 15, 1933. The terms of this covenant are too well known to call for repetition at any length. Briefly, they included the surrender by Japan of her mandate over the ex-German Pacific islands north of the Equator, and the assumption by the United States of responsibility for their future administration. Both countries formally undertook to abstain from any endeavours to exercise political or economic control over China or her contiguous territories, and both agreed to consult together with a view to joint action against any third Power that might seek to acquire such control in the future. Territory which had changed hands during the war was to remain *in statu quo*. This clause applied, in reality, only to the United States, which had forcibly recovered all her original possessions in the Western Pacific, besides having seized the Caroline, Pelew, Mariana, and Marshall islands; but its insertion proved a salve to Japan's dignity. While no indemnity was demanded by the United States, a separate protocol embodied provisions for commercial reciprocity which have already yielded beneficial results to both the signatory Powers.

Now that peace has been re-established on a sound and apparently permanent basis, the historian may be permitted to marvel at the folly of Japan in wantonly attacking a country with whom she had no real cause for enmity, and whose friendship was, indeed, essential to her own welfare. As a result of this unprovoked conflict, Japan was brought to the verge of ruin, nor is it conceivable that she will regain her former status as a first-rank Power during the present generation.

If the United States emerged victorious from the fray, it cannot be said that she derived any substantial benefit beyond the elimination of that menace of war which had been for many years a perpetual source of anxiety to her statesmen. Her shipping trade was virtually destroyed, and as yet it shows no sign of recovery. The enormous expenditure in which she had been involved left its inevitable aftermath of high taxation and consequent social unrest. War is never a paying proposition from any national point of view, and the great conflict of which the salient phases are described in the foregoing pages has proved, in its material aspects at least, scarcely less disastrous to victors than to vanquished.

APPENDIX I

THE UNITED STATES NAVY

Tables of the Principal Effective Ships complete during 1931–32.

(Those marked * were lost during the War.)

Year of Launch.	Name.	Normal Displacement in tons.	Designed Speed in knots.	Armour over Vital parts.	Armament.
		18 BATTLESHIPS.			
1921 1920 1921	*Colorado Maryland West Virginia*	32,600	21	16–18 in.	Eight 16 in. twelve 5 in.; eight 3 in. AA.; two torpedo tubes.
1919	*California Tennessee*	32,300	21	14–18 in.	Twelve 14 in., 50 cal.; twelve 5 in.; eight 3 in. AA.; two torpedo tubes.
1917	*Idaho Mississippi New Mexico*	32,000	21	14–18 in.	
1915	*Arizona Pennsylvania*	31,400	21	14–18 in.	Twelve 14 in., 45 cal.; fourteen 5 in.; eight 3 in. AA.; two torpedo tubes.
1914	*Nevada Oklahoma*	27,500	20·5	13½–18 in.	Ten 14 in., 45 cal.; twelve 5 in.; eight 3 in. AA.; two torpedo tubes.
1912	*New York Texas*	27,000	21	12–14 in.	Ten 14 in., 45 cal.; sixteen 5 in.; eight 3 in. AA.; four torpedo tubes.
1911	*Arkansas *Wyoming*	26,000	20·5	11–12 in.	Twelve 12 in., 50 cal.; sixteen 5 in.; eight 3 in. AA.; two torpedo tubes.
1910 1909	**Florida* *Utah*	21,825	20·75	11–12 in.	Ten 12 in., 45 cal.; sixteen 5 in.; eight 3 in. AA.; two torpedo tubes.

Year of Launch.	Name.	Normal Displacement in tons.	Designed Speed in knots.	Armour over Vital parts.	Armament.

8 AIRCRAFT CARRIERS.

Year of Launch.	Name.	Normal Displacement in tons.	Designed Speed in knots.	Armour over Vital parts.	Armament.
1929 {	Alaska / Montauk / Curtiss (new)	23,000	27	—	Two 8 in.; six 5 in. AA.
1925 {	Lexington / Saratoga	33,000	34·5	—	Eight 8 in.; twelve 5 in. AA.
1920	*Curtiss (old)	15,000	10·5	—	Four 5 in.
1912	Langley	12,700	15	—	Four 5 in.
1920	Wright	11,000	15	—	Two 5 in.; two 3 in. AA.

(The auxiliary vessels *Harvard*, *Houston* and *Shafter* were also employed as temporary aircraft carriers.)

26 MODERN CRUISERS.

Year of Launch.	Name.	Normal Displacement in tons.	Designed Speed in knots.	Armour over Vital parts.	Armament.
1927	*Albany				
1929	Atlanta				
1929	*Cleveland (new)				
1927	*Columbia				
1928	Columbus				
1928	Denver (new)				
1929	Galveston (new)				
1928	Hartford	10,000	34	—	Nine or twelve 8 in.; six 3 in. AA.; six torpedo tubes.
1927	Indianapolis				
1927	Kansas City				
1929	Los Angeles				
1927	*Minneapolis				
1928	Olympia (new)				
1927	Portland				
1928	*Troy				
1929	Wilmington				
1921	Cincinnati				
1921	*Concord				
1922	Detroit				
1923	*Marblehead				
1924	Memphis	7,500	33·7	—	Twelve 6 in.; four 3 in. AA.; ten torpedo tubes.
1921	Milwaukee				
1920	Omaha				
1922	Raleigh				
1921	Richmond				
1923	*Trenton				

21 OBSOLETE CRUISERS.

Year of Launch.	Name.	Normal Displacement in tons.	Designed Speed in knots.	Armour over Vital parts.	Armament.
1906	Charlotte				Four 10 in.; sixteen 6 in. (*Seattle*, four 6 in.); twelve 3 in.; four torpedo tubes.
1906	*Missoula	14,500	22	5–9 in.	
1905	Seattle				

Year of Launch.	Name.	Normal Dis-place-ment in tons.	Designed Speed in knots.	Armour over Vital parts.	Armament.
1903 1903 1904 1903 1903	*Frederick Huntington Huron Pittsburgh Pueblo	13,680	22	6 in.	Four 8 in.; four-teen 6 in.; two 3 in. AA.; two torpedo tubes.
1904 1905	*Charleston S . Louis	9,700	21·5	4 in.	Twelve 6 in. Six 3 in.
1891	Rochester†	8,150	21	4–6 in.	Four 8 in.; eight 5 in.; two 3 in. AA.
1907	Birmingham Chester Salem	3,750	24	—	Four 5 in.; three 3 in.
1903 1901 1903 1902 1902	Chattanooga *Cleveland (old) *Denver (old) Des Moines *Galveston (old)	3,200	16·5	—	Eight 5 in.; one 3 in. A.A.
1896	New Orleans	3,430	20	—	Eight 5 in.; one 3 in. AA.
1892	Olympia† (old)	5,865	21·5	—	Ten 5 in.; two 3 in. AA.

† Both *Rochester* and *Olympia* were found too worn out to be used for any effective purpose during the War.

16 MINELAYERS.

These included the *Aroostook, Shawmut, Baltimore, San Francisco,* together with 12 destroyers converted into light minelayers.

275 DESTROYERS.

The majority of these were of the 34-knot "flush deck" type, averaging 1,200 tons displacement, and armed with four 4 in. and two 3 in. AA. guns, and twelve torpedo tubes.

111 SUBMARINES.

These included 12 of the powerful " V " type, 3 of " T " type, 50 of the " S " series, 27 of " R " series, and 19 of earlier types, all of which were practically obsolete and useless for oceanic operations.

GENERAL.

The numbers of Patrol Vessels, Minesweepers, Submarine, Aircraft and Destroyer Tenders, Repair Ships, Oilers, Colliers and other auxiliaries varied at different periods of the War, a large number of mercantile vessels being taken over and converted for sundry purposes in the course of 1931–32.

APPENDIX II

THE IMPERIAL JAPANESE NAVY

Tables of the Principal Effective Ships complete during 1931–32.

(Those marked * were lost during the War.)

Year of Launch.	Name.	Normal Displacement in tons	Designed Speed in knots.	Armour over Vital parts.	Armament.
		7 Battleships.			
1921	*Kaga (vide p. 259)	40,000	23	14 in.	Ten 16 in.; twenty 5·5 in.; four 3 in. AA.; eight torpedo tubes.
1920 1919	*Mutsu Nagato	33,800 33,600	} 23	13–14 in.	Eight 16 in.; twenty 5·5 in.; four 3 in. AA.; eight torpedo tubes.
1917 1916	Hiuga Ise	31,460 31,260	} 23	12 in.	Twelve 14 in.; twenty 5·5 in.; six torpedo tubes.
1914 1915	Fuso Yamashiro	30,600 30,800	} 22	12 in.	Twelve 14 in.; sixteen 6 in.; four 3 in. AA.; six torpedo tubes.
		5 Battle Cruisers.			
1923	Akagi (vide p. 259)	44,000	33	12 in.	Eight 16 in.; twenty 5·5 in.; four 3 in. AA.; eight torpedo tubes.
1913 1912 1913 1912	*Haruna Hiyei *Kirishima *Kongo	27,613 27,500 27,613 27,500	} 27·5	8–10 in.	Eight 14 in.; sixteen 6 in.; four 3 in. AA.; eight torpedo tubes.

Year of Launch.	Name.	Normal Displacement in tons.	Designed Speed in knots.	Armour over Vital parts.	Armament.

4 AIRCRAFT CARRIERS.

Note.—Former Aircraft Carriers *Kaga* and *Akagi* were re-transformed into capital ships, as listed above).

Year of Launch.	Name.	Normal Displacement in tons.	Designed Speed in knots.	Armour over Vital parts.	Armament.
1928 1929 1928	*Matsushima Mishima Okinoshima	5,833	25	—	Three 4·7 in.; two 3 in. AA.
1921	Hosho	9,500	25	—	Four 4·7 in.; two 3 in. AA.

(Auxiliary Vessel *Hakata* was also employed as an Aircraft Carrier.)

33 MODERN CRUISERS.

Year of Launch.	Name.	Normal Displacement in tons.	Designed Speed in knots.	Armour over Vital parts.	Armament.
1926 1928 1927 1929 1928 1928 1926 1926 1929 1929 1929 1929	*Ashigara *Chitose Haguro Hashidate Itsukushima *Kasagi Myoko Nachi Otowa Takasago Yonezawa Yoshino	10,000	34	—	Eight or ten 8 in.; six 3 in. AA.; twelve torpedo tubes.
1925	Aoba Furutaka Kako Kinugasa	7,100	34	—	Six 8 in.; four 3 in. AA.; eight torpedo tubes.
1923 1921 1923 1922 1921 1924 1922 1923 1922	Abukuma Isudzu Jintsuu Kinu Nagara Naka Natori Sendai Yura	5,570	33	—	Seven 5·5 in.; three 3 in. AA.; eight torpedo tubes.
1920 1920 1919 1920 1920	Kiso Kitakami Kuma *Ohi Tama	5,500	33	—	Seven 5·5 in.; two 3 in. AA.; eight torpedo tubes.
1923	Yubari	3,100	33	—	Six 5·5 in.; four torpedo tubes.
1918	*Tatsuta Tenryu	3,500	31	—	Four 5·5 in.; one 3 in. AA.; six torpedo tubes.

Year of Launch.	Name.	Normal displacement in tons.	Designed Speed in knots.	Armour over Vital parts.	Armament.
		14 Obsolete Cruisers.			
1902	*Kasuga*	7,750	20	6 in.	One 10 in.; two 8 in.; fourteen 6 in.; ten 3 in.; four torpedo tubes.
1903	*Nisshin	7,750	20	6 in.	Four 8 in.; fourteen 6 in.; ten 3 in.; four torpedo tubes.
1899	*Idzumo	9,750	20·75		Four 8 in.; eight 6 in.; twelve 3 in.; four torpedo tubes.
1900	*Iwate	9,750	20·75	7 in.	
1899	*Azuma	9,426	21		
1899	*Yakumo	9,735	20·5		
1898	*Asama*	9,700	21·5		
1898	*Tokiwa*	9,700	21·5		

(Last two of above ships were temporarily rearmed for bombardment operations—*vide* p. 84.)

Year of Launch.	Name.	Normal displacement in tons.	Designed Speed in knots.	Armour over Vital parts.	Armament.
1900	*Aso*	7,800	21	8 n.	Two 8 in.; eight 6 in.; sixteen 3 in.; two torpedo tubes.

(This vessel was fitted for minelaying work.)

Year of Launch.	Name.	Normal displacement in tons.	Designed Speed in knots.	Armour over Vital parts.	Armament.
1911	*Chikuma* *Hirago* *Yahagi*	4,950	26	—	Eight 6 in.; four 3 in.
1907	*Tone*	4,105	23	—	Two 6 in.; ten 4·7 in.
1902	*Tsushima*	3,420	20	—	Six 6 in.; ten 3 in.

12 Minelayers.

The majority of these were of small size and importance.

108 Destroyers.

The above figure represents the total number understood to have been in service at the outset of hostilities. More than half of these exceeded 1,200 tons in displacement and 34 knots in speed. By the end of the War it has been calculated that some 50 more destroyers had been built, all of large size. Almost all Japanese destroyers carried 4·7 in. guns as their main armament.

126 Submarines.

Six of these were of the famous Submarine Cruiser type, described on pp. 65–66. The majority of the remainder were of the first class, exceeding 1,000 tons surface displacement.

General.

Full information concerning the number of Patrol Vessels, Minesweepers, Parent Ships for destroyers and submarines, Repair Ships, Oilers, Colliers, and other auxiliaries is difficult to obtain, as so many mercantile vessels were taken up for varying periods during the War.

INDEX OF PERSONAL NAMES

Note.—Those marked with an asterisk lost their lives in the course of the War.

INDEX OF SHIP NAMES

Note.—Ships marked with an asterisk were lost during the War.

" Dummy Battleships " are referred to on pp. 209, 210, 240, 241, 246, 247, 248, 253, 262, 263, 267, 268, 269, 273, 274, 276.